Entrepreneurial Strategies

STRATEGIC MANAGEMENT SOCIETY BOOK SERIES

The Strategic Management Society Book Series is a cooperative effort between the Strategic Management Society and Blackwell Publishing. The purpose of the series is to present information on cutting-edge concepts and topics in strategic management theory and practice. The books emphasize building and maintaining bridges between strategic management theory and practice. The work published in these books generates and tests new theories of strategic management. Additionally, work published in this series demonstrates how to learn, understand, and apply these theories in practice. The content of the series represents the newest critical thinking in the field of strategic management. As a result, these books provide valuable knowledge for strategic management scholars, consultants, and executives.

Published

Strategic Entrepreneurship: Creating a New Mindset
Edited by Michael A. Hitt, R. Duane Ireland, S. Michael Camp and Donald L. Sexton

Creating Value: Winners in the New Business Environment
Edited by Michael A. Hitt, Raphael Amit, Charles E. Lucier and Robert D. Nixon

Strategy Process: Shaping the Contours of the Field
Edited by Bala Chakravarthy, Peter Lorange, Günter Müller-Stewens and Christoph Lechner

The SMS Blackwell Handbook of Organizational Capabilities: Emergence, Development and Change
Edited by Constance E. Helfat

Mergers and Acquisitions: Creating Integrative Knowledge
Edited by Amy L. Pablo and Mansour Javidan

Strategy in Transition
Richard A. Bettis

Restructuring Strategy: New Networks and Industry Challenges
Edited by Karel O. Cool, James E. Henderson and René Abate

Innovating Strategy Process
Edited by Steven W. Floyd, Johan Roos, Claus D. Jacobs and Franz W. Kellermanns

Entrepreneurial Strategies: New Technologies and Emerging Markets
Edited by Arnold C. Cooper, Sharon A. Alvarez, Alejandro A. Carrera, Luiz F. Mesquita and Roberto S. Vassolo

Forthcoming

Strategic Networks: Learning to Compete
Edited by Michael Gibbert and Thomas Durand

Entrepreneurial Strategies:
New Technologies in Emerging Markets

Edited by
Arnold C. Cooper, Sharon A. Alvarez,
Alejandro A. Carrera, Luiz F. Mesquita
and Roberto S. Vassolo

Blackwell
Publishing

© 2006 by Blackwell Publishing Ltd

BLACKWELL PUBLISHING
350 Main Street, Malden, MA 02148-5020, USA
9600 Garsington Road, Oxford OX4 2DQ, UK
550 Swanston Street, Carlton, Victoria 3053, Australia

The right of Arnold C. Cooper, Sharon A. Alvarez, Alejandro A. Carrera, Luiz F. Mesquita and Roberto S. Vassolo to be identified as the Authors of the Editorial Material in this Work has been asserted in accordance with the UK Copyright, Designs, and Patents Act 1988.

First published 2006 by Blackwell Publishing Ltd

1   2006

Library of Congress Cataloging-in-Publication Data

Entrepreneurial strategies : new technologies and emerging markets / edited by Arnold Cooper . . . [et al.].
     p.   cm.—(Strategic Management Society book series)
    Includes bibliographical references and index.
    ISBN-13: 978-1-4051-4167-3 (alk. paper)
    ISBN-10: 1-4051-4167-0 (alk. paper)
    1. Industrial management—Developing countries.   2. Entrepreneurship—Developing countries.
3. International business enterprises—Developing countries.   I. Cooper, Arnold C.   II. Series.

    HD70.D44E58 2006
    658.4′21091724—dc22
                                    2005032606

A catalogue record for this title is available from the British Library.

For further information on
Blackwell Publishing, visit our website:
www.blackwellpublishing.com

Contents

Notes on Contributors

Alvarez, Sharon A. is an assistant professor of management and human resources at the Fisher College of Business, Ohio State University. Professor Alvarez's current research focus is on entrepreneurial theory, high technology alliances between entrepreneurship firms and larger established firms, entrepreneurial decision making and women entrepreneurs. She is active with the venture capital and entrepreneurship community in the Columbus area, and was founder and academic director of the Center for Entrepreneurship. Her previous experience includes work with such companies as Hiram Walker, LTD, Celsius Energy and Texaco, Inc. She has started and owned a small business, has served on the board of directors for small businesses and consults in the biotechnology industry.

Barney, Jay B. is the Bank One Chair for Excellence in Corporate Strategy. His research focuses on the relationship between costly-to-copy firm skills and capabilities and sustained competitive advantage. He has published more than 50 articles in top-tier journals such as the *Academy of Management Review, Management Science,* the *Sloan Management Review* and the *Journal of Management;* serves on the editorial boards of the *Strategic Management Journal, Columbia Journal of World Business* and the *Journal of Business Venturing;* and has been associate editor for the *Journal of Management* and senior editor for *Organization Science.* Dr Barney has delivered scholarly papers at more than 40 universities worldwide; has published three books; and has been honored for his research and teaching, including election as a Fellow of the Academy of Management. His consulting work focuses on large-scale organizational change and strategic analysis.

Brito, Luiz A. is an assistant professor at the Operations Management Department of the Fundação Getúlio Vargas Business School (FGV-EAESP) in São Paulo, Brazil. His research interests are the determinants of firm performance and its links to operations and business strategy as well as variance component analysis. He has worked for several years as a business consultant in Brazil and several other countries in South America.

Carrera, Alejandro A. is a professor and chair of the Business Policy and Strategy department at the IAE School of Management and Business, Universidad Austral. He received his DBA from the IESE Business School, at the Universidad de Navarra. His research interests include food chain competitiveness, corporate strategies of business groups in emerging economies, entrepreneurship and corporate governance of small and medium enterprises.

Chacar, Aya S. is an assistant professor at Florida International University. Her research and teaching are on business and corporate strategy and the management of innovation and change. Her research has been singled out twice for publication in the yearly Academy of Management Proceedings.

Cooper, Arnold C. is the Louis A. Weil, Jr. Professor of Management, Krannert Graduate School of Management, Purdue University. He has served on the faculties or as a visiting scholar at the Harvard Business School, Stanford University, The Wharton School, Manchester Business School (England), and IMEDE Management Development Institute (Switzerland). His current research interests include: influences upon entrepreneurship and the performance of new firms, strategic responses to technological threats, and relationships between strategy and performance. He has also studied the management of technology. He has consulted on problems relating to strategic planning, general management, and management of new and small firms.

Ireland, R. Duane is the Foreman R. and Ruby S. Bennett Chair in Business Administration at Texas A & M University where he also serves as Head of the Management Department. He has authored or co-authored many books and book chapters and published numerous articles in journals such as the *Academy of Management Journal, Academy of Management Review, Academy of Management Executive, Strategic Management Journal, Administrative Science Quarterly, Decision Sciences, Journal of Management, Entrepreneurship Theory and Practice and Journal of Management Studies,* among others. Dr Ireland has received awards for best paper from the *Academy of Management Journal* (2000), *Academy of Management Executive* (1999), and the US Association for Small Business and Entrepreneurship (USASBE).

Madanmohan, T. R. is an associate professor of technology and operations management at the Indian Institute of Management Bangalore and an adjunct research professor at Eric Sprott School of Business, Carleton University, Canada. He received a BE in Civil Engineering from Gulbarga University, in 1985, and a PhD in Management Studies from the Indian Institute of Science, Bangalore, in 1992. His research interests include open standards and open source, pharmaceutical industry and service operations. He is a member of the IEEE Engineering Management Society, Operations Research Society of India, and Society of Operations Management.

McDermott, Gerald A. is an assistant professor at the Management Department of the Wharton School. His research interests focus on institutional change and development, origins and change in networks, comparative political economy, and economic and political development. He has several publications in prestigious journals such as the *Academy of Management Review, Industrial and Corporate Change*, and *Small Business Economics.*

Mesquita, Luiz F. is an assistant professor of strategy at the School of Global Management and Leadership, Arizona State University. His PhD is from Purdue University. His research, which focuses on inter-firm knowledge transfer, vertical-alliances and performance and interdependencies coordination among clustered-firms, has been accepted in prestigious research outlets, such as the *Academy of Management*

Review and the *Academy of Management Executive*. Professor Mesquita is fluent in English, Portuguese and Spanish, and has lived for several years in the US, Brazil and Argentina. He has worked/lectured at Fortune 500 companies and has also been Research Project Director for the Inter-American-Development Bank. Professor Mesquita is an active member of both the Strategic Management Society and the Academy of Management.

Peng, Mike W. is the Provost's Distinguished Professor of Global Strategy at the University of Texas at Dallas. He received his PhD from the University of Washington. Dr Peng was previously an associate professor at the Fisher College of Business, Ohio State University. He is the author of numerous articles and three books, including, most recently, *Global Strategy* (Thomson South-Western, 2006). He has served on the editorial boards of the *Academy of Management Journal, Academy of Management Review, Journal of International Business Studies,* and *Strategic Management Journal,* as a guest editor for the *Journal of Management Studies,* and as an editor for the *Asia Pacific Journal of Management.*

Rocha, Hector O. is an assistant professor of management at the IAE School of Management and Business, Universidad Austral. Dr Rocha's research focuses on three interrelated areas: the theoretical foundations and practical implications of core assumptions in economics and management; the role of clusters and entrepreneurship in fostering socio-economic development at the regional and national levels; and the role of the private sector and its collaboration with the public sector in the promotion of human development and the alleviation of poverty.

Vasconcelos, Flávio C. is a professor at the Management Department of the Fundação Getúlio Vargas Business School (FGV-EAESP) in São Paulo, Brazil. His research interests focus on the convergence of business strategy and institutional theory. He has over 25 articles published in peer reviewed journals and has authored two books.

Vassolo, Roberto S. is an assistant professor of business policy and strategy at the IAE School of Management and Business, Universidad Austral. He received his PhD in strategic management from Purdue University. His research interests include strategic alliances in the technological exploration process, real options theory, and the analysis of strategic alliance portfolios and mutual forbearance in exploration contexts.

Vissa, Balagopal is an assistant professor of entrepreneurship at INSEAD, Singapore. His research interests focus on how new venture networks influence their performance and how new venture teams can leverage their network ties, especially in emerging economy settings. His research also addresses how business groups in emerging economies such as India can influence the success of their affiliated firms. His teaching evolves around business strategy and entrepreneurship and he currently teaches elective courses offered by the entrepreneurship area.

Webb, Justin W. is a PhD candidate in the Mays Business School at Texas A&M University. Strategic management and entrepreneurship are his areas of interests in the PhD program. He has published several chapters in scholarly books. His research interests include strategic entrepreneurship, managing resources, and sustaining organizational value.

Yin, Xiaoli is an assistant professor of management at the College of Business of San Francisco State University. She obtained her PhD in Organization Behavior and Sociology at Northwestern University. Her research interests focus on network theory and alliance decisions. Professor Xiaoli is a recipient of the CEER award for her outstanding research.

Figures

Tables

CHAPTER ONE

Entrepreneurship and Innovation in Emerging Economies

Sharon A. Alvarez, Luiz F. Mesquita and Roberto S. Vassolo

The evolving twenty-first century may well be termed a time of uncertainty. Cycles of boom and bust in the rising global competitive landscape have presented firms with complexities and increasing difficulties to predict the future, as new technologies, products and methods of production are destroyed and replaced by even newer ones. Such dramatic changes have led practitioners to broaden their speculation about emerging trends in management, organization, and strategy, often questioning the adequacies of practices hailed in recent years. Emerging managerial practices are often found to be astoundingly dissimilar and habitually conflicting; yet the essential matter for managers today still seems to come down to one thing: coping with dramatic uncertainty (Barkema et al., 2002).

Paradoxically, while uncertain conditions have their own unique managerial challenges, these conditions also foster unique situations and opportunities that can be exploited by entrepreneurs and entrepreneurial firms (Audretsch, 1995). Entrepreneurship and innovation have come to be perceived as engines of economic and social development in many nations throughout the global competitive landscape (Acs and Audretsch, 2003; Holcombe, 2003). In fact, entrepreneurship and innovation have become essential managerial features for young and old firms, for large and small firms, for service companies and manufacturing firms as well as high-technology ventures (Thomke, 2003). Thus, because the very essence of entrepreneurship and innovation in these firms relates to identifying and exploiting new environmental conditions where new goods and services can satisfy evolving needs in the market (Meyer et al., 2002), it is not surprising that the importance of entrepreneurship and the management of innovation has grown over time, at par with the evolving complexity of the new global competitive landscape.

The sources of uncertainty and the factors leading to entrepreneurial activity, however, differ dramatically not only from industry to industry and firm to firm, but most conspicuously from country to country. Specifically, while in developed economies companies face uncertainties which are mostly related to technological and process development of new products and ideas, the conditions of uncertainty in the business environments of emerging economies are often magnified by phenomena of macroeconomic and institutional instabilities. Such phenomena are often observed to evolve into conditions of currency fluctuations, political disorders and even prevarication of existing property rights defensive laws. Yet, emerging economies are seeing record rates of entrepreneurship and innovation relative to developed economies. For example, the empirical evidence of the Global Entrepreneurship Monitor (GEM) studies find that emerging economies in continents as far apart as Latin America (e.g. Argentina, Brazil), Africa (e.g. Uganda) and Asia (e.g. China, India) have greater total entrepreneurial activity (TEA) than other countries of similar size but with more stable environments (GEM, 2005).

While an increasing number of scholarly and managerial publications address the phenomena of entrepreneurship and innovation, it is unclear how these many different sources of uncertainty, so pervasive in emerging economies, shape and affect entrepreneurial opportunities as well as how they affect entrepreneurial decision making. Understanding such links can be not only beneficial to multinationals entering emerging markets through wholly owned investments or partnerships but also to national entrepreneurs and public policy makers. In order to shed more light on such links, we have crafted this book. Specifically, our goal is to help academics, policy makers and business practitioners understand how the different conditions of uncertainty in emerging economies affect entrepreneurial opportunities in the market place, as well as how entrepreneur-managers navigate through these emerging market specific conditions.

To describe how firms produce and manage innovation in emerging economies, we consider several topics in this book, as follows.

Part I: Entrepreneurial Theory and Uncertain Environments

Chapter 2 by Alvarez and Barney begins to lay the foundation for a theory of the firm that addresses why firms would form when value creation is the central question. They challenge whether current theories of the firm such as transactions cost economics and incomplete contracts appropriately address firm formation under conditions of uncertainty when the source of this uncertainty is value creation. While Alvarez and Barney acknowledge that both of these theories have much to say about appropriation issues and conditions of uncertainty as they pertain to appropriation, they point out that neither theory sufficiently address fundamental issues of firm formation in the early stages of the value creation process.

Future research on less developed countries can use this theory of the firm as a lens to understand value creation in settings when such conditions as property rights are unstable such as in China. Moreover, this theory can be applied when problems of creation cannot be separated from problems of appropriation because the problems associated with potential appropriation are not only in the form of opportunistic behavior from individuals but perhaps from governments as well.

Finally the chapter has some novel ideas about why organizing a firm under conditions of value uncertainty is important. Certainly a research question that can be derived from this theory is: if different cultural norms are applied where opportunistic behavior is not acceptable and the society itself polices against this type of behavior, do firms still exist and why would they exist if not to create value?

In chapter 3, Peng offers findings which are consistent with the Alvarez and Barney theory of uncertainty that the more dynamic, hostile, and complex the environment, the higher the level of innovation, risk-taking, and "proactivity" among the most successful entrepreneurial firms in transition economies. Specifically, Peng explicitly addresses the increase of entrepreneurial activity in the transition economies of Central and Eastern Europe, the former Soviet Union and East Asia. In this chapter, the author strongly posits that the rise in entrepreneurship in these economies is the result of uncertainty from political change and changes in business practices as a result, also pointing out that entrepreneurial firms in these economies are formed – despite poor property rights protections – in order to create wealth.

The chapter suggests that network ties in these economies replace many institutional safeguards that are typically found in developed countries. Peng suggests that in an environment where personal ties figure prominently, entrepreneurs without deep and strong network relations may have a lot of difficulties in getting things done. However, network ties are necessary but not sufficient for good performance, good management practices such as hiring, motivating and retaining talented employees also give these firms an advantage at value creation.

Finally, Peng addresses the issue of value appropriation by entrepreneurs. He suggests that some of this value might be appropriated not by the entrepreneurs creating the value but by other entrepreneurs and even by government officials. Peng further suggests that this type of appropriation behavior might induce either short-term goals on the part of entrepreneurs or even be a deterrent to entrepreneurial behavior.

In chapter 4, Ireland and Webb add to the list of concerns outlined in Peng and also expands their scope to a broader international perspective. Specifically, the authors look at a specific form of entrepreneurship in international contexts, termed as "international entrepreneurship," as a way of explaining the process through which firms discover and exploit opportunities that lie outside a firm's domestic markets in the pursuit of global competitive advantages. Their perspective adds to existing literature which often takes firms as "born global," and does not enable a more thorough analysis of the entrepreneurial initiatives of entering international markets.

Ireland and Webb enrich our understanding of entrepreneurship in emerging economies in that they describe the roles of resource bundles formed with financial capital, human capital, and social capital in the exploration and exploitation of entrepreneurial opportunities in emerging economies. They posit that while certain resource bundles are necessary to flexibly accommodate the identification of entrepreneurial opportunities in the dynamic uncertainty associated with emerging economies, other resource bundles are more appropriate for undertaking entrepreneurial efforts in an international context. Because large and small firms may differ in regards to their resource bundles, they may differently possess certain competencies that enhance their competitive advantage in different phases of their international entrepreneurship efforts. Thus, large firms, who often own ample financial resources and experiential knowledge of routines are often more successful in exploiting opportunities. On the other hand, smaller firms who often lack "deep pockets" are more likely to be successful when leveraging human-technical and social capitals to maneuver through the maze of changing institutional forces in emerging markets and more quickly and flexibly identify opportunities while engaging in exploration-oriented actions.

Part II: National Context and New Enterprises

Previous empirical studies notice important differences on entrepreneurship and innovation across countries. In order to shed light on the nature and relationships explaining these differences, our book incorporates several different empirical perspectives. Chapter 5 by Cooper and Yin surveys the literature about entrepreneurship and innovation across countries, and examines the factors that bear upon the creation of innovative and growth oriented firms. They stress the relevance of the GEM studies as a source of information about the relationship between entrepreneurship and innovation in emerging economies. One of the apparent paradoxes of emerging economies is their important amount of entrepreneurial activity. However, as the GEM studies show, this higher rate of entrepreneurship is partially explained as "entrepreneurship by necessity" as opposed to "entrepreneurship by opportunity." Entrepreneurship by opportunity leads to growth-oriented firms, which are more willing to attract venture capitalist and are more innovative. Therefore, an important percentage of the entrepreneurial activity in emerging economies will face severe problems of survival.

In spite of these limitations, new and small firms in developing countries will operate with some advantages. Cooper and Yin identify at least two: proximity to focal markets will allow them to better identify market opportunities, and production in such countries will permit firms to take advantage of lower factor costs. It is still unclear, however, whether these advantages are enough to lead to growth-oriented innovative firms. Nonetheless, as Cooper and Yin conclude, *most new ventures will not be very innovative or lead to much growth, regardless of the country setting.* For new entrepreneurial ventures in emerging economies, much will depend upon the human and financial capital they can bring to the entrepreneurial process.

As these resource conditions may vary country by country, the question that naturally evolves is to what extent performance differences can be sustained across different markets. In other words, to what extent does "country" matter, as an explanatory factor for competitive success? In chapter 6, Brito and Vasconcelos present an important methodological study assessing this question. Following a long tradition in strategic management of measuring the firm and the industry effect on performance (Rumelt, 1991; Schmalensee, 1985; McGahan and Porter, 1997; Brush and Bromiley, 1997) they incorporate another variable – the country effect. Although most previous studies decomposing performance variances focus on industry and firm effects, Brito and Vasconcelos' novel methodological approach enables us to confirm what economic and strategic management theorists have long posited – that local works as an important determinant of firm heterogeneity.

Although they find that country *does* matter, their study also enables one to assess *how much* country matters. Their conclusion is that country effects are not the main factor in explaining performance variance. Factors associated with the individual firm, such as entrepreneurial drive and mind-set for example, are still the most important source of explanation for performance. Country effects compete in the second rank of factors like industry membership. Moreover, country effects also vary across economic sectors. Specifically, they find that country effect is low in sectors like Transportation and Services and rich by up to 20 percent of total performance in sectors like Agriculture.

As these studies suggest that entrepreneurial mind-sets and entrepreneurship management can help firms gain an edge in the higher volatility of emerging economies, in chapter 7 Rocha investigates how a firm's positioning within a social network can explain different performances. Rocha uses a meta-study to explore if clusters are conducive to new entrepreneurial activities in Latin American countries. As the study assesses, clusters are not only an agglomeration of firms, but also networks within geographical boundaries. From a theoretical perspective, clusters foster entrepreneurship for multiple reasons like lowering entry and exit barriers and fostering competitive climate. However, the empirical evidence in Latin America is not conclusive on this relationship. Rocha hypothesizes that clusters foster entrepreneurship in traditional manufacturing or specialized suppliers' clusters such as software, given the more flexible governance structures in these types of industries. Instead, clusters inserted in value chains with vertical structures not embedded in the local community, such as some automotive clusters, are likely to hinder firm creation.

Rocha also explores the relationship between entrepreneurship, clusters, and economic development in Latin America. Its unique conditions are the emergent nature and especial configuration of its clusters and the higher level of entrepreneurial activity in terms of both necessity and opportunity driven entrepreneurship.

In chapter 8, McDermott complements the previous chapter by analyzing how a country's policy makers' approach to institution building interacts with network reproduction and, therefore, with social capital. Since firms are embedded in a concrete socio-political establishment, the distribution of public power affects economics networks. McDermott examines how existing institutional and political factors in the Czech Republic inhibit or enhance network adaptation to external technological and economic shocks in the mechanical engineering industry. Therefore, this study stresses that the political approaches that governments take to build new institutions alter not only their network authority structures but their network stability and reconfiguration.

Emerging economies suffer from institutional volatility, a fact which in turn seems to erode social capital. Given these changes, McDermott's study highlights the importance of providing alternative institutional arrangements to mediate disputes and share risks. Under this framework, to the extent that political leaders are able to empower and monitor a variety of public actors to experiment with new institutional roles, network firms appear to be more likely to extend their time horizons and pursue negotiated modes of reorganizations. On the other hand, to the extent that political leaders seek to insulate and centralize public power, fragmentation and winner-take-all strategies are likely to prevail in the network. This study gains especial relevance given the spur in liberalization of emerging economies across Asia, Latin America, and Eastern and Central Europe.

Vissa and Chacar, in chapter 9, stress the positive impact of social ties on new ventures performance in emerging economies, since such ties are often substitutes for underdeveloped institutions. Analyzing the software industry in India, they show that external network contacts provide informational advantages that, giving the uncertainty of managing a new venture, results in superior strategic decision making and, therefore, in superior venture performance. Uncertainty is mitigated and the informational advantage is enhanced by trustworthiness. Therefore, trustworthiness emerges as an important moderator between external network contacts and new business performance in an environmental context with weak institutions like that of emerging economies.

Moving towards network markets in India, in chapter 10, Madanmohan explores the growth process by which recently established firms attain substantial size and they keep growing. The study points out different capabilities endowments required at different stages of the life of a high-tech venture. At initial stages, the key organizational capability is employee recruitment and training and strategy setting. In more developed stages, the key capabilities are quick imitation and strategic extension. Thinking in the long run, however, firms not only need to have the right capabilities at the right moment, but also be in condition to update this set when they move at a different development stage. This is a core dynamic capability that new start ups should develop since their creation if they want to achieve sustainability.

Conclusions

In the first paragraphs of this introduction, we stressed that uncertainty is a double-edge sword that a successful entrepreneur in emerging economies should know how to handle. Innovation characterizes growth-oriented ventures, and entrepreneurs should develop critical capabilities to succeed in hostile environments. Our primary concern involved in selecting the chapters of this book, thus, has been with categorizing different sources of uncertainty which are more peculiar to emerging economies and illustrating how different managerial mind-sets, different entrepreneurial strategies in deploying resource bundles as well as different positioning tactics relative to changing environmental conditions enable a firm to sustain competitive advantages.

As a final comment, let us paraphrase Cooper and Yin: "Overall, entrepreneurship has demonstrated that it can be a major force in economic development. As millions of entrepreneurs all over the world start their businesses and try to develop them, countries benefit from their creativity, their energy, and their dreams."

References

Acs, Z. J. and Audretsch, D. (Eds.) 2003. *Handbook of Entrepreneurship Research: An Interdisciplinary Survey and Introduction*. (Vol. 1). The Netherlands: Kluwer Academic Publishers.

Audretsch, D. 1995. *Innovation and Industry Evolution*. London: MIT Press.

Barkema, H. G., Baum, J. A. C., and Mannix, E. 2002. Management challenges in a new time. *Academy of Management Journal*, 45(5): 916–30.

Brush, T. H., and Bromiley, P. 1997. What does a small corporate effect mean? A variance components simulation of corporate and business effects. *Strategic Management Journal*, 18(10): 825–35.

GEM. 2005. *Global Entrepreneurship Monitor.* http://www.gemconsortium.org/.

Holcombe, R. G. 2003. The origins of entrepreneurial opportunities. *Review of Austrian Economics*, 16: 25–54.

McGahan, A. and Porter, M. 1997. How much does industry matter, really? *Strategic Management Journal*, 18 (Summer special issue): 15–30.

Meyer, G. D., Neck, H. M., and Meeks, M. D. 2002. The entrepreneurship-strategic management interface. In M. A. Hitt, R. D. Ireland, S. M. Camp and D. L. Sexton (Eds.), *Strategic Entrepreneurship: Creating a New Mindset.* Oxford: Blackwell Publishers, 19–44.

Rumelt, R. 1991. How much does industry matter? *Strategic Management Journal*, 12(3): 167–85.

Schmalensee, R. 1985. Do markets differ much? *American Economic Review*, 75(3): 341–51.

Thomke, S. 2003. R&D comes to services. *Harvard Business Review*, 81(4): 70–9.

Thompson, J. D. 1967. *Organizations in Action: Social Science Bases of Administration.* New York: McGraw-Hill.

PART I

Entrepreneurial Theory and Uncertain Environments

CHAPTER TWO

Can Organizing a Firm Create New Economic Value?

Sharon A. Alvarez and Jay B. Barney

For some time now, economists (Smith, 1778; Marshall, 1930), strategic management scholars (Penrose, 1959), and entrepreneurship scholars (Knight, 1921; Schumpeter, 1934) have studied how various productive resources in an economy can be used to create new economic value. The ability of a variety of these resources – including labor, capital, and technology – to be sources of new economic value has already been examined by several scholars (Smith, 1778; Walras, 1954; Williamson, 1985). This chapter examines the ability of another productive resource in the economy – the firm as an organizing entity – to be a source of such value creation.

Unfortunately, the currently most influential theory that explains why firms come into existence – opportunism-based transactions cost economics – focuses on how organizing a firm can reduce transactions costs in completing an exchange rather than on how organizing a firm can create new economic value (Williamson, 1975; 1985).[1] Despite a few efforts to extend opportunism-based logic from cost minimization to value maximizing (e.g., Riordan and Williamson, 1985; Zajac and Olsen, 1993), most theoretical and empirical work that applies this theoretical tradition is still based on the assumption that "efficiency" is more important than "strategizing" in understanding why firms are created (Williamson, 1991).

This chapter acknowledges that the creation of firms often depends on the ability of these governance devices to reduce transactions costs in completing an exchange. However, when it is possible for new value in an exchange to be created, failing to recognize the impact that organizing a firm can have on realizing this potential might lead to misleading conclusions about whether or not a firm should be used to manage a given exchange.

Following Zajac and Olsen (1993), the purpose of this chapter is to extend current opportunism-based transactions cost logic to incorporate the notion that adopting a firm to manage an economic exchange can, in some settings, create new economic value. The chapter does this by analyzing the governance consequences of recognizing that exchanges can be characterized by market uncertainty as well as by behavioral uncertainty. The theory of the firm that is derived from this effort specifies conditions under which the creation of a firm is necessary if an exchange is to create new economic value. The chapter concludes by discussing the relationship between this theory of the firm, opportunism-based transactions cost theories of the firm, and incomplete contract theories of the firm.

Opportunism-based Transactions Cost Economics[2]

The theoretical and empirical literature in opportunism-based transactions cost economics is vast, and no effort will be made to review this literature. Rather, the objective here is to summarize the basic arguments of this theory, especially as they relate to the conditions under which firms are created to manage economic exchanges.

Opportunism-based transactions cost economics takes as its unit of analysis a transaction between two economic entities. The theory examines the different ways that such a transaction can be managed, including markets, intermediate governance mechanisms, and hierarchies (or firms). The main driver of the choice among these governance devices is hypothesized to be what might be called "behavioral uncertainty," or the inability of one economic entity to evaluate the motives and objectives of another economic entity at low cost. In particular, high levels of behavioral uncertainty imply that the willingness of an exchange partner to behave opportunistically, if given the opportunity to do so, cannot be evaluated at low cost. In this context, opportunism is defined as "profit seeking with guile" (Williamson, 1975), and might include a broad range of adverse selection, moral hazard, or hold-up activities (Barney and Ouchi, 1986).

Given high levels of behavioral uncertainty, the theory further hypothesizes that profit seeking, but boundedly rational economic entities, will assume that those with whom they are contemplating an exchange will, if given the opportunity, behave opportunistically. Whether or not an economic entity has the opportunity to behave opportunistically is hypothesized to depend on the level of transaction specific investment that parties to an exchange must make if they are to complete that exchange. Transaction specific investments have more value in a particular transaction than they do in alternative transactions.

If it is possible to write and enforce a contract that fully specifies all the ways that parties to an exchange may behave opportunistically, then that exchange can be managed through some sort of market or intermediate market form of governance. But if such a contract is too costly to write or enforce, an exchange will have to be managed with hierarchical governance. Hierarchical governance, or a firm, is also a type of contract. However, this contract gives some people associated with an exchange the right to monitor and control the behavior of other people associated with that exchange, as long as those behaviors are not controlled by other contracts, by custom, or by law. Thus, in this sense, a firm is said to exist when rights to make decisions not otherwise specified in a relation are given to some individuals associated with an exchange, but not others.

The advantage of hierarchical governance under conditions of high behavioral uncertainty is that this form of contract does not have to anticipate all the different ways that parties to an exchange may behave opportunistically. Rather, through close monitoring, unanticipatable forms of opportunism can be identified over the life of the exchange, and appropriate remedies to ensure all parties to this exchange are treated fairly can be implemented.

Opportunism-based Transactions Cost Economics and New Value Creation

This opportunism-based transactions cost theory of the firm has received significant criticism in the literature. Some scholars have argued that this theory overstates the likelihood that exchange partners will be willing to behave opportunistically, if given the opportunity (Donaldson, 1990). Others have argued that this assumption leads firms to vertically integrate too much, and thus is bad for practice (Ghoshal and Moran, 1996). Still others have argued that those who are given the right to monitor and control behaviors in a firm often have interests that conflict with efficiently realizing the full value of an exchange (Jensen and Meckling, 1976). Finally, several scholars have pointed out that, over time, exchange partners can come to understand the motives and objectives of each other, and thus this basic theory needs to be augmented by some learning dynamics (Barney and Hansen, 1994).

While all these criticisms have some validity, and have stirred controversy in this area of research for some time, these potential limitations of the opportunism-based transactions cost theory of the firm are not the primary issue here. The primary issue to be discussed in this chapter is that this theory assumes that the only purpose of making governance choices in managing an economic exchange is to minimize the lost economic value that could have existed if this exchange was managed efficiently. That is, opportunism-based transactions cost theory takes the value to be created by an exchange as given, and seeks to identify that governance device that will enable parties to this exchange to extract as much of this value, at the lowest cost, possible.

This is an important and legitimate research question. Unfortunately, it is not the research question that underlies several management research disciplines, including strategic management and entrepreneurship. These fields of work are interested not only in how to manage an exchange so as to extract as much value from it as possible, they are also interested in where this value comes from in the first place, and in particular, how organizing a firm can affect the total value created in an exchange (Rumelt et al., 1991).

Riordan and Williamson (1985) recognized this limitation of opportunism-based transactions cost economics and developed a model to examine the governance implications when transactions specific investments in an exchange are allowed to have two effects. The first effect – higher transactions specific investments lead to higher threats of opportunism – is the traditional effect in the theory. The second effect – higher transactions specific investments can increase the productive efficiency of an exchange – is not considered in the traditional model. Unfortunately, Riordan and Williamson's (1985) model adopted the assumption that the governance choices in question were being made in very competitive conditions, conditions where the ability of any investments, specific or not, to generate new economic value in an exchange is extremely limited (Besanko et al., 1996). Thus, since the structure of their model truncated any possible value enhancing effects of transactions specific investments, it is not surprising that Riordan and Williamson (1985) conclude that the threat of opportunism from transaction specific investment is a more important determinant of governance choices than any value enhancement from these investments.

Thus, while Riordan and Williamson (1985) recognized the important limitation of opportunism-based transactions cost economics, their model fails to fully resolve this weakness. This is the objective of this chapter.

Introducing Market Uncertainty into Opportunism-based Transactions Cost Economics

Of course, the reason that opportunism-based transactions cost economics cannot be used to analyze how organizing a firm can create new economic value is that this theory is built entirely around understanding how the firm helps resolve transactional problems associated with behavioral uncertainty. The ability to create new economic value in an exchange depends on the existence of what might be called "market uncertainty," or the inability of parties to an exchange to know the full future value of investments in that exchange, ex ante. Any theory of the firm that examines how the creation of a firm might create new economic value must focus on how the firm helps resolve transactional problems associated with high market uncertainty.

Value creation and market uncertainty

It is not hard to show that when there is no market uncertainty, it is unlikely for an exchange to create new value (Barney, 1986). In such settings, the future value of any current investments in an exchange are fully known, and parties to an exchange will receive payments based on these expectations. In such exchanges, there are no "surprises," either positive or negative.

When market uncertainty is high, however, the actual value created from an exchange may vary significantly from any value that might be anticipated at the time an investment is made. If that value is greater than what was expected, at least some parties to an exchange may receive payments for investing in that exchange greater than what they would otherwise have expected. These payments are economic rents (Rumelt, 1987), and are an indication that new value has been created in an exchange.

Of course, the value realized in an exchange characterized by high market uncertainty may be lower than what was expected, in which case parties to an exchange may experience a real economic loss. The existence of this possibility, together with the possibility of new value creation in high market uncertainty settings, can create strong incentives for at least some parties to an exchange characterized by high levels of market uncertainty to carefully monitor and control that exchange, in ways that are discussed in more detail below.

Also, even though the creation of new economic value under conditions of high market uncertainty cannot be fully anticipated at the time investments in an exchange are made, it does not follow that any such value that is actually created represents only an economic entity's good luck (Barney, 1986). These issues will also be explored in more detail later.

Transactions problems under high market uncertainty

Just as conditions of high behavioral uncertainty can create transactional problems for those looking to engage in economic exchanges, so too can high market uncertainty create transactional problems for those looking to engage in economic exchanges under these conditions. At least two such problems exist. Since at the time investments in these exchanges are made, their future value is not fully known, the first important issue that must be addressed in order for an exchange of this type to go forward is: "who in this exchange will have the incentives to invest to create the potential for generating new economic value?" Second, assuming these investments are made and turn out to be valuable, another important question that must be resolved before this exchange goes forward is: "who will appropriate any new economic value created from an exchange?"

The creation problem

Opportunism-based transactions cost theory takes the economic value that is to be created from an exchange as given, and focuses only on how to realize this full value. However, under conditions of high market uncertainty, the value created by an exchange is not given, it must be created by investments that are made and nurtured by parties to an exchange over time.

Note that it is rarely the case that these investments to create new economic value are made all at once. Rather, they typically require the systematic nurturing of investments over time, as parties to an exchange monitor how the value in an exchange is evolving and increase, decrease, or modify their investments in that exchange accordingly. In this sense, the ability of an exchange under conditions of high market uncertainty to actually create economic value depends, at least in part, on the willingness and ability of parties to that exchange to monitor and adjust their investments in this exchange over time.

It is in this sense that any value created in an exchange operating under conditions of high market uncertainty does not necessarily have to be attributed entirely to an economic entity's good luck. While the full value of these investments cannot be known at the time they are initially made, their value can become known over time. Moreover, the skillful monitoring and nurturing of these investments can increase the chances that they will generate new economic value.

The appropriation problem

Of course, parties to an exchange will be unwilling to make and nurture these uncertain investments unless they can be assured of receiving some payment from doing so. This payment would be drawn from any economic rents that an investment in an exchange under these conditions might generate. And while the willingness and ability of parties to this type of exchange to monitor and nurture an investment can increase the chances that it will actually generate new economic value, such value is far from certain. Thus, in addition to knowing how any new economic value created by an investment would be appropriated, parties to an exchange will also want to know how any economic losses associated with that exchange will be allocated before they would be willing to engage in these kinds of transactions.

Governance to solve these transactional problems

It is not hard to see that market contracts, and even most forms of intermediate market contracts, will usually not solve these two transactional problems under conditions of high market uncertainty. Both these types of contract fail because, under conditions of high market uncertainty, it is not possible, ex ante, to specify the kinds of investments – including their nature, their timing, and how they will need to be adjusted over time – that will be required to actually create value. And because the nature of these investments cannot be known, ex ante, who should receive what level of compensation for investing in an uncertain exchange can also not be known.

Notice that these problems exist with market and intermediate market contracts even if there is no behavioral uncertainty associated with this exchange. Imagine, for example, that two parties to an exchange have a history of cooperative relations, and thus that the threat of opportunism in this exchange is quite low (Barney and Hansen, 1994). In this setting, it is still difficult, if not impossible, to write a contract specifying who should make what kinds of investments, and when, in an exchange characterized by high levels of market uncertainty. The answers to these questions are simply not known when an exchange of this type is first being contemplated. And if such contractual details cannot be specified ex ante, then it is also impossible to know what an appropriate allocation of any economic value or loss that might be created should be.

Of course, it may very well be the case that a particular exchange is characterized by both high market and high behavioral uncertainty. How governance choices will be made in this setting will be discussed in more detail below.

Assuming that parties to an exchange under conditions of high market uncertainty cannot anticipate all that must be anticipated if they are to write a market or intermediate market contract to manage this exchange, what alternatives do they have? Obviously, these parties can agree to write a contract that specifies those details of the relationship that can be specified, and leaves the remaining details to be worked out over time. This contract could also specify how these remaining details will be worked out, i.e., who will make the decision, how the decisions will be implemented, and so forth.

Of course, such a contract is, at its heart, a firm. Recall the definition of a firm discussed earlier in this chapter: a contract that gives some people associated with an exchange the right to monitor and control the behavior of other people associated with that exchange, as long as those behaviors are not controlled by other contracts, by custom, or by law. Thus, under conditions of high market uncertainty, parties to an exchange will prefer hierarchical forms of governance to market or intermediate forms of governance, because hierarchical governance enables parties to an exchange to monitor and adjust the investments in such exchanges in ways that maximize the probability that this exchange will actually create value.

These hierarchical contracts can vary along several dimensions. Differences in these contracts might suggest different kinds of firms. For example, some of these contracts might not specify in very much detail the process through which decisions about how to invest in an uncertain exchange over time should be made. The firms that are created by such contracts will be managed in a very different way than firms that are based on contracts that detail explicitly how investment decisions are going to be made. However, despite these differences, both of these contracts can be thought of as firms in the sense defined earlier.

Who should control decision making in a firm?

While firms may vary in the extent to which they specify who in an exchange has the right to make and implement decisions about continuing investment in that exchange, some obvious patterns are likely to emerge. For example, the costs of negotiating each and every decision between two equally powerful parties in a firm can be very high. Moreover, these costs can be high even if there is virtually no behavioral uncertainty in an exchange. Such costs reflect the cost of collecting and analyzing information about how an investment is evolving, and then agreeing about what this information means for decision making. Even well-informed, non-opportunistic economic entities can legitimately disagree about the implications of information that has been collected about the evolution of a transaction under conditions of high market uncertainty. This is even more likely when different parties to an exchange bring different resources to that exchange. To avoid these ongoing negotiation costs, it would not be surprising for one party to an exchange to accept more responsibility in directing ongoing investment decisions than another party.

But which party to this type of exchange should adopt this role? Incomplete contracts theory suggests that the party to an exchange who has more to gain if an uncertain investment actually generates new economic value should have the responsibility for making non-contractually specified decisions in a transaction (Hart and Moore, 1988). Not only does this solution avoid serious negotiation costs, it also helps address the creation and appropriation transactions problems identified with these uncertain exchanges earlier.

In particular, by giving the entity with the most to gain from an exchange residual rights of control in that exchange, the party who has the strongest incentive to ensure that that exchange actually generates value is also in the position to most completely influence how investment decisions are made in that transaction. They are also in the best position to ensure that they are able to appropriate the value they should appropriate if value is successfully created.

Incomplete contract theory is somewhat less clear about how to identify which parties to an uncertain exchange stand to gain the most from that exchange (Maskin and Tirole, 1999a). Indeed, if the answer to this question could be known with great certainty, then it is not clear how much market uncertainty actually exists in an exchange.

Recent work in strategic management can help resolve this dilemma. In particular, while the resource-based view (Barney, 1991) cannot specify, with certainty,

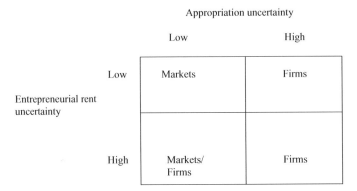

Figure 2.1   Governance choices when appropriation and ex-ante entrepreneurial rent uncertainty can both vary

whether or not a particular exchange characterized by high market uncertainty will create value, it can be used to answer a related question: Which parties to such an exchange are more likely to enjoy sustained competitive advantages should this uncertain exchange turn out to be valuable? The party who would enjoy the largest sustained competitive advantage should an uncertain investment turn out to be valuable would have the most to gain from insuring that this investment's potential value be realized. Thus, this logic suggests that residual decision rights in a firm should be allocated to those entities that are most likely to gain and sustain competitive advantages, should this uncertain investment actually create value.

Resource-based logic also suggests the kinds of resources that are likely to generate such sustained competitive advantages if they turn out to be valuable. These are the rare and costly to imitate resources described in Dierickx and Cool (1989) and Barney (1991), and include socially complex, causally ambiguous, and path dependent resources and capabilities. Those who control these kinds of resources in a firm should have residual decision rights in a firm.

Of course, it may well be the case that more than one party to an exchange characterized by high market uncertainty could possess these kinds of resources and capabilities. In this setting, decision-making power may have to be shared – despite the attendant negotiation costs – at least until the relative value of these sets of resources and capabilities in a particular exchange becomes better known.

The Governance Effects of Behavioral and Market Uncertainty

Of course, that market uncertainty can have an impact on governance choices does not suggest that behavioral uncertainty is unimportant in making these choices. A more complete model of governance must consider behavioral and market uncertainty simultaneously. A simple framework for doing so is presented in Figure 2.1.

Most of the governance choices in Figure 2.1 come directly out of either opportunism-based transactions cost economics or the current analysis of governance choices under high market uncertainty. For example, under conditions of low behavioral uncertainty and low market uncertainty, both theories suggest that market forms of governance will be preferred over hierarchical forms of governance. Market contracts are sufficient to protect against potential problems with opportunism in this setting, and the extra expense of hierarchical governance to monitor and nurture an uncertain investment is unnecessary when that investment is not uncertain.

Similar logic applies to exchanges that are characterized by high behavioral uncertainty and low market uncertainty. While hierarchy is not required to manage an investment of certain value over time, it is needed to solve potential opportunism problems. And both theories predict that hierarchical governance will be preferred under conditions of high behavioral uncertainty and high market uncertainty.

However, the two theories do make contradictory predictions under conditions of low behavioral uncertainty and high market uncertainty. Opportunism-based transactions cost economics suggests that, because of low behavioral uncertainty, market contracts will be sufficient to manage an exchange. However, the analysis in this chapter suggests that the challenges associated with creating and appropriating value associated with a transaction that is characterized by high market uncertainty require hierarchical governance.

The possibility that these two theories of the firm might make contradictory predictions in at least one setting depends, of course, on the possibility that a given transaction can be both low in behavioral uncertainty and high in market uncertainty. While the overall correlation between these types of uncertainty is ultimately an empirical question, at the very least, it is possible to point to examples of transactions that are characterized by low behavioral uncertainty and high market uncertainty.

Consider, for example, starting a new business in the Silicon Valley of the 1990s. The efficient reputational network in Silicon Valley during this time period has been described in a variety of sources (Saxenian, 1996). As discussed originally by Klein, Crawford, and Alchian (1978), these kinds of networks create strong disincentives for individuals to behave opportunistically, for to do so reduces the likelihood that an individual will be invited to join in future economic enterprises. Thus, the level of behavioral uncertainty in this setting is quite low. However, because starting a new business is a very uncertain enterprise, the level of market uncertainty in exchanges associated with starting this business is very high. This is precisely the situation identified in Figure 2.1 where the two theories make contradictory predictions.

It is interesting to note that, in this specific Silicon Valley context, most efforts to create new businesses were organized through the creation of firms, despite the relatively low levels of behavioral uncertainty in this setting. While an interesting anecdote, these observations hardly constitute a rigorous test of these two theories. They do suggest, however, that behavioral uncertainty and market uncertainty need not always move together, and thus that the contradictory predictions of these two theories can, in principle, be examined.

Of course, any real tests of the empirical implications of these two theories will have to incorporate complexities stemming from adding intermediate forms of governance to the governance choices that are available to those looking to manage an economic exchange. Put differently, Figure 2.1 adopts the simple markets versus hierarchies distinction originally developed by Williamson (1975). While this simplification helps describe the fundamental logic of these two theories, it does ignore the reality of the "swollen middle" of governance (Hennart, 1993).

Discussion

The ideas discussed in this chapter have a variety of implications for theory and research in strategic management, entrepreneurship, and management scholarship more generally. Some of these implications are discussed below.

What is a firm?

Any theory of the firm must first deal with a difficult definitional problem – defining what a firm is. A variety of approaches have been used to try to define the concept of a firm. For example, some authors have emphasized common goals as a defining characteristic of a firm (Thompson, 1967). Others have emphasized common cultural attributes as the defining characteristic of a firm (Deal and Kennedy, 1982). Still others have used legal reporting requirements to define a firm (Coleman, 1974).

The approach to defining the concept of a firm adopted in this chapter builds on the notion that a firm is a "nexus of contracts" (Alchian and Demsetz, 1972; Jensen and Meckling, 1976). However, if firms are just "bundles of contracts," then firms are no different to markets or other forms of contracting. To avoid losing the firm as a distinctive theoretical construct, it is necessary to go beyond recognizing that firms are a "nexus of contracts" to specify the kinds of contracts that constitute a "firm" versus the kinds of contracts that constitute a "non-firm."

This chapter observes that what separates firm contracts from non-firm contracts is the idea of residual rights of control. That is, a firm exists when one party to an exchange is given the right to make decisions about that exchange that are not otherwise specified in contracts, by custom, or by law. This is clearly a contract, but it is a contract that has clear and identifiable properties.

Interestingly, three separate theoretical traditions have adopted similar definitions of the firm. Opportunism-based transactions cost economics has adopted this contractual definition of a firm, although it assumes that the only aspects of an exchange not specified, ex ante, through other contracts, custom, or by law have to do with sources of opportunism in an exchange (Madhok, 2002). Incomplete contract theory in economics also adopts this definition of a firm (Maskin and Tirole, 1999b), as do some efforts by resource-based theorists to develop a resource-based theory of the firm (Conner and Prahalad, 1996).

Ultimately, a definition of a concept is not "right or wrong," it is either "fruitful or unfruitful" (Merton, 1957). Fruitful definitions enable the development of theories with testable implications. That this contractual definition of the firm has been found fruitful in three separate theoretical traditions, and that it has also been fruitful in the context of this chapter, suggests that it has significant potential if it was more broadly applied in management research.

The swollen middle

Earlier, it was suggested that Figure 2.1 significantly simplifies the actual governance choices facing economic entities because it eliminates the "swollen middle" of intermediate governance devices. While this may be an appropriate simplification in the beginning of developing a new theoretical perspective, in the long run, the complexities of incorporating intermediate governance devices into the theory developed here will need to be addressed. However, even in this early stage of theory development, it may be possible to use the transactional problems created by behavioral uncertainty and market uncertainty to more completely understand intermediate governance choices.

Consider, for example, the possibility that some intermediate governance mechanisms are more effective at resolving transactional problems associated with behavioral uncertainty while others may be more effective at resolving transactional problems associated with market uncertainty. While most transactions will probably be characterized by some level of behavioral and market uncertainty, it will also often be the case that one or another of these types of uncertainty will be more important in a particular exchange. Which of these two types of uncertainty are more important in an exchange may be an important determinant of the specific intermediate governance mechanism that is chosen to manage an exchange.

It is beyond the scope of this chapter to develop this theory of intermediate governance in any detail. However, one of the challenges associated with applying traditional opportunism-based transactions cost logic to intermediate governance choices is that this theory hypothesizes a single critical independent variable – the level of transaction specific investment as an indicator of the threat of opportunism in an exchange – while intermediate governance devices seem to vary in their form and structure along several dimensions. By incorporating a second independent variable, market uncertainty, into the analysis of intermediate governance choices, it may be possible to develop a more nuanced theory that matches multiple dimensions of transactions with multiple dimensions of intermediate governance.

Toward a strategic theory of the firm

As suggested earlier in this chapter, one of the fundamental problems facing organizational and strategic management scholars has to do with a mismatch between opportunism-based transactions cost economic theories of the firm – which take the value of an exchange as given – and the academic interests of strategic management scholars – who are interested in understanding how this value is created and can be maximized. Put differently, for some time now, strategic management scholars have been in a difficult position of adopting a theory of the firm (opportunism-based transactions cost economics) that assumes that the dependent variable they are most interested in understanding (economic rents) does not exist.

In this context, it is not surprising that several strategic management scholars have made efforts to develop a strategic theory of the firm, where the purpose of the creation of firms is not just to minimize transactions cost, but also to maximize exchange value. Examples of these efforts include Conner and Prahalad (1996), Liebeskind (1996), and Grant (1996). The current chapter extends this previous work.

Which, if any, of these strategic theories of the firm will come to dominate the strategic management literature cannot, of course, be known at this time. That said, the theory developed in this chapter does have at least one advantage over previous theories: its structure and implications parallel a theory of the firm that is gaining broad acceptance in other disciplines. This other theory of the firm is known as incomplete contracts theory (Grossman and Hart, 1986). And while empirical work on incomplete contracts theory continues to lag, conceptual development of this theoretical perspective continues at a rapid pace (Maskin and Tirole, 1999b). In many circles, incomplete contracts theory is seen as the logical successor to opportunism-based transactions cost economic theories of the firm (Holmstrom and Tirole, 1989).

However, while incomplete contract theory parallels and supports the effort to develop a strategic theory of the firm in this chapter, the theory developed here is not identical to incomplete contract theory. For example, while incomplete contract theory argues that the economic entity that has the most to gain from investing in an uncertain exchange should have the residual rights of control, the theory developed here articulates the conditions under which one party to an exchange is more or less likely to have the most to gain from making these investments.

To the extent that incomplete contract theory, or any other theory of the firm for that matter, facilitates our understanding of how organizing a firm can create economic value, its insights should be incorporated into a strategic theory of the firm. However, to the extent that other theories of the firm fail to adopt the economic value creation problem as a central issue, strategic management scholars will need to develop their own theories of the firm.

Toward an entrepreneurial theory of the firm

For some time, the field of entrepreneurship has been mired in discussions about what does or does not constitute entrepreneurial phenomena (Shane and Venkataraman, 2000). One dimension of this discussion has been whether or not entrepreneurial phenomena must be manifest through the creation of a firm in order to be an object of research in the field of entrepreneurship (Gartner, 1985; Alvarez and Barney, 2002).

The theory developed here helps shed some light on this question. If entrepreneurship is about the creation of new economic value, and if new economic value can only be created under conditions of high market uncertainty, it follows that most entrepreneurial activity will, in fact, be managed through the creation of firms. This is because the hierarchical governance of firms helps to resolve the transactional difficulties that face those looking to create new economic value.

Put differently, the theory developed here suggests that the study of entrepreneurship will frequently involve the study of entrepreneurial firms, because those seeking to create new economic value will generally adopt the firm as the mechanism through which to realize this value. Current debates about whether the study of entrepreneurship should or should not be restricted to the study of entrepreneurial firms become less important in the context of these observations.

More generally, the theory developed here suggests not only a strategic theory of the firm, but also an entrepreneurial theory of the firm. This theory suggests that firms are not created to minimize transactions cost – although it acknowledges that this may be an important issue some of the time – but instead are created to generate new economic value. The search for opportunities to create and appropriate economic rents will lead entrepreneurs to make investments in settings characterized by high market uncertainty, and when these investments are made, to erect firms to manage them. Thus, the essential attributes of entrepreneurial behavior – discovering opportunities and exploiting opportunities – can both be incorporated into a single theory of the firm.

Acknowledgments

We would like to thank Josh Lerner, David Hirshleifer, Anil Makhija, The Bridge conference at University of Indiana, The SMS conference at Universidad Austral, University of Texas Austin, Washington University, and University of Richmond. We especially thank our close colleagues Jay Dial, Michael Leiblein, Jeff Reuer, Doug Bosse, for offering encouragement, support, and insight during the writing of this chapter.

Notes

1 Of course, there are other current theories of the firm besides opportunism-based transactions cost theory (see Hart, 1995). However, there is little doubt that opportunism-based transactions cost theory is the most influential of these theories in the management literature. Thus, the discussion of the ability of alternative theories to address the issues raised in this chapter will focus mostly on opportunism-based transactions cost theory.
2 The term "transactions cost" can refer to a broad set of phenomena that increase the cost of engaging in an economic transaction or to a specific theory that focuses on a particular class of these costs, namely, transaction specific investments that generate the threat of opportunism in an exchange (Williamson, 1975; 1985). All theories of the firm are "transactions cost" theories in the first sense of this term (Coase, 1937), since all these theories rely on various costs of using the market system to explain the existence of firms. However, not all theories of the firm are "transactions cost" theories in the second sense of the term, since many focus on other costs of using the market system besides transaction specific investments and the threat of opportunism (Coase, 1937). Throughout this chapter, the following conventions will be adopted: the term "transactions cost" will be used to refer to the broad range of phenomena that can have the effect of increasing the cost of using market forms of exchange; the term "opportunism-based transactions cost" will be used to refer to the specific theory that hypothesizes that transaction specific investment and the threat of opportunism are the primary determinants of the emergence of the firm.

References

Alchian, A. A., and Demsetz, H. 1972. Production information costs and economic organization. *American Economic Review*, 62: 777–95.

Alvarez, S. A., and Barney, J. B. 2002. Resource-based theory and the entrepreneurial firm. In A. Hitt, R. D. Ireland, S. M. Camp and D. L. Sexton (Eds.), *Creating a New Mindset: Integrating Strategy and Entrepreneurship Perspectives.* New York: John Wiley.

Barney, J. B. 1986. Strategic factor markets: Expectations, luck and business strategy. *Management Science,* 42: 1231–41.

Barney, J. B. 1991. Firm resources and sustained competitive advantage. *Journal of Management,* 17: 99–120.

Barney, J. B., and Hansen, M. 1994. Trustworthiness as a source of competitive advantage. *Strategic Management Journal,* 15: 175–90.

Barney, J. B., and Ouchi, W. G. 1986. *Organizational Economics: Toward a New Paradigm for Studying and Understanding Organizations.* San Francisco: Jossey-Bass.

Besanko, D., Dranove, D., and Shanley, M. 1996. *The Economics of Strategy.* New York: John Wiley.

Coase, R. H. 1937. The nature of the firm. *Economica,* 4: 386–405.

Coleman, J. S. 1974. *Power and the Structure of Society.* New York: Norton.

Conner, K. R., and Prahalad, C. K. 1996. A resource-based theory of the firm: Knowledge versus opportunism. *Organization Science,* 7(5): 477–501.

Deal, T. E., and Kennedy, A. A. 1982. *Corporate Cultures.* Reading, MA: Addison-Wesley.

Dierickx, I., and Cool, K. 1989. Asset stock accumulation and sustainability of competitive advantage. *Management Science,* 35: 1504–11.

Donaldson, L. 1990. A rational basis for criticisms of organizational economics: A reply to Barney. *Academy of Management Review,* 15: 394–401.

Gartner, W. B. 1985. A conceptual framework for describing the phenomenon of new venture creation. *Academy of Management Review,* 10(4): 696–707.

Ghoshal, S., and Moran, P. 1996. Bad for practice: A critique of the transaction cost theory. *Academy of Management Review,* 21(1): 58–72.

Grant, R. M. 1996. Toward a knowledge-based theory of the firm. *Strategic Management Journal,* 17 (Winter Special Issue): 109–22.

Grossman, S., and Hart, O. 1986. The cost and benefits of ownership: A theory of vertical and lateral integration. *Journal of Political Economy,* 94: 691–719.

Hart, O. D. 1995. *Firms, Contacts, and Financial Structure.* Oxford: Clarendon Press.

Hart, O. D., and Moore, J. 1988. Incomplete contracts and renegotiation. *Econometrica,* 56(4): 755–86.

Hennart, J. F. 1993. Explaining the swollen middle: Why most transactions are a mix of market and hierarchy. *Organization Science* 4(4): 529–47.

Holmstrom, B. R., and Tirole, J. 1989. The theory of the firm. In R. Schmalensee and R. D. Willig, (Eds.), *Handbook of Industrial Organization,* Amsterdam: North-Holland, 61–133.

Jensen, M., and Meckling, W. H. 1976. Theory of the firm: Managerial behavior, agency costs and ownership structure. *Journal of Financial Economics,* 3: 305–60.

Klein, B., Crawford, R. G., and Alchian, A. A. 1978. Vertical integration, appropriable rents, and the competitive contracting process. *Journal of Law and Economics,* 21(2): 297–327.

Knight, R. H. 1921. Cost of production and price over long and short periods. *Journal of Political Economy,* 29: 332.

Liebeskind, J. P. 1996. Knowledge, strategy, and the theory of the firm. *Strategic Management Journal,* 17 (Winter Special Issue): 93–107.

Madhok, A. 2002. Reassessing the fundamentals and beyond: Ronald Coase, the transaction cost and resource-based theories of the firm and the institutional structure of production. *Strategic Management Journal,* 23(6): 535–50.

Marshall, A. 1930. *Principles of Economics.* 8th edn. London: Macmillan.

Maskin, E., and Tirole, J. 1999a. Unforeseen contingencies and incomplete contracts. *Review of Economic Studies*, 66(226): 83–115.

Maskin, E., and Tirole, J. 1999b. Two remarks on the property-rights literature. *Review of Economic Studies*, 66(226): 139–50.

Merton, R. K. 1957. *Social Theory and Social Structure*. New York: Free Press.

Penrose, E. T. 1959. *The Theory of the Growth of the Firm*. Oxford: Blackwell.

Riordan, M. H., and Williamson, O. E. 1985. Asset specificity and economic organization. *International Journal of Industrial Organization*, 3: 365–78.

Rumelt, R. P. 1987. Theory, strategy, and entrepreneurship. In D. J. Teece (Ed.), *The Competitive Challenge: Strategies for Industrial Innovation and Renewal*. Cambridge, MA: Ballinger, 137–58.

Rumelt, R., Schendel, D., and Teece, D. 1991. Strategic management and economics. *Strategic Management Journal*, 12: 5–29.

Saxenian, A. 1996. *Regional Advantage: Culture and Competition in Silicon Valley and Route 128*. Cambridge, MA: Harvard University Press.

Schumpeter, J. A. 1934. *Theory of Economic Development: An Inquiry into Profits, Capital, Credit, Interest and the Business Cycle*. Cambridge, MA: Harvard University Press.

Shane, S., and Venkataraman, S. 2000. The promise of entrepreneurship as a field of research. *Academy of Management Review*, 25(1): 217–26.

Smith, A. 1778. *An Inquiry into the Nature and Causes of the Wealth of Nations*. London, Printed for W. Strahan; and T. Cadell.

Thompson, J. D. 1967. *Organization in Action*. New York: McGraw-Hill.

Walras, L. 1954. *Elements of Pure Economics*. London: Allen and Unwin.

Williamson, O. E. 1975. *Markets and Hierarchies: Analysis and Antitrust Implications*. New York: Free Press.

Williamson, O. E. 1985. *The Economic Institutions of Capitalism*. New York: Free Press.

Williamson, O. E. 1991. Strategizing, economizing, and economic organization. *Strategic Management Journal*, 12: 75–94.

Zajac, E. J., and Olsen, C. P. 1993. From transaction costs to transactional value analysis: Implication for the study of interorganizational strategies. *Journal of Management Studies*, 30: 131–45.

CHAPTER THREE

How Entrepreneurs Create Wealth in Transition Economies*

Mike W. Peng

The rise of entrepreneurship throughout the transition economies of Central and Eastern Europe (CEE), the newly independent states (NIS) of the former Soviet Union, and East Asia has fundamentally transformed these economies, and caught worldwide attention. Entrepreneurs and the start-ups they found create wealth and push these economies to a higher level of competitiveness through their sheer energy, relentless strategies, and sometimes controversial practices. Although there are numerous country- and region-specific studies,[1] there have been few attempts that shed light on the overall development of entrepreneurship in transition economies from Shanghai to St. Petersburg. While there are many cultural, political, and economic differences permeating these countries, publications such as those by the World Bank (1996) and OECD (1996) have grouped them under the collective label of "transition economies." Increased knowledge about the wealth-creation process throughout transition economies can greatly enrich global entrepreneurship practice and research.

The Rise of Entrepreneurship

Entrepreneurship during the socialist era

Entrepreneurs are the founders of new businesses.[2] Despite harsh political conditions, entrepreneurship existed in virtually all of these countries before major transitions took place in the 1980s (Morris, 1998). Before the transition, the private sector, which had a number of peculiar labels, such as the "gray," "second," and "underground" economy, was usually small, labor-intensive, and often informal. By the 1980s, most socialist governments started to loosen restrictions on the private sector, resulting in an initial wave of entrepreneurship. At that time, however, these coun-

* First published as M. W. Peng, 2001. How entrepreneurs create wealth in transition economies. *Academy of Management Executive*, 15(1): 95–108. Reprinted by permission.

tries were reluctant to legalize private property. The government still imposed a limit on the size of a private firm, such as seven employees in Hungary and eight in China (which was later lifted in the 1990s). What is remarkable is the rapid rise of entrepreneurship in such an ambiguous environment, with little protection of private property. Wherever and whenever the government had relatively few restrictions on the private sector, pockets of entrepreneurship, such as those in South China, would start to develop.[3]

A golden era during the transition

After a period of slow but steady growth in the 1980s, private entrepreneurship blossomed in the 1990s. The most fundamental driving force was the removal of the yoke of communism throughout CEE and the NIS. The other underlying force was the continued deterioration of the state sector. We may regard the lure of capitalism as a pull factor, and the failure of state-owned enterprises (SOEs) as a push factor. A combination of the pull and push factors resulted in the abolition of many restrictions on private firms. In turn, these transitions opened the floodgates of entrepreneurship, which rose to undermine the foundation of the socialist economy.

Since the mid-1990s, the majority of the GDP has been contributed by the private sector throughout CEE and the NIS (e.g., approximately 80 percent in Hungary, 75 percent in the Czech Republic, and 70 percent in Russia; see EBRD, 1998, p. 26). At the same time, the nonstate sector in China has quietly but steadily become the backbone of the economy, contributing approximately 70 percent of total industrial output. The growth of the private sector has created jobs and at least partially compensated for the decline of SOEs. During the 1990s in CEE, about 5 percent of the adult working population attempted to start new firms or become self-employed, a figure very similar to the percentage of nascent entrepreneurs in the United States and Western Europe.[4] The 1990s was indeed a golden era for entrepreneurial start-ups throughout transition economies.

Who Are These Entrepreneurs?

What drives people to become entrepreneurs has remained an intriguing puzzle around the world, and perhaps more so in transition economies. Four types of entrepreneurs have emerged: farmers, gray individuals, former cadres, and professionals.

Farmers

Although private farming was eradicated in most socialist countries, Poland never nationalized its agriculture, and its private farmers owned more than 70 percent of the land in 1987. Even in countries where private farming had not been allowed before, the loosening of government regulations spurred a great deal of private farming. However, most private farmers would not bother to register their undertaking as a company. Over time, some of them organized along more formal lines, and attempted to grow beyond the family holdings. While most of them remain small, some of the better-managed ones have become larger and more visible. For example, the largest private company in China during the 1990s, the Hope Group, could trace its roots to private farming (Au and Sun, 1998).

Gray individuals

Because there were very few possibilities under state socialism to lawfully organize entrepreneurial ventures, unlawful ways emerged in a gray economy.[5] The socialist era left a legacy of disregard of the supremacy of the law. Too few formal laws governed economic behavior, and there was little legitimacy for the laws that did exist, which were routinely ignored. Thus, despite its lack of legality, the gray economy was widely tolerated and accepted by the public.

During the transition, frontier-style overnight accumulation of wealth through gray activities became possible. Ranging from small-scale tax evasion and bribery to large-scale mafia practices, all of these activities may be in violation of some laws or regulations.[6] Since the emerging legal and regulatory frameworks are under-developed, their enforcement leaves numerous loopholes. As a result, these gray entrepreneurs emerge to take advantage of loopholes as intermediaries connecting individuals and organizations with economic exchanges that otherwise would not have taken place.

While strictly speaking violating laws and regulations, these individuals do not necessarily belong to criminal organizations, although some of them certainly do. Most of these people are entrepreneurs in a classical sense: "persons who add value by brokering the connection between others" (Burt, 1997, p. 342). They blur the boundaries separating different sectors by taking advantage of the information and resource asymmetry across different sectors. In turn, they profit from these arbitrage opportunities (Peng, 1998; Peng et al., 2000; Peng and Ilinitch, 1998). For example, they can trade foreign exchange through black markets, obtain business licenses from officials, and enforce contracts through security services. Some of these services are clearly of a criminal nature, such as resolving contractual disputes through assassination by the Azerbaijian mafia active in Russia, resulting literally in cut-throat competition in some cases (Peng, 2000, p. 192). The size of the overall gray economy is, of course, very difficult to estimate. Tentative figures in the mid-1990s (Table 3.1) put the total size of the unofficial gray economy at approximately 11–12 percent of the GDP in the Czech Republic and Poland, about 30 percent in Bulgaria and Hungary, 40–50 percent in Russia and Ukraine, and, in the extreme case, over 60 percent in Azerbaijian and Georgia (Johnson et al., 1997).[7]

Cadres

Cadres, former communist party leaders and officers, are widely believed to benefit from the transition by becoming entrepreneurs. People with more education are found, in general, to do better in market economies than those with less education (Cooper and Dunkelberg, 1987). Cadres, who as a group are better educated than the general population, are thus likely to be in an advantageous position during the transition. Power accumulated under state socialism can be converted into assets of

Table 3.1 Share of the unofficial economy as a percentage of total GDP

Country (% of private sector share of total GDP in 1998)*	Percentage of the unofficial, gray economy share of total GDP**						
	1989	1990	1991	1992	1993	1994	1995
Central and Eastern Europe							
Bulgaria (50)	22.8	25.1	23.9	25.0	29.9	29.1	36.2
Czech Republic (75)	6.0	6.7	12.9	16.9	16.9	17.6	11.3
Hungary (80)	27.0	28.0	32.9	30.6	28.5	27.7	29.0
Poland (65)	15.7	19.6	23.5	19.7	18.5	15.2	12.6
Romania (60)	22.3	13.7	15.7	18.0	16.4	17.4	19.1
Newly Independent States of the Former Soviet Union							
Azerbaijian (45)	12.0	21.9	22.7	39.2	51.2	58.0	60.6
Belarus (20)	12.0	15.4	16.6	13.2	11.0	18.9	19.3
Estonia (70)	12.0	19.9	26.2	25.4	24.1	25.1	11.8
Georgia (60)	12.0	24.9	36.0	52.3	61.0	63.5	62.6
Kazakhstan (55)	12.0	17.0	19.7	24.9	27.3	34.1	34.3
Latvia (60)	12.0	12.8	19.0	34.3	31.0	34.2	35.3
Russia (70)	12.0	14.8	23.5	32.8	36.7	40.3	41.6
Ukraine (55)	12.0	16.3	25.6	33.6	38.0	45.7	48.9

*EBRD (1998, p. 26).
**Johnson et al. (1997, p. 183).

high value in a transition economy. During privatization, for example, strategically located cadres can take advantage of their positions in acquiring state property, as in the spontaneous privatization throughout CEE and the NIS. Cadres can also tap into their personal networks to acquire valuable resources from their former colleagues still in the government, maneuvering across different sectors as intermediaries who seek rents for their services.

In one case, a former Chinese cadre, who quit his post at the State Planning Commission in 1989, operated a $120 million company by 1995. The firm comprised a futures-and-commodities trading operation, a clinic to treat nearsightedness with lasers, and a collection of high-tech start-ups (Peng, 2000, p. 172). One of the key reasons the former cadre did so well was that he had access to powerful friends and contacts in many government agencies. In another case, during the first period of major transitions in Hungary (1989–91), cadre-entrepreneurs more than doubled their personal income, while noncadre-entrepreneurs and the entire population increased their income by 73 percent and 59 percent, respectively (Rona-Tas, 1994; see also Bird et al., 1998).

Professionals

Professional-entrepreneurs are entrepreneurs who previously held professional positions not directly related to the party state, such as lawyers, managers, engineers, and professors. In transition economies, they enhance the technology and professionalism of private firms, which traditionally concentrate on low-tech, labor-intensive sectors such as farming, restaurants, and retail shops. Professionals also increase the legitimacy of private firms. Less educated farmers and gray individuals with dubious backgrounds and activities do not inspire much confidence among the public. Cadre-entrepreneurs are widely viewed with suspicion and resentment by the public. Professionals, on the other hand, are better educated and have few connections with the party state or the gray economy. The added legitimacy to professionally run private firms, in turn, is likely to attract more experienced professionals and recent college graduates, thus fueling the development of these firms.

A group of defense scientists in 1991 started Vimpelcom, a high-tech start-up that later became Russia's largest cellular-telecom provider and the first Russian company to earn a full listing on the New York Stock Exchange. Combining defense industry know-how, contacts in the telecom industry, and the lack of Soviet-era baggage that typically plagued many privatized firms, Vimpelcom was built from the ground up with Western-style management and accounting principles that made it easy to present the three years of US standard audits required to list in New York (Peng, 2000, pp. 175–6).

On the other hand, the development of products and services with more technology content requires more long-term investment, such as R&D. Unfortunately, the general environment in transition economies, characterized by policy instability and regulatory chaos, is not conducive to such investment.[8] Moreover, professional-entrepreneurs' lack of connections with other sectors may be a liability rather than an asset. In an environment where personal ties figure prominently, entrepreneurs without deep and strong network relations may have a lot of difficulties in getting things done.

In sum, economic transitions have provided powerful incentive for all sorts of entrepreneurs to mushroom. They tend to specialize in different fields, taking advantage of their particular strengths. Farmer-entrepreneurs usually focus on food and vegetable production, farm produce distribution, and low-tech manufacturing. Gray individuals are likely to specialize in various intermediary services, both legal and illegal. Cadre-entrepreneurs are known for their interest in relationship-intensive industries, such as trading, entertainment, and property development. Professionals-turned-entrepreneurs tend to be more interested in such knowledge- and technology-based ventures as computer software and architecture design.

Major Entrepreneurial Strategies

Recent research focusing on transition economies has highlighted three major entrepreneurial strategies: prospecting, networking, and boundary blurring.[9] While they are not the only viable strategies in transition economies, individually or in combination, they do appear to be associated with the most successful entrepreneurs in these countries. These strategies are not necessarily unique to transition economies; prospecting and networking, for example, have been widely practiced by entrepreneurs elsewhere. What is interesting in transition economies is the importance of these strategies, whereby alternatives (e.g., acquisitions) are few. On the other hand, blurring the boundaries of public and private sectors in multiple directions does appear to be a unique challenge to global entrepreneurship practice and research. Therefore, the discussion below starts with a most generic strategy, and moves progressively to highlight more unusual strategies.

Prospecting

Prospectors are firms with a changing market, a focus on innovation and change, and a flexible organizational structure headed by younger, more aggressive managers, all of which are characteristic of entrepreneurial firms in transition economies (Miles and Snow, 1978). In contrast, defenders are firms with a narrow market, a stable customer group, and an established organizational structure managed by older, more conservative executives. Compared with larger SOEs and recently privatized ex-SOEs, which tend to be defenders, private firms are usually smaller and have a higher level of market orientation, agility, and flexibility. Often headed by younger individuals, start-ups also tend to adopt a simple organizational structure, which allows them to react quickly to opportunities. Start-ups also have little inherited organizational baggage from the socialist era, low fixed costs, and the ability to attract the most talented people.

Another way to view this strategy is to treat these start-ups as underdogs that have very little choice but to adopt guerrilla warfare tactics. Underdog firms cannot compete against the larger and more established rivals head-on. Instead, smaller firms conserve scarce resources for crucial battles. They use speed and stealth to create disruptions by preempting competitors, and to be the first movers while forcing their competitors to be defenders or reactors. Such a quick movement often gives entrepreneurial start-ups substantial first-mover advantages by allowing them to build up a market share and increase brand-name awareness in new niche markets.

Poland's Optimus Computer exemplifies such a strategy. Founded in 1988, this start-up held 35 percent of the Polish PC market by 1995. The owner attributed his success to a guerrilla strategy that sought first-mover advantages when the PC revolution was starting to gain momentum in that country in the early 1990s. Optimus thrived by always moving ahead of the competitors in terms of products and services. Specifically, while competitors imported models approaching the end of their product life cycle, Optimus provided locally assembled, low-cost PCs equipped with the latest versions of Intel chips, Samsung monitors, and Microsoft operating systems (Peng, 2000, pp. 179–80).

This prospector or guerrilla strategy has several limitations. The industries that entrepreneurs enter tend to have relatively low entry barriers and less capital intensity. As a result, they often focus on labor-intensive farming, light manufacturing, and small-scale services, and shy away from large-scale, technology- and capital-intensive industries. (Optimus Computer is an exception.) While their larger rivals find it difficult to compete on speed and stealth, successful start-ups often attract a large number of other private firms to follow the first movers. Because of the nature of these industries (e.g., their low entry barriers), the first movers are often unable to defend themselves and, consequently, fail to sustain a competitive advantage. Therefore, entrepreneurial firms have a tendency to be footloose, exiting existing industries or niches and searching for new opportunities elsewhere. Finally, while the prospector or guerrilla strategy may be viable during the initial phase of the transitions, when there are a large number of unfilled niches, it is questionable whether this strategy can be pursued in the long run, when the economy becomes more developed and mature.

Networking

To some extent, entrepreneurial firms around the world rely on networking as a strategy. In transition economies, virtually every firm needs to pay attention to its networks, which are necessitated by the institutional environment.

The lack of certain market-supporting institutions often leads managers and entrepreneurs to develop networks to perform basic functions, such as obtaining market information, interpreting regulations, and enforcing contracts. In an environment in which formal institutional constraints such as laws and regulations are weak, informal institutional constraints, such as those embodied in interpersonal networks, connections, and ties cultivated by managers and entrepreneurs (e.g., *blat* [connections] in Russia and *guanxi* [relationships] in China), help to at least partially overcome the infrastructure deficiencies by facilitating economic exchanges among members (Boisot and Child, 1996; Khanna and Palepu, 1997, 1999).

Compared with other firms such as SOEs, privatized firms, and foreign entrants, a networking strategy is perhaps more important for private start-ups. What is noteworthy about entrepreneurial networking is its urgency, intensity, and impact. Private firms initially suffer from a lack of legitimacy as new organizations because of their liability of age, which prompts stronger urgency for them to rapidly establish network ties with the environment. Specifically, they have to cultivate two sets of networks. The first is with entrepreneurs and managers at other firms, such as suppliers, buyers, and competitors, which may be useful in most economies. A second set of networks, with government officials, may be more unique to transition economies, because harassment from various government officials remains a constant danger. In Russia, for example, every private company must provide 28 quarterly reports to the tax authorities. In China, most private firms have to pay nearly 50 kinds of different taxes. Taxation and regulatory policies are often contradictory, and even the most scrupulous entrepreneurs cannot be in consistent compliance. It is not surprising that entrepreneurs clearly understand the importance of having good relationships with government officials, especially those in tax bureaus. In China, for example, the impact of network linkages with officials on firm performance is more important than those with entrepreneurs at other firms (Peng and Luo, 2000).

A second characteristic that distinguishes entrepreneurial networking is its intensity (Morris, 1998; Morris and Sexton, 1996). In order to ensure survival, smaller firms often have to intensify their networking activities with larger, more legitimate, and more powerful players. Moreover, a large number of them are in service industries, which, in general, are more relationship-intensive than manufacturing industries. Legal frameworks in transition economies are less developed in the service sector than in manufacturing, necessitating intense networking efforts.

Because of the small size of these start-ups, the contributions of individual entrepreneurs' personal networks tend to have a stronger impact on firm performance. In comparison, the impact of similar networks cultivated by managers at larger firms may be less pronounced because of the sheer size of these firms. Moreover, being private owners, entrepreneurs can directly pocket the residual income if their firms perform well, thereby providing powerful incentives for them to network through entertainment, gift giving, and/or bribery.

A case in point are the struggles of the entrepreneurs heading China's Lucky Transportation, a trucking company servicing the construction industry. Several state-owned construction and trucking firms formed an informal enterprise group aiming at internal collaboration and excluding nonmembers. In order to grow, Lucky Transportation had to become a member of the group by cultivating personal ties between its entrepreneurs and other managers in the group, as well as with government officials. The entrepreneurs worked hard to be their friends, taking them out to dinner, and occasionally giving them such gifts as red envelopes, known to contain cash.[10] Eventually, Lucky Transportation was accepted as a member of the group, enabling it to achieve significant growth – over 500 percent growth in sales during its first three years, 1992–95 (Peng, 1997).

On the other hand, it is important to note the limitations of a networking strategy. One common and erroneous belief is to exaggerate the importance of personal networks. Possessing effective personal networks may be necessary but not sufficient for good performance (Peng and Luo, 2000, p. 498). After all, a start-up needs to deliver value-added in the marketplace by having strengths in such traditional areas as product or service quality, advertising, and delivery. This is increasingly important in light of the drive toward more normal, market-based competition in these countries.

Boundary blurring

Closely associated with networking, two specific types of boundary blurring exist, involving the blurring of boundaries separating public and private sectors, and of those separating legal and illegal sectors.

Blurring public–private boundaries

A surprisingly large number of entrepreneurial start-ups are not privately owned companies in a classical sense. Called collective enterprises, these nonstate, nonprivate start-ups are especially visible in the Chinese economy, and since the early 1990s have become the largest contributor to the GDP, over and above the purely private sector and the SOE sector. Collective enterprises, specifically, are non-SOEs subordinate to local governments and owned and operated collectively (Bruton et al., 2000; Luo et al., 1998). Local governments benefit from these firms, which not only generate jobs, but also provide income streams and tax revenues over which local governments can have discretion. In contrast to CEE, outright privatization of these firms had not occurred in China until the late 1990s. However, hidden or informal privatization has been widespread. Specifically, entrepreneurs can bid for long-term leases to control these firms. Although such lease agreements do not entitle lease-holders to formal property rights, these agreements are widely viewed by the entrepreneurial lease-holders, as well as by the employees and the public, as *de facto* property rights.

These public-private hybrid firms, therefore, represent a gradual evolution from public to private ownership. On the other hand, a large number of pure, private start-ups move in the opposite direction by choosing to register themselves as collective firms in an effort to appear to have some public ownership, or "wear a red cap." Given the residual antagonism against private entrepreneurs, many entrepreneurs are concerned about renewed hostility directed against them and the possible appropriation of their assets. Lucky Transportation is such a collective company that is a private firm in disguise.

In an environment still institutionally unfriendly to private ownership, it makes good sense for many entrepreneurs not to advertise the private nature of their firms. Even when discriminatory policies are removed, purely private firms are still at a great disadvantage in obtaining state-controlled resources such as bank credit. For example, frustrated by its inability to access credit, Carpenter Tan, a highly successful private start-up in China, had to use advertisements in national media to plead to the banks, all of which were state-owned. The campaign stirred up a nationwide debate on why it was so hard for private firms to raise capital. This contrasts sharply with the situation in developed economies, where banks advertise to promote their loans. Paradoxically, while refusing to support Carpenter Tan, the banks continued to supply capital to numerous money-losing SOEs that hardly paid interest, let alone principal. Although there was no discriminatory policy banning loans to private firms, bankers practiced self-imposed and unfair sanctions against private firms. While it was normal for banks not to recover anything from loans to SOEs, any loan loss associated with private firms would automatically lead to suspicions that the loan officer was guilty of embezzlement and collusion with entrepreneurs. "So why do I want to take any risk to provide loans to private firms?" one loan officer asked (Peng, 2000, pp. 186–8).

Unfortunately, the experience of Carpenter Tan is not alone. Table 3.2 reveals a striking pattern of under-funding for non-SOEs in China: while their 1996 share in total industrial output and value-added rose to 71.5 percent and 91.2 percent, respectively, their share of total bank loans remained below 16 percent.[11] Non-SOE firms needed bank loans, but in most cases, their loan applications were simply denied, while banks continued to channel precious financial resources to SOEs. Nevertheless, because of the clout of local governments, changing to a collective status may allow private firms to gain better access to critical resources such as loans.

While some collective firms embody the evolution away from public ownership, other collective enterprises represent a movement away from private ownership. Given the general movement toward clearer specification of property rights throughout transition economies and the ambiguous property rights surrounding these firms, the question becomes: can ambiguous property rights sometimes be efficient? The answer is a qualified yes (Li, 1996; Nee, 1992). Under the particular circumstances of the transition, such a collective hybrid strategy may lead to the best of the two worlds. On paper at least, these firms still retain public ownership, and many local governments take these firms under their wings by shielding them from harassment from other intrusive government agencies and helping them obtain needed resources. At the same time, through creeping privatization, most of these firms behave more like pure, private firms. In short, the public-private hybrid

Table 3.2   The nonstate sector in China: Contributions and shares of bank financing*

	Percentage of industrial output	Percentage of industrial value-added	Percentage of total bank loans
1987	40.3	51.2	17.4
1988	43.2	52.4	17.0
1989	43.9	47.5	15.7
1990	45.4	62.2	15.0
1991	47.1	56.3	14.8
1992	51.9	67.5	14.4
1993	56.9	68.7	15.8
1994	66.9	80.1	15.6
1995	69.1	94.7	15.8
1996	71.5	91.2	15.9

* The nonstate sector covers registered, pure private firms; collective (public–private hybrid) firms; and foreign-invested firms. In other words, it includes all non-SOEs.
Source: Peng (2000, p. 187).

represents an interesting and previously unencountered phenomenon in global entrepreneurship practice and research, and deserves further attention from practitioners, researchers, and policymakers.

Blurring legal–illegal boundaries
In some CEE and NIS countries, the blurring of the legal–illegal boundaries has reached epic proportions. Russia seems to stand out as the most corrupt major economy in the world. While the true extent of the gray and/or illegal economy in Russia is difficult to assess, one estimate says approximately 70 to 80 percent of private companies may be paying extortion money to organized, mafia-type criminal gangs (Manev et al., 1998). Rising organized crime has occurred in just about every transition economy. Taking advantage of the entrepreneurial boom, many criminal organizations operate under the title of fully legal business firms with impeccable offices, letterheads, and bank accounts. Consider Multigroup, a small start-up founded in Bulgaria in 1989. By 1996, it became a giant, with 8,000 employees, $1.5 billion in annual sales, and offices in a dozen countries from Russia to the Philippines. Despite its success, public opinion in Bulgaria widely suspects Multigroup of being an efficient scheme of siphoning off public money from the communist era and laundering it to the benefit of ex-communist officials (Manev et al., 1998).

To acknowledge the blurring of legal–illegal boundaries does not mean to celebrate it. However undesirable, the emergence of these gray organizations may be a natural by-product of economic transitions. In the absence of a strong formal legal and regulatory regime, informal constraints such as rules and regulations imposed by the mafia rise to fill the vacuum as a form of self-government to provide some public goods, such as protection from thieves and contract enforcement. In many cases, the mafia seems to have more effective contract enforcement mechanisms – the collection of payments and the delivery of punishment such as the cut-throat method discussed earlier – than the weak court and regulatory systems. To the extent that criminal organizations are able to provide better enforcement services than the predatory government, then there will continue to be a demand for such services (Hay and Shleifer, 1998).

While such a boundary-blurring strategy may be viable during the initial, chaotic phase of the transition, the sustainability of this strategy in the long run remains to be seen. Lawlessness cannot work in the long run, and as transition economies gradually establish more legislation and regulations backed by credible law enforcement, these gray organizations will have to confront increasing pressures for legitimization. The CEO of Bulgaria's Multigroup perhaps provided the best advice on a future strategy that might be called tail cutting: "The lizard survives if it cuts off its tail. It's time for our [illegal] economic groups to cut off their illegal tails."

While analytically distinct, these three entrepreneurial strategies are not necessarily separate in practice, and are often employed concurrently by start-ups. In other words, a start-up can adopt a prospector or guerrilla strategy, while engaging in intense networking that blurs the public–private and/or legal–illegal boundaries.

What Can Be Learned?

The development of entrepreneurship throughout transition economies has generated important lessons for entrepreneurs in these economies, as well as for foreign entrepreneurs and managers interested in these emerging markets.

Lessons for entrepreneurs in transition economies

Dealing with environmental turbulence
At the dawn of the new millennium, the political, social, and economic environment in many transition economies continues to be characterized by turbulence, which is not likely to stop soon. In CEE and the NIS, the transition brought hyperinflation in the early 1990s, which was tamed only by the mid-1990s. Then came the Russian crash in 1998, which not only sparked a collapse of Russia's financial system, but also forced countries across the region to brace themselves against contagion. In China, although the constitution was finally amended in 1999 to catch up with reality by acknowledging the private sector's important role in the economy,[12] the government has continued to behave unpredictably. In 1998, it banned direct marketing without any public consultation, despite nearly $200 million invested by American firms such as Amway, Avon, and Mary Kay, and an estimated involvement of 20 million Chinese entrepreneurs. In 1999, the government in a similar manner announced a ban on all foreign investment in Chinese Internet-content providers, most of which are entrepreneurial start-ups.[13]

Despite its complexity and unpredictability, environmental turbulence seems to be a major catalyst for entrepreneurial activity in transition economies. The more dynamic, hostile, and complex the environment, the higher the level of innovation, risk-taking, and proactivity among the most successful entrepreneurial firms (Morris, 1998, p. 66).

Three ways of dealing with environmental turbulence in transition economies can be identified:

- *Establish alliances with larger, more legitimate, and more powerful players.* This is the heart of networking and boundary-blurring strategies discussed earlier. Partners in these alliances can include more established domestic firms, as well as foreign entrants and certain government agencies. From foreign entrants, entrepreneurial firms can gain access to financial assets and learn managerial and technical capabilities (Hitt et al., 2000). Teaming with government agencies allows start-ups to tap into the resources of these partners, thus helping deter environmental turbulence for entrepreneurs. Lucky Transportation's efforts to register as a collective firm and join an enterprise group in China serve as a case in point. For the same reason, many private Internet start-ups in China have investment from government-run Internet providers.
- *Take collective action to promote entrepreneurial development.* As a new organizational form, private start-ups are misunderstood by many people in certain transition economies, who associate these firms with criminal organizations. Entrepreneurs should mobilize to form industry or business owners' associations in order to lobby the new government, the media, and the public about the wealth-creation role they play in the economy. Of course, similar to lizards sacrificing their tails, gray organizations with criminal or dubious backgrounds may have to cut off their illegal tails in order to advance their legitimate interests.
- *Create linkages with established educational institutions.* Collaboration with educational institutions confers legitimacy on entrepreneurs among the future generation of employees and entrepreneurs. Entrepreneurs can also access researchers in these institutions, whose findings may further disseminate the role of entrepreneurship in transition economies. As a result, many start-ups, after they survive the first stage, often establish linkages with educational institutions through scholarships, internships, and research support. The importance of such linkages is especially noted by professional-entrepreneurs, such as those running Russia's Vimpelcom.

Transforming raw entrepreneurship into strategic leadership
While these tactics for dealing with environmental turbulence focus on strategic alliances and collective actions, recent research suggests that smaller, entrepreneurial firms may face an inherent disadvantage when collaborating with larger and more powerful players (Alvarez, 1999). Entrepreneurs may have better odds for success if they can develop capabilities that allow them to stand on their own and grow the firm (Peng and Heath, 1996). One key enabler is to focus on strategic leadership, defined as the "ability to anticipate, envision, maintain flexibility, think strategically, and work with others to initiate changes that will create a viable future for the organization" (Ireland and Hitt, 1999). This capability has been argued to be a major factor differentiating the winners from the losers in the new competitive landscape of the twenty-first century.

With little exaggeration, most early entrepreneurial strategies in transition economies can be viewed as highly opportunistic, making the first move to fill many unfilled gaps. This is precisely the heart of a prospector or guerrilla strategy. As transitions deepen and competition becomes more saturated, a higher level of entrepreneurial capability – namely, strategic leadership – will be required to transform such raw entrepreneurship. Specifically, entrepreneurs need to:

- *Develop and communicate a long-term strategic vision.* While entrepreneurs might operate without a clearly articulated strategy when the organizational size is small, developing an explicit, long-term strategic vision becomes more critical for increasingly larger organizations. Such an ability seems to characterize the best-performing start-ups, such as China's Hope Group and Russia's Vimpelcom. Increasingly, the need to strategize is felt among entrepreneurs interested in taking their business to a new height.
- *Build dynamic core competencies.* The days when entrepreneurs could hit and run in the early stages of the transition seem to be passing. The new competition requires sustained investment in core-competencies-based strongholds that can be defended and strengthened, often leading to a deep-niching strategy for many entrepreneurial firms. These core competencies have to be dynamic, and be continuously updated and extended. Facing gigantic multinationals targeting these economies, the built-in flexibility of entrepreneurial firms resulting from their small size and informal structure may be especially helpful (Dawar and Frost, 1999). Poland's Optimus Computer can serve as a vivid case in point.
- *Focus on human capital.* Given their thin resource base, entrepreneurial firms must compete on resourcefulness, the ability to do more with less. Making the most of the human capital of their employees becomes critical. Entrepreneurs should seek to not only hire, train, and invest in the best talents, but also to make sure that such human capital stays within the firm as it grows. A hurdle that entrepreneurial firms like China's Hope Group need to overcome is family-style management, which tends to rule out criticism of the boss and discourages creativity. Few employees aspiring for top posts will be satisfied with an organization that will not allow them a role in business strategies. The ability to motivate and retain talented employees may become a source of competitive advantage for entrepreneurial firms.
- *Make effective use of new technology.* While the technological base of most established firms in transition economies is obsolete, many entrepreneurial firms are uniquely positioned to leapfrog by acquiring some of the latest technology in sophisticated manufacturing and services. Recent examples are the numerous Internet start-ups popping up in these economies. These new start-ups change the low-tech, labor-intensive image of many entrepreneurial firms in transition economies, and push both the scope and pace of technological progress to new levels. Given the lackluster performance of many SOEs and privatized ex-SOEs in these economies, entrepreneurial start-ups may offer these countries the best hope of catching up with the global technological race.

In sum, these lessons for current and would-be entrepreneurs in transition economies call for continuous management of environmental turbulence and fundamental transformation from raw entrepreneurship to strategic leadership. Similarly, important lessons can be drawn for foreign entrants.

Lessons for foreign entrants

Up to this point, most of the interactions that foreign firms have with local firms in transition economies are with larger SOEs as joint-venture partners or ex-SOEs as acquisition targets (Si and Bruton, 1999; Uhlenbruck and de Castro, 1998; Yan and Gray, 1994). As the entrepreneurial sector becomes more established in these countries, however, some of these firms will become attractive partners or targets for foreign entrants. Without much research to draw from, the lessons for foreign entrepreneurs and managers interested in working with entrepreneurs in transition economies are more tentative and speculative. In general, foreign entrants need to:

- *Treat entrepreneurial partners sensibly.* Even for foreign companies experienced in the region, very few have so far dealt with smaller, entrepreneurial firms. How to treat these entrepreneurial firms differently from SOEs remains a major task for interested foreign entrants. Some of the assumptions that foreign companies hold with regard to SOEs – such as that they have inefficiency and governance problems – may not be applicable to start-ups. Typically, the first step in restructuring firms in transition economies is a very costly, difficult, and time-consuming process of conversion from SOEs to market players. This process may not be necessary when working with private firms. The new breed of entrepreneurial ventures, which are smaller, younger, and more aggressive, can be regarded as the opposite of SOEs in market orientation. Therefore, foreign entrants may need to unlearn some of the ungeneralizable prior notions about firms in transition economies (e.g., the need to teach Marketing 101 and Finance 101), when working with entrepreneurial start-ups. Smaller firms in transition economies may provide unique resources attractive to the larger, more resource-rich foreign entrants, such as market knowledge and specialized skills (Hitt et al., 2000). At the same time, new ventures in transition economies may share certain similarities with SOEs and recently privatized firms, such as a short-term mentality and a lack of interest in continuous learning. Therefore, foreign firms' experience in transforming SOEs, such as ABB in Poland, may be helpful (Oblej and Thomas, 1998). In particular, foreign entrants may need to simultaneously restructure both hard (structures) and soft (human resources) aspects of the acquired firms, instead of handling one aspect at a time in a piecemeal fashion.[14]
- *Take collective action to promote mutual interest.* The stronger and more effective the collective actions of foreign entrants, the more likely their goals – which usually include market opening and legal reforms in transition economies – will be accomplished. Industry and trade associations representing foreign business interests in transition economies, such as the US–China

Business Council and the Working Committee on Eastern Europe of the European Council for Small Business, have become increasingly visible. For example, facing the Chinese government's bans on direct marketing and Internet investment in 1998 and 1999, respectively, American direct-marketing companies and Internet venture-capital firms pressed their cases through US trade negotiators in China's World Trade Organization talks, and eventually obtained significant concessions from the Chinese side.

- *Establish alliances.* The rationale behind foreign entrants' need to use alliances is similar to that of domestic entrepreneurs. However, such an alliance strategy does not necessarily lead to joint ventures. In certain knowledge-intensive industries, foreign entrants may have little choice but to establish wholly owned subsidiaries to protect their intellectual assets. Nevertheless, wholly owned subsidiaries can still pursue alliance strategies with larger and more powerful players. When encountering extensive software piracy in China, Microsoft, through its wholly owned subsidiary, chose to collaborate with the Ministry of Electronics to develop new software, instead of challenging the government head-on. Microsoft figured that once the government has a stake in the sales of legitimate Microsoft products, it may also have a strong interest in using its clout to crack down on sales of counterfeit software. In essence, Microsoft followed its entrepreneurial counterparts in China by wearing a "red cap" in order to accomplish its goals.

Research suggests that foreign-led turnaround and restructuring of firms in transition economies, which so far have been limited to current and ex-SOEs, can succeed despite the difficulties (Estrin and Meyer, 1998; Meyer and Moller, 1998; Oblej and Thomas, 1998). Such development is encouraging for foreign companies interested in restructuring entrepreneurial firms in transition economies. After all, the founding principles (e.g., private ownership, profit maximization) between foreign firms and entrepreneurial firms in the region have a better fit than the radical contrasts between foreign firms and SOEs. Given the expected increase of foreign firms' dealings with entrepreneurial firms in transition economies, following some of the tentative lessons above should increase the odds for successful interactions over those with SOEs.

Some caveats

The outlook for entrepreneurship in transition economies is not always rosy. Entrepreneurship does not always create wealth. Many entrepreneurs in transition economies have not created wealth, but appropriated or redistributed wealth in their favor. Given that many entrepreneurial undertakings are clouded by gray activities, how entrepreneurship can be developed in an ethical and legal manner that is sustainable in the long run is important (Puffer and McCarthy, 1995). Although in the short run, some gray or illegal activities serve a role that is economically functional, accepting these activities as a legitimate and natural by-product of economic transitions is dangerous in the long run. While providing arbitrage profits to certain intermediaries, such as former cadres, these activities may create new distortion in the economy, deter foreign investment, and generate public resentment toward all entrepreneurs, legitimate or otherwise (Gray and Kaufmann, 1998).

Since individual entrepreneurs, however enlightened, may be unable to deter the tide of gray activities, policymakers need to seriously curtail these activities by clearly delineating and enforcing the rules of the game (Baumol, 1990; North, 1990). It is fair to say that most transition economies have made considerable, if not uniform, progress in establishing basic institutional frameworks. However, they have usually achieved greater progress in the extensiveness than in the effectiveness of the laws and regulations. The private enforcement of contracts, sometimes through illegal means, has emerged as a response to the failure of the state to provide and enforce its own rules. Therefore, cracking down on the illegal enforcement services of the gray economy will not succeed until public law enforcement is sufficiently developed.

Governments should also minimize the possibility of harassment against entrepreneurs by rent-seeking officials. Instead of being viewed as a softer invisible hand, the government is often viewed as a greedy, grabbing hand in countries such as Russia (Frye and Shleifer, 1997). Facing such a predatory regime, many existing entrepreneurs may continue to be drawn into the gray economy and interested only in short-term profits, and many more would-be entrepreneurs will simply give up on their ideas. Simplification of tax rules and reduction of marginal rates will draw more firms out of the unofficial gray economy. They will also make it less likely for rent-seeking officials to succeed, because transparency of the rules creates little room to maneuver.

Creative Destruction

Despite different paces and results, the entrepreneurial transformation of transition economies takes on increasing importance. How do entrepreneurs and the start-ups they found create wealth in these environments traditionally hostile to entrepreneurship? A short answer is that they accomplish this through aggressive prospector and guerrilla strategies, extensive networking, and active boundary-blurring. The lessons that can be learned all center on enhancing entrepreneurial start-ups' competitive advantage and, by extension, promoting the entrepreneurial spirit of these economies. Since entrepreneurship inevitably implies a deviation from customary behavior in any country (Brenner, 1987), entrepreneurs in transition economies are not without controversy, leading to caveats about some of the practices of the new competition.

This chapter has opted for a generalization approach. While the lessons are derived from a multinational triangulation process based on the experience of practitioners, advice from officials and advisors guiding the transitions, and the findings of scholars, overgeneralization must be avoided. Every transition economy is different. The lessons for Poland's relatively more developed economy are not likely to be the same as those for Vietnam's or Belarus's less developed economies. For large countries such as China and Russia, regional differences within a country are also enormous, again making overgeneralization dangerous. The history of economic transitions in the past two decades suggests that what transition economies need is not a set of standard lessons, recipes, or packages, but rather institutional and organizational experimentation to allow for the evolutionary emergence of entrepreneurship (Spicer et al., 2000; see also Gartner, 1985; Hisrich and Fulop, 1995).

Entrepreneurs create wealth throughout transition economies using a "creative destruction" process that Joseph Schumpeter first highlighted. In essence, start-up firms create an alternative organizational form that challenges and may eventually destroy the state sector. Although entrepreneurs are pursuing their private gains and are not concerned with official ideology, they collectively become participants in a great social movement whose invisible hand pushes a bankrupt, socialist regime aside. Such wide-ranging transitions manifest the staggering, creative and destructive power of entrepreneurship and competition – both for the entrepreneurs who participate in the transitions and for the economies that embrace them.

Acknowledgments

This research draws on a larger project funded, in part, by the Center for International Business Education and Research, Center for Slavic and East European Studies, Fisher College of Business Research Committee, and Office of International Studies, The Ohio State University; Hong Kong Research Grants Council (project HKUST6174/98H/CUHK/EI16); and French Center for Research on Contemporary China (CEFC). I thank Jay Barney, Paul Beamish, John Child, and Oded Shenkar for their encouragement; Sharon Alvarez, Kevin Au, Trevor Buck, Jean-Francois Huchet, Igor Filatotchev, Philippe Lasserre, Yuan Lu, Yadong Luo, Klaus Meyer, Niels Mygind, Snejina Michailova, Torben Pederson, Agnes Peng, Ming-Jie Rui, Justin Tan, Denis Wang, Zhong-Ming Wang, Verner Worm, Mike Wright, Ming Zeng, the two reviewers, the guest editors (especially Mike Hitt), and the *AME* editor, Sheila Puffer, for their helpful comments; and Seung Hyun Lee and Heli Wang for research assistance. Finally, I thank Simon Johnson, Bruce Kogut, Karen Newman, Don Sexton, and Andrew Spicer for promptly answering my inquires.

Notes

1 Examples of country-specific publications include Audretsch (2000), Chang and MacMillan (1991), and Puffer (1994). Examples of region-specific works include Mugler (2000) and OECD (1996).
2 This definition of entrepreneurship can be found in Gartner (1985), Low and MacMillan (1988), and Lumpkin and Dess (1996). The emphasis of this chapter, private entrepreneurship at smaller start-ups, is different from corporate entrepreneurship. See Spicer et al. (2000) and Wright et al. (1998).
3 Local governments in south China, such as those in Guangdong Province, are more accommodating and friendly to entrepreneurs. See Chang and MacMillan (1991).
4 The CEE figure is reported by Mugler (2000). The US and Western European percentages can be found in Aldrich (1999, p. 75).

5   The value-neutral term "gray economy" is used here for compositional simplicity. Other terms include labels such as the second, semiprivate, shadow, underground, and unofficial economy.

6   While mafia practices are clearly unethical and illegal in both transition and developed economies, using personal favoritism and grease payments to get things done and ignoring tax laws and regulations, which tend to be considered unethical in developed economies, are often regarded as largely acceptable and even ethical in transition economies. Some unquestioned (and hence ethical) practices in the West, such as layoffs and whistleblowing, are considered to be unethical in Russia. See Puffer and McCarthy (1995).

7   Similar estimates were provided by Schneider and Enste (2000). A more radical estimate suggested that the unreported, gray economy in Russia may be larger than the official economy. See Shama and Merrell (1997).

8   In general, small firms – regardless of locations – tend to be unwilling to invest in R&D. However, in Eastern Germany, they are less than half as likely to undertake R&D as their Western counterparts in unified Germany. See Audretsch (2000).

9   Such research focusing on China includes Peng (1997), Peng and Luo (2000), Tan (1996), and Xin and Pearce (1996). CEE research includes Johnson et al. (1997) and Mugler (2000). The NIS research can be found in Charap and Webster (1993), McCarthy et al. (1993), Puffer et al. (2000), and Zhuplev et al. (1998).

10 Although bribery was used in this case, it is not a practice to be recommended. Most entrepreneurs such as those running Lucky Transportation resent having to resort to bribery to get things done. However, if they refuse to pay while competitors do, then entrepreneurs who do not pay bribes may be disadvantaged in terms of market opportunities and resources. This dilemma is similar to the one confronting many US firms abroad, which are constrained by the Foreign Corrupt Practices Act. See Hill (2000, p. 70) and Vogl (1998, especially p. 30).

11 The nonstate firms in Table 3.2 include not only registered, pure private firms, but also collective (private-public hybrid) firms, and foreign-invested firms. Therefore, it may safely be inferred that the percentage of loans obtained by registered private firms is substantially smaller than the meager 15.9 percent figure obtained by all three categories on nonstate firms in 1996.

12 China's new revolution. *Business Week*, September 27, 1999, pp. 72–8.

13 Ultimatum for the Avon Lady. *Business Week* (Asian edn), May 11, 1998, p. 22; Big brother and the e-revolution. *Business Week*, October 4, 1999, pp. 132–42.

14 A dissenting view is that too much change at one time may inhibit organizational learning and, consequently, hurt firm performance. See Newman (2000).

References

Aldrich, H. 1999. *Organizations Evolving*. London: Sage.

Alvarez, S. 1999. Entrepreneurial alliances: Prescriptions for alliance success with larger firms. PhD dissertation, University of Colorado, Boulder.

Au, K., and Sun, L. 1998. Hope Group: The future of private enterprises in China. *Asian Case Research Journal*, 2: 133–48.

Audretsch, D. A. 2000. Entrepreneurship in Germany. In D. Sexton and H. Landstrom (Eds.), *The Blackwell Handbook of Entrepreneurship*. Oxford: Blackwell, 107–27.

Baumol, W. 1990. Entrepreneurship: Productive, unproductive, and destructive. *Journal of Political Economy*, 98: 893–921.

Bird, E., Frick, J., and Wagner, G. 1998. The income of socialist upper classes during the transition to capitalism: Evidence from longitudinal East German data. *Journal of Comparative Economics*, 26: 211–25.

Boisot, M., and Child, J. 1996. From fiefs to clans and network capitalism: Expanding China's emerging economic order. *Administrative Science Quarterly*, 41: 600–28.

Brenner, R. 1987. National policy and entrepreneurship. *Journal of Business Venturing*, 2: 95–101.

Bruton, G., Lan, H., and Lu, Y. 2000. China's township and village enterprises: Kelon's competitive edge. *The Academy of Management Executive*, 14: 19–27.

Burt, R. 1997. The contingent value of social capital. *Administrative Science Quarterly*, 42: 339–65.

Chang, W., and MacMillan, I. 1991. A review of entrepreneurial development in the People's Republic of China. *Journal of Business Venturing*, 6: 375–9.

Charap, J., and Webster, L. 1993. Constraints on the development of private manufacturing in St. Petersburg. *Economics of Transition*, 1: 299–316.

Cooper, A., and Dunkelberg, W. 1987. Entrepreneurship research: Old questions, new answers, and methodological issues. *American Journal of Small Business*, 11: 1–20.

Dawar, N., and Frost, T. 1999. Competing with giants: Survival strategies for local companies in emerging markets. *Harvard Business Review*, March–April: 119–29.

EBRD (European Bank for Reconstruction and Development) 1998. *Transition Report 1998*. London: EBRD.

Estrin, S., and Meyer, K. 1998. Opportunities and tripwires for foreign investors in Eastern Europe. *Thunderbird International Business Review*, 40: 209–34.

Frye, T., and Shleifer, A. 1997. The invisible hand and the grabbing hand. *American Economic Review*, 87: 354–58.

Gartner, W. 1985. A conceptual framework for describing the phenomenon of new venture creation. *Academy of Management Review*, 10: 139–61.

Gray, C., and Kaufmann, D. 1998. Corruption and development. *Finance and Development*, March: 7–10.

Hay, J., and Shleifer, A. 1998. Private enforcement of public laws: A theory of legal reform. *American Economic Review*, 88: 398–403.

Hill, C. 2000. *International Business*, 3rd edn. Boston: Irwin.

Hisrich, R., and Fulop, G. 1995. Hungarian entrepreneurs and their enterprises. *Journal of Small Business Management*, 33: 88–94.

Hitt, M., Davin, M., Levitas, E., Arregle, J., and Borza, A. 2000. Partner selection in emerging and developed market contexts: Resource-based and organizational learning perspectives. *Academy of Management Journal*, 43: 449–67.

Ireland, R. D., and Hitt, A. 1999. Achieving and maintaining strategic competitiveness in the 21st century: The role of strategic leadership. *The Academy of Management Executive*, 13(1): 43–57.

Johnson, S., Kaufmann, D., and Shleifer, A. 1997. The unofficial economy in transition. *Brookings Papers on Economic Activity*, 2: 159–238.

Khanna, T., and Palepu, K. 1997. Why focused strategies may be wrong for emerging markets. *Harvard Business Review*, July–Auguest: 41–51.

Khanna, T., and Palepu, K. 1999. The right way to restructure conglomerates in emerging markets. *Harvard Business Review*, July–August: 125–34.

Li, D. 1996. A theory of ambiguous property rights in transition economies. *Journal of Comparative Economics*, 23: 1–19.

Low, M., and MacMillan, I. 1988. Entrepreneurship: Past research and future challenges. *Journal of Management*, 14: 139–61.

Lumpkin, G., and Dess, G. 1996. Clarifying the entrepreneurial orientation construct and linking it to performance. *Academy of Management Review*, 21: 135–72.

Luo, Y., Tan, J., and Shenkar, O. 1998. Strategic response to competitive pressure: The case of town and village enterprises in China. *Asia Pacific Journal of Management*, 15: 33–50.

Manev, I., Manolova, T., and Yan, A. 1998. The governance, legality and interdependence of firms in transforming economies. Working paper, School of Management, Boston University.

McCarthy, D. J., Puffer, S. M., and Shekshnia, S. V. 1993. The resurgence of an entrepreneurial class in Russia. *Journal of Management Inquiry*, 2: 125–37.

Meyer, K., and Moller, I. 1998. Managing deep restructuring: Danish experiences in Eastern Germany. *European Management Journal*, 16: 411-21.

Miles, R., and Snow, C. 1978. *Organizational Strategy, Structure, and Process*. New York: McGraw-Hill.

Morris, M. 1998. *Entrepreneurial Intensity*. Westport, CT: Quorum.

Morris, M., and Sexton, D. 1996. The concept of entrepreneurial intensity: Implications for company performance. *Journal of Business Venturing*, 36: 5–14.

Mugler, J. 2000. The climate for entrepreneurship in European countries in transition. In D. Sexton and H. Landstrom (Eds.), *The Blackwell Handbook of Entrepreneurship*. Oxford: Blackwell, 150–75.

Nee, V. 1992. Organizational dynamics of market transition: Hybrid forms, property rights, and mixed economy in China. *Administrative Science Quarterly*, 37: 1–27.

Newman, K. 2000. Organizational transformation during institutional upheaval. *Academy of Management Review*, 25: 602–19.

North, D. 1990. *Institutions, Institutional Change, and Economic Performance*. New York: Norton.

Oblej, K., and Thomas, H. 1998. Transforming former state-owned companies into market competitors in Poland: The ABB experience. *European Management Journal*, 16: 390–9.

OECD (Organization for Economic Cooperation and Development) 1996. *The Development of Entrepreneurship in Transition Economies*. Paris: OECD.

Peng, M. W. 1997. Firm growth in transitional economies: Three longitudinal cases from China, 1989–96. *Organizational Studies*, 18: 385–413.

Peng, M. W. 1998. *Behind the Success and Failure of US Export Intermediaries*. Westport, CT: Quorum.

Peng, M. W. 2000. *Business Strategies in Transition Economies*. Thousand Oaks, CA: Sage.

Peng, M. W., and Heath, P. 1996. The growth of the firm in planned economies in transition: Institutions, organizations and strategic choice. *Academy of Management Review*, 21: 492–528.

Peng, M. W., Hill, C., and Wang, D. 2000. Schumpeterian dynamics versus Williamsonian considerations: A test of export intermediary performance. *Journal of Management Studies*, 37: 167–84.

Peng, M. W., and Ilinitch, A. 1998. Export intermediary firms. A note on export development research. *Journal of International Business Studies*, 29: 609–20.

Peng, M. W., and Luo, Y. 2000. Managerial ties and firm performance in a transition economy: The nature of a micro-macro link. *Academy of Management Journal*, 43: 486–501.

Puffer, S. 1994. Understanding the bear: A portrait of Russian business leaders. *The Academy of Management Executive*, 8(1): 41–54.

Puffer, S., and McCarthy, D. 1995. Finding the common ground in Russian and American business ethics. *California Management Review*, 37: 29–46.

Puffer, S. M., McCarthy, D. J., and Naumov, A. I. 2000. *The Russian Capitalist Experiment: From State-owned Organizations to Entrepreneurships*. Cheltenham: Edward Elgar.

Rona-Tas, A. 1994. The first shall be last? Entrepreneurship and communist cadres in the transition from socialism. *American Journal of Sociology*, 100: 40–69.

Schneider, F., and Enste, D. 2000. Shadow economies: Size, causes, and consequences. *Journal of Economic Literature*, 38: 77–114.

Shama, A., and Merrell, M. 1997. Russia's true business performance. *Journal of World Business*, 32: 320–32.

Si, S., and Bruton, G. 1999. Knowledge transfer in international joint ventures in transition economies: The China experience. *The Academy of Management Executive*, 13(1): 83–90.

Spicer, A., McDermott, G., and Kogut, B. 2000. Entrepreneurship and privatization in Central Europe: The tenuous balance between destruction and creation. *Academy of Management Review*, 25: 630–49.

Tan, J. J. 1996. Regulatory environment and strategic orientations: A study of Chinese private entrepreneurs. *Entrepreneurship Theory and Practice*, 21: 31–41.

Uhlenbruck, N., and de Castro, J. 1998. Privatization from the acquirer's perspective. A mergers and acquisitions based framework. *Journal of Management Studies*, 35: 619–40.

Vogl, F. 1998. The supply side of global bribery. *Finance and Development*, June: 30–3.

World Bank 1996. *World Development Report: From Plan to Market*. Washington DC: World Bank.

Wright, M., Hoskisson, R., Filatotchev, I., and Buck, T. 1998. Revitalizing privatized Russian enterprises. *The Academy of Management Executive*, 12: 74–85.

Xin, K., and Pearce, J. 1996. *Guanxi:* Good connections as substitutes for institutional support. *Academy of Management Journal*, 39: 1641–58.

Yan, A., and Gray, B. 1994. Bargaining power, management control, and performance in US-China joint ventures. *Academy of Management Journal*, 37: 1478–517.

Zhuplev, A., Konkov, A., and Kiesner, F. 1998. Russian and American small business: Motivations and obstacles. *European Management Journal*, 16: 505–16.

CHAPTER FOUR

International Entrepreneurship in Emerging Economies: A Resource-based Perspective

R. Duane Ireland and Justin W. Webb

Entrepreneurship, a phenomenon encompassing acts of organizational creation, renewal, or innovation occurring within or outside an existing firm (Sharma and Chrisman, 1999), has long been of interest to scholars and business practitioners. Widespread benefits for economies and individual firms competing within them (McDougall and Oviatt, 2000) may be a key determinate of this interest.

As a specific form of entrepreneurship and international business, international entrepreneurship, which is a key part of the analysis presented in this chapter, is receiving increasing attention from entrepreneurship researchers and business people committed to competitive success (McDougall and Oviatt, 2000). Zahra and George (2002b, p. 261) define international entrepreneurship as, "the process of creatively discovering and exploiting opportunities that lie outside a firm's domestic markets in the pursuit of competitive advantage." As this definition suggests, international entrepreneurship is (1) an organization-wide phenomenon, (2) a dynamic process rather than a static action, (3) an important part of a firm's culture, (4) a process involving both exploring for opportunities in international markets and their subsequent exploitation in those markets, and (5) the set of actions taken with the intention of helping the firm create value for its stakeholders, especially the shareholders (Dimitratos and Plakoyiannaki, 2003). Entrepreneurship and international business are closely interrelated, in that venturing into foreign markets is an entrepreneurial act (Ibeh and Young, 2001; Lu and Beamish, 2001). And, just as research regarding firms' attempts to engage in international diversification is adding a new dimension to the diversification literature (Bergh, 2001), studies about international entrepreneurship should increase our understanding about entrepreneurship.

The majority of the early international entrepreneurship research has focused on "born globals," a label used to describe new ventures that choose to enter international markets at an early age, sometimes even at the time of their founding (Autio et al., 2000; Bloodgood et al., 1996; Oviatt and McDougall, 1997; Rhee, 2002; Zahra et al., 2000b). International entrepreneurship is also used to describe the actions of established corporations, such as multinationals exercising entrepreneurial actions to enter and compete in international markets (Birkinshaw, 1997; Tallman and Li, 1996; Zahra and Garvis, 2000). While previous research has sought to identify resources and competitive conditions linked to achieving success in international markets, the results of these efforts have not meaningfully enhanced our understanding of how to successfully apply international entrepreneurship in the specific context of emerging economies. Being able to successfully engage in international entrepreneurship in emerging economies is important (given the size of these economies), yet challenging, in that the environmental turbulence in emerging economies greatly magnifies the uncertainties that are associated with entrepreneurial efforts taken in them.

As Dimitratos and Plakoyiannaki (2003) note, the international entrepreneurship literature remains in its infancy. Given the paucity of research dealing with the phenomenon and its growing importance, the purpose of our work is to contribute to an emerging field of inquiry, international entrepreneurship, as practiced within an increasingly important setting in the global marketplace – emerging economies.

Theory Development

The resource-based view is a theoretical lens that is commonly used to understand issues examined in the international business literature (Peng, 2001a). As an extension of this theory, the knowledge-based view of the firm argues that growth within companies is achieved through entrepreneurial activities that are first used to create and then to exploit knowledge (Kazanjian et al., 2002). Competitively relevant knowledge is developed through exploration processes and is effectively exploited when the firm innovatively batches what it knows into knowledge stocks (Grant, 1996; Kazanjian et al., 2002; March, 1991). The continuous refinement of a firm's knowledge stocks through entrepreneurial activities provides it with strategic flexibility, which allows the organization to innovatively exploit opportunities surfacing as a result of the rapidly changing conditions that are a part of today's competitive landscape (Hitt and Reed, 2000). Evidence suggests that innovation is a key driver to increasing a firm's performance in global environments (Franko, 1989; Hitt et al., 1998; Hitt and Reed, 2000; Zahra et al., 2000b). From a resource-based view, knowledge is the key resource allowing firms to develop innovations that are rare, valuable, inimitable, and nonsubstitutable and to develop competitive advantages as a result of doing so (Barney, 1991).

Several studies provide evidence of the competitive advantage yielded by the possession and use of specific, relevant knowledge in a firm's internationalization activities (Bloodgood et al., 1996; Zahra et al., 2000b, 2003). However, limited research has been conducted to study how to manage resources, including knowledge, in ways that create competitive advantages (Ireland et al., 2002; Sirmon and Hitt, 2003). In addition, minimal attention has been given to the environmental conditions uniquely present in emerging economies that define the success of firm-specific resource bundles. We discuss these issues in this chapter. More specifically, in developing our arguments, we address the issues of managing resources within the unique environmental conditions associated with emerging economies.

While engaging in entrepreneurial actions, ranging from those necessary to launch a start-up venture through the stages of a product's life cycle, firm-specific resources must be acquired, shaped, and leveraged in order for firms to continuously use them in ways that facilitate competitive success as change continuously occurs in the firm's external environment (Bergmann-Lichtenstein and Brush, 2001). Forming and using optimal resource bundles require an understanding of the relationships linking specific resource types. Herein we focus on the symbiotic relationships among a firm's internal knowledge stocks (human capital) and external knowledge stocks (social capital). The ability to realize the full potential of investments in either of these assets is dependent upon the concurrent level of the other one (Webb et al., 2004). Because of the symbiotic resource relationships between a firm's human capital and its social capital, the organization's ability to integrate knowledge gained from its international investments is largely a function of its existing knowledge structure (Anand, 2002; Webb et al., 2004).

Firms must also be able to cope with the dynamism and uncertainty that characterize competition in emerging economies as well as the increased costs associated with exploration and exploitation functions in an international context. Financial capital enhances the firm's flexibility as it purchases or provides other resources. Therefore, along with human capital and social capital, we examine financial capital as the third primary resource that firms must consider when managing their resources while seeking competitive success in dynamic, uncertain emerging economies. Our specific application of the general issue of effectively managing firm resources is concerned with resource management in larger, established firms as well as in smaller, entrepreneurial ventures taking entrepreneurial actions in emerging economies.

Evidence suggests that in general, small entrepreneurial ventures are able to effectively identify opportunities in the external environment but are less skilled in terms of developing the competitive advantages needed to exploit the opportunities (Ireland et al., 2001). In contrast, large, established firms are less effective in identifying opportunities when they surface in the external environment but are more capable of forming competitive advantages (Ireland et al., 2003) to exploit known opportunities. Resource-based theory implies that certain aspects of large firms and entrepreneurial ventures' respective resource structures contribute to these relative skill sets. Small entrepreneurial ventures, for example, are constrained by their lack of resources and experience (Calof, 1993; Freeman et al., 1983; Hannan and Freeman, 1984; Levinthal and Fichman, 1988; Stinchcombe, 1965), suggesting that a "resource-efficient" approach (one in which resources are used efficiently "to do things right") may be appropriate to verify that the firm is leveraging part of its resource bundle to create competitive advantage. Conversely, larger, established firms may be somewhat hindered by the size and the long history of their resource bundles, in that "size" and "time" can create core rigidities, reduced experimentation, reduced incentive intensity, increased strategic transparency, and inflexibility (Mosakowski, 2002). These features limit the ability of established firms to quickly and consistently identify opportunities as they surface in the external environment. Therefore, managing resources effectively to verify that the firm is "doing the right things" to leverage its resource bundle in ways that foster the identification of opportunities is critical for competitive success in larger, established organizations.

Hitt et al. (2001) argued that entrepreneurship is about creation (i.e., exploration) while strategic management is about how competitive advantages are established and maintained in order to benefit from what the firm has created (i.e., exploitation). Building on this earlier work, Ireland et al. (2003) modeled strategic entrepreneurship, which they defined as the taking of entrepreneurial action through use of a strategic perspective.

Herein, we rely on resource-based theory to extend the Ireland et al. (2003) strategic entrepreneurship model in order to describe the use of international entrepreneurship (in the form of an international entrepreneurship strategy) as a means of competing successfully in emerging economies. To do this, we first specify emerging economies' unique attributes. We do this first largely because others have argued that variables moderate the relationship between entrepreneurship and some other construct. For example, Covin and Slevin (1989) and Luthans et al. (2000) have reported that the relationship between entrepreneurial posture and firm performance is moderated by external variables. Next, we integrate the management of resources (Sirmon and Hitt, 2003) into the context of using entrepreneurial actions in emerging economies. Resulting from this effort is a set of activities through which small, entrepreneurial ventures and large, established firms can manage resources in *relatively more* efficient and *relatively more* effective manners, respectively. We argue that concentrating on or emphasizing either resource efficiency (in small, entrepreneurial ventures) or resource effectiveness (in larger, more established firms) increases the probability that firms will be able to successfully use entrepreneurial action as a means of competing in emerging economies. *Resource efficiency* is concerned with using the firm's resources to *do things right* to create competitive advantages while *resource effectiveness* is concerned with using the firm's resources to *do the right things* so that the firm is able to consistently identify entrepreneurial opportunities.

Our analysis focuses on an *emphasis* of either resource efficiency or resource effectiveness – not the exclusive use of either. Indeed, both resource efficiency and resource effectiveness are linked to firm success. Our purpose is to describe how an appropriate emphasis on resource efficiency or resource effectiveness within either small entrepreneurial ventures or larger, established firms allows each type of firm to improve its ability to simultaneously exploit current advantages while exploring for future advantages in ways that maximize the probability of successfully using entrepreneurial actions when competing in emerging economies.

Complexities Associated with International Entrepreneurial Activities in Emerging Economies

Numerous environmental conditions create uncertainties for firms undertaking entrepreneurial activities in emerging economies. These uncertainties are derived primarily from economic, social, and political instabilities (Zahra et al., 2000a). With respect to economic instabilities, high interest rates, restrictive taxation policies, and inflation that occurred in Asia, South America, and Mexico during the last decade are examples of instabilities that create uncertainties (Luthans et al., 2000). In these instances, firms with less than ample financial capital may not be able to effectively explore for and then exploit identified entrepreneurial opportunities in promising, yet volatile, emerging economies. The reason for this is that the cost of failure for firms without ample financial capital can be catastrophic. Social instabilities, a second source of environmental uncertainty, develop from various situations including the lack of qualified workers, office space, and reliably delivered utilities (Paradine, 1996). In emerging economies characterized by social instabilities, firms requiring specific knowledge and skills may find it too difficult or cost prohibitive when seeking to develop the levels of intellectual capital required for competitive success. Additionally, some regions may lack the technological infrastructure that is needed to support a firm's human capital as it engages in various activities, including entrepreneurial activities. As witnessed in markets such as those in Yugoslavia and Kazakhstan, political complications are a third example of a potential source of uncertainty in emerging economies. These issues stem from multiple sources, such as considerable administrative discretion and corruption, few formal laws, and political upheavals (Luthans et al., 2000; Mueller and Goic, 2002). Too much rapid, widespread change and overall environmental uncertainty in the norms and values institutionalized in an emerging economy's system of economic activity may stifle an organization's ability to learn through experience, inhibiting necessary organizational transformation and, consequently, the effectiveness of entrepreneurial activities (Newman, 2000).

An additional factor increasing the complexity of operating in emerging economies is the fact that these economies are in different stages of development, stem from different sociocultural roots or political systems, and have undergone different patterns of transition (Mueller and Goic, 2002). In combination, these conditions suggest that firms seeking to engage in international entrepreneurship in emerging economies should expect to encounter difficulties if they were to try to apply what they have learned in one economy to other emerging economies. In slightly different words, the outcomes of organizational learning may be idiosyncratic to individual cultures.

Complexity also exists for firms competing in non-domestic economies in having to cope with liabilities of foreignness (Johanson and Vahlne, 1977; Zaheer, 1995; Zaheer and Mosakowski, 1997), which are costs associated with a firm's lack of familiarity with a new environment as well as the costs incurred to coordinate the management of resources over larger spatial distances. Liabilities of foreignness also stem from external factors, including a lack of legitimacy in foreign countries, economic nationalism, and restrictions placed on the firm by its host country. A lack of legitimacy can inhibit a firm's ability to form productive relationships – relationships with potential to lead to valuable, market-specific knowledge – with emerging economy organizations. However, even if these types of relationships can be formed, institutionalized restrictions in an emerging economy can dilute an identified opportunity's value by engendering financial limitations or social liabilities. Thus, non-domestic firms facing these types of liabilities of foreignness are competitively disadvantaged relative to local companies (Zaheer, 1995).

Despite the multiple uncertainties and disadvantages of international entrepreneurship in emerging economies, vast opportunities also exist. Indeed, although unpredictable changes in the external environment create uncertainty, these changes simultaneously create new and perhaps novel information flows, resulting in knowledge of new entrepreneurial opportunities (Shane and Venkataraman, 2000). Firms capable of dynamically managing their resource bundles are more favorably positioned to overcome environmental uncertainty and liabilities of foreignness and to identify entrepreneurial opportunities.

We suggest that competitive advantages flow from the successful management of three characteristics of a resource bundle – appropriate levels of financial slack, strategic flexibility, and the ability to innovate. The value of ample financial capital has been suggested in several venues. Financial slack enables a firm to absorb environmental shocks. In addition, financial slack allows the firm to absorb the costs of ineffective organizational actions taken to innovate and to develop the skills needed to flexibly respond to environmental conditions (Sharfman et al., 1988). Evans and Leighton (1989) also suggested that entrepreneurs are more willing to accept the risks of exploiting entrepreneurial opportunities when they have access to greater financial capital. To exploit competitive advantages, firms must also develop strategic flexibility by constantly renewing their knowledge stocks and by increasing their awareness of potential environmental changes. When strategically flexible, firms are better able to adaptively exploit opportunities stemming from environmental changes (Hitt and Reed, 2000). Enhancing innovation by developing diverse sets of knowledge (Nonaka, 1994) that are capable of absorbing and integrating new information flows (Cohen and Levinthal, 1990) also contributes to the formation of new competitive advantages. Moreover, continuously using diverse knowledge sets increases the likelihood that bisociation will occur. Bisociation is the development of novel combinations of information that can then be exploited (Koestler, 1964; Smith and Di Gregorio, 2002). Using novel combinations of information can lead to new competitive advantages.

In the next section, we examine the key resources needed to support the effective use of international entrepreneurship in emerging economies.

Resources and the Use of International Entrepreneurship in Emerging Economies

Financial capital

Financial capital is the money available to the firm from both internal and external sources. In younger, entrepreneurial firms, internal financial capital can be pulled from a number of sources, such as founders' savings and equity contributions, while external financial capital is the money available from trade credit, bank loans, and equity from outside investors, friends, and relatives (Chandler and Hanks, 1998). Larger, established organizations have greater access to external financial capital in the form of long-term debt and equity markets (Davidson and Dutia, 1991).

The organizational slack provided by ample levels of financial capital acts as a buffer to changes in the external environment, conditions created by internal fluctuations, and organizational failures. Moreover, because it can be used to acquire other resources, ample financial capital offers the highest levels of strategic flexibility, which in turn, is linked to successful innovation efforts and competition in emerging markets (Sharfman et al., 1988). Moreover, ample financial resources enable a firm to identify and exploit opportunities arising from new information flows (Ireland et al., 2003).

Although financial capital supports innovation, as noted above, too much financial capital may hinder a firm's innovation capabilities, in that too much financial slack can create complacency and a lack of discipline in using innovations to pursue environmental opportunities (Nohria and Gulati, 1996). Thus, the value of financial capital is maximized when it is allocated to support *effectiveness* (to allow the firm to take actions through which entrepreneurial opportunities will be identified) and *efficiency* (to allow the firm to take actions to develop the competitive advantages needed to exploit identified opportunities) (Webb et al., 2004).

Human capital

Human capital is the value of all the knowledge and skills owned or controlled by a firm (Hitt and Ireland, 2002). Human capital can be divided into two subcategories – intellectual capital and structural capital. Intellectual capital is the sum of employees' educations, experiences, specific identifiable skills, and the resulting value created within a firm, possibly through patents or some other form of trade secret. Structural capital signifies the value of information technologies that securely store and transmit the intellectual capital, enabling the efficient use of knowledge within the firm (Hitt and Ireland, 2002). Jointly, these asset stocks act as a fundamental driver of firm success on multiple levels. For example, human capital enables a firm to innovate efficiently (Loch et al., 1996), provides strategic flexibility (Hitt and Reed, 2000), enhances a firm's capacity to identify attractive opportunities (Davidsson and Honig, 2003; Shane and Venkataraman, 2000), increases a firm's ability to recognize value from new information and apply it to commercial ends (Cohen and Levinthal, 1990), and is associated with higher levels of profitability (Zirger and Maidique, 1990). Nevertheless, there may exist an optimal level of human capital (Webb et al., 2004), and a firm can over invest in its own human capital. The possibility of over investing in human capital suggests that as a resource, human capital should be allocated to support both *efficiency* and *effectiveness*, and, as is discussed next, that its ability to create value is maximized when this happens.

Social capital

Social capital is the "the set of resources, tangible or virtual that accrue to an actor through the actor's social relationships, facilitating the attainment of goals" (Knoke, 1999, p. 2). Social capital is an asset that is embedded in relationships (Liao and Welsch, 2003). There are two primary subcategories of social capital. Internal social capital consists of the relationships existing within the firm, adding value to the firm by facilitating interunit resource exchange, the creation of human capital, and cross-functional team effectiveness (Adler and Kwon, 2002). External social capital represents the value of all the linkages between the firm and outside entities such as individuals, other firms, universities, or financial institutions. In the case of external social capital, value is derived from strengthened supplier relations, greater and quicker accessibility to new markets, technologies, skills, and financial capital, and a reputation of legitimacy (Adler and Kwon, 2002). Both human capital and social capital contribute to efficiency and effectiveness. However, on a relative basis, human capital enhances the firm's ability to innovate efficiently while social capital enhances the firm's ability to innovate effectively (Loch et al., 1996). Nevertheless, as with financial and human capital, social capital can become a liability if a firm over invests in this asset, suggesting that its value is maximized when it is allocated to support *efficiency* and *effectiveness* (Anand, 2002; Webb et al., 2004).

Resource symbiosis

Although financial capital, human capital, and social capital are each valuable to the performance of a firm engaging in international entrepreneurship in an emerging economy, there are relationships among them that can increase or decrease the value of future investments into each of these resources (Webb et al., 2004). Understanding and managing the symbiotic relationships among financial, human, and social capital increases the likelihood the firm will be able to successfully use international entrepreneurship to compete in emerging economies.

Absorptive capacity and bounded rationality mediate the value of the firm's investments in its bundles of resources. Recently, Zahra and George (2002a, p. 185) conceptualized absorptive capacity as "a dynamic capability pertaining to knowledge creation and utilization that enhances a firm's ability to gain and sustain a competitive advantage." Absorptive capacity and bounded rationality are both important to our work in that understanding symbiotic relationships among resources facilitates the firm's efforts to invest in and structure its future resource bundles in forming competitive advantages. In dynamic, uncertain emerging economies, for example, where firms are subjected to significant quantities of disparate types of information, the ability to handle and integrate resource investments to adequately support efficiency and effectiveness, absorbing valuable knowledge and discarding insignificant information in the process of doing so, creates needed flexibility and leads to the forming of competitive advantages.

As a characteristic of a firm's existing human capital, absorptive capacity mediates the value of future investments in human capital and social capital (Cohen and Levinthal, 1990; Tsai, 2001) that are made to help the firm establish and sustain competitive advantages. Existing levels of human capital facilitate the absorption and integration of new knowledge. A firm's human capital must have the available capacity to absorb a certain volume of information as well as a level of requisite variety to absorb new diverse knowledge (Cohen and Levinthal, 1990; Nonaka, 1994). If a firm does not have the absorptive capacity to integrate knowledge garnered from a social network, the firm's investment in that network may not generate optimal value. For example, firms engaging in international entrepreneurship in non-domestic, emerging economies must possess both the technical knowledge needed to develop innovations that are appropriate to the markets they are serving as well as the skills required to market (i.e., to distribute and support) the use of those innovations in a culturally sensitive manner. If the firm lacks appropriate levels of technical and marketing-related knowledge, it may have a deficit in the ability of its human capital to absorb external knowledge. If this is the case, additional investments in the firm's human capital may be needed to further develop its absorptive capacity so it can gain the skills needed to innovate and successfully market the products resulting from the innovations.

Because of bounded rationality, individuals do not have the time or the mental capacity to absorb and fully evaluate every potential consequence of each possible new resource combination (Simon, 1982a; 1982b). This is especially true in emerging economies where firms constantly experience significant external environmental changes, but do not have the time to fully analyze each and every change. Bounded rationality stems from both the volume of available information as well as from the pieces of information that are not readily present (Dequech, 2001). In cases in which firms perceive a gap in the knowledge required to effectively innovate, they can choose to undertake a search for new information at an unknown cost – of financial and social capital – and for an indefinite period of time to complement existing knowledge stocks (Dequech, 2001). However, these actions could potentially affect the quality of the firm's decisions as well if it is unable to acquire the necessary knowledge resources at an acceptable cost. On the other hand, the firm could pursue opportunities by utilizing heuristics or routines gained from experience, but this has the potential to introduce errors or biases (Augier et al., 2001). This second option could potentially be destructive in emerging economies because the context of past experiences leading to routines and heuristics within a firm may be drastically different compared to the firm's current context due to frequent, widespread changes in the external environment. Therefore, some routines may not remain applicable for extended periods of time for firms using international entrepreneurship as a means of competing in emerging economies.

Managing Resources while Using International Entrepreneurship in Emerging Economies

As we noted previously, on a relative basis, small, entrepreneurial ventures are more effective than larger, established firms in terms of identifying new opportunities. In contrast, large, established organizations, compared to smaller entrepreneurial ventures, are relatively less skilled in exploring for entrepreneurial opportunities, but relatively more skilled in terms of developing competitive advantages to exploit identified opportunities. Relatively, then, we argue that small entrepreneurial ventures using international entrepreneurship in emerging economies should emphasize resource efficiency (which is concerned with using financial capital, human capital, and social capital to create and exploit competitive advantages) when managing its resources. This "resource efficient" approach to managing resources focuses on "doing things right" (i.e., concentrating on exploiting resources to form and use competitive advantages). In contrast, larger, established firms using international entrepreneurship in emerging economies should emphasize resource effectiveness (which is concerned with using financial capital, human capital, and social capital to explore entrepreneurial opportunities) when managing its resources. This "resource

Table 4.1 Resource management in international entrepreneurship

To increase	Financial capital	Human capital	Social capital
Resource effectiveness (Exploration – A greater emphasis for large firms)	Acquire additional funds to support boundary spanning activities	Further develop intellectual capital	Emphasize the use of external social capital
Resource efficiency (Exploitation – A greater emphasis for small firms)	Use financial controls to ensure efficient use of available financial capital	Emphasize structural capital	Emphasize the use of internal social capital

effectiveness" approach to managing the firm's resources focuses on "doing the right things" (i.e., concentrating on exploring for entrepreneurial opportunities). Symbiotically managing their resources in these ways finds small entrepreneurial ventures using their resources to complement their inherent exploration skills and larger, established firms managing their resources to complement their well-developed exploitation skills.

We highlight the actions smaller and larger firms should take to symbiotically manage their resources in Table 4.1. The actions in each part in Table 4.1 do not imply exclusivity. In other words, every firm must simultaneously manage its total set of financial, human, and social capital to create value while engaging in marketplace competition. Thus, our argument is that the contents of each part in Table 4.1 present actions for which there is a *greater* need of focus in order to enhance a firm's capabilities in terms of either exploration (in the instance of larger, established organizations) or exploitation (in the case of smaller, entrepreneurial ventures) when using international entrepreneurship to compete in emerging economies. For example, while further development of intellectual capital (through training, for example) should be the primary focus of human capital investments during the exploration phase, structural capital investments will also be necessary to support the intellectual capital, although these investments will be comparatively less significant to the creation of optimal resource effectiveness. However, for firms seeking to more efficiently manage their resources, in order to improve their exploitation skills, structural capital should be emphasized.

Next, we discuss how the component parts of an entrepreneurial orientation (mindset, culture, and leadership) affect the management of resources in ways that facilitate organizations' efforts to successfully use their resource bundle when relying on entrepreneurial actions as a means of pursuing competitive success in emerging economies.

Entrepreneurial orientation

Although conducted simultaneously, exploration and exploitation consist of two distinct sets of actions that, in many cases, necessitate use of common resources owned or controlled by the firm (March, 1991). Because of a number of factors, exploratory functions in larger, established firms tend to be less effective compared to those in smaller, entrepreneurial ventures. Structures, strategy, and on-going routines in established firms consistently counteract forces to innovate, thereby stifling creativity (Burgelman, 1983; Dougherty and Hardy, 1996; Hannan and Freeman, 1984). For example, a segmentalist orientation in established firms leads managers to dissect and distribute tasks to individual units rather than foster organization-wide collaboration (Dougherty and Hardy, 1996; Hlavacek and Thompson, 1973). Similarly, reward systems punish individuals who fail to focus on their established responsibilities (Dougherty and Hardy, 1996), and organizational routines limit communication between various functional units (Dougherty, 1990). These characteristics call for larger, established organizations using international entrepreneurship in emerging economies to adopt a "resource-effective" approach in order to boost exploration and create a greater balance with their complementary, well-developed exploitative (i.e., efficiency oriented) competencies. Exploration is equally important to the success of smaller, entrepreneurial firms. However, in these companies, human and social capital characteristics enable successful exploration efforts, meaning that on a relative basis, the resource-effective approach is more applicable to the large firm. The intent in the large firm is to form or mimic the entrepreneurial venture or smaller firms' characteristics that enable them to identify opportunities and flexibly redirect resources in directions suggested by them.

Firms with an entrepreneurial orientation, or "the processes, practices, and decision-making activities that lead to new entry" (Lumpkin and Dess, 1996, p. 136), excel in terms of exploration. However, we believe that an entrepreneurial orientation also benefits the firm seeking to develop a competitively relevant balance between exploration and exploitation when allocating resources in its resource bundle. In slightly different words, an entrepreneurial orientation facilitates decision makers' efforts to explain to others in the firm that resources must be used to support both exploration and exploitation and that in certain instances, resources must be allocated in a manner that emphasizes either exploration or exploitation. An entrepreneurial orientation is characterized by five dimensions – autonomy provided to individuals or teams within a firm, the propensity for the firm to engage in and support innovativeness, affinity for risk-taking behavior, the tendency for proactiveness towards future needs or changes, and the competitive aggressiveness of the firm (Lumpkin and Dess, 1996). An entrepreneurial orientation tends to form in organizations characterized by an entrepreneurial mindset, entrepreneurial culture, and entrepreneurial leadership (Ireland et al., 2003).

Entrepreneurial mindset

An entrepreneurial mindset is a growth-oriented perspective that takes advantage of uncertainty and change by promoting flexibility, creativity, continuous innovation, and renewal (Ireland et al., 2003). This approach requires a reallocation of knowledge responsibilities in established organizations to enhance the entrepreneurial alertness of the firm. Entrepreneurial alertness is a superior insight in recognizing valuable opportunities (Alvarez and Barney, 2002; Kirzner, 1997), and it is enhanced through knowledge of the general environment (McGrath and MacMillan, 2000). The superior insight resulting from one being entrepreneurially alert often occurs in organizations and individuals possessing an entrepreneurial mindset. In other words, developing a growth-oriented perspective to frame how one views uncertainty and the opportunities resulting from it increases the likelihood of both organizations and individuals becoming entrepreneurially alert.

As a fundamental component for creating an entrepreneurial mindset, an opportunity register is a structural component of human capital in which a firm's identified opportunities are recorded (McGrath and MacMillan, 2000). By providing an intra-firm view of opportunities, it enables a group in one area to potentially exploit prospective knowledge identified in another (Ireland et al., 2003). In addition, the register provides a framework that a firm can employ for balancing resource investments in multiple opportunities, thereby minimizing waste, increasing the likelihood of identifying the *right* opportunity, and enhancing strategic flexibility (Ireland et al., 2003; Mosakowski, 2002).

For large firms undertaking entrepreneurial efforts in emerging economies, there are two primary avenues of organizational learning for enhancing entrepreneurial alertness – human capital and external social capital enhancements. The advantages gained from organizational learning have been found to be equally important to companies launching international ventures as they are to firms with on-going operations in non-domestic venues (Luo and Peng, 1999). However, the optimal learning method is dependent upon existing knowledge stocks and financial resources and the dynamic uncertainty of the environment. As one form of organizational learning, human capital can be increased through operating in the emerging economy for a period of time, with a diversity of experience facilitating entrepreneurship in hostile, dynamic environments and long-term experience assisting actions taken in hostile, complex climates (Luo and Peng, 1999). The length of experience enables firms to identify valuable market segments and product-differentiating features (Luo and Peng, 1999; Mitchell et al., 1992). This experience offsets some of the liabilities of foreignness that affect firms competing in foreign economies, enabling them to identify valuable opportunities specific to an emerging economy. Diversity in experience exposes the firm to vast knowledge bases that enhance the breadth of its opportunity register (Luo and Peng, 1999).

The ability to create enhanced human capital stocks is dependent on the firm's available slack resources and the uncertainty of the external environment (Webb et al., 2004). In markets that are highly unstable and dynamic, a firm may opt to undertake organizational learning by obtaining external social capital (Dimitratos and Plakoyiannaki, 2003; Ireland et al., 2003). Forming partnerships with local firms facilitates knowledge acquisition and strengthens a firm's performance in foreign ventures (Makino and Delios, 1996; Peng, 2001b). In addition, especially in emerging economies where formal institutional constraints are weak, interpersonal ties may facilitate economic exchange and increase firm performance (Peng, 2001b; Peng and Heath, 1996). Nevertheless, the ability for a firm to absorb and utilize knowledge acquired from local partners will depend on the existing absorptive capacity and bounded rationality of the firm's human capital (Cohen and Levinthal, 1990; Dequech, 2001).

Entrepreneurial culture and leadership

Organizational culture consists of shared values and beliefs that establish behavioral norms within a firm, forming accepted, unseen guidelines for communication, expectations, and other organizational functions (Dess and Picken, 1999; Ireland et al., 2003). Entrepreneurial leaders are responsible for forming and nurturing an organizational culture that embraces entrepreneurial actions. This type of culture, which is called an entrepreneurial culture, embodies continual, organization-wide searches for new opportunities and renewal of the business (Covin and Slevin, 1991; McGrath and MacMillan, 2000). Thus, entrepreneurial leaders are individuals who lead others in ways that result in continuous identification and exploitation of opportunities (Covin and Slevin, 2002).

As the previous comments suggest, an effective entrepreneurial leader works to form a culture in which opportunity-seeking and advantage-seeking behaviors are appropriately emphasized. In general, and as we have noted, actions on which larger, established firms tend to concentrate are concerned with developing competitive advantages. Therefore, entrepreneurial leaders in these firms need to re-balance human capital and internal social capital assets as well as financial resources to adjust the organizational culture so that it will support appropriate levels of the more entrepreneurial, opportunity-seeking behaviors in a setting in which advantage-seeking behaviors are dominant. This can be a difficult task, in that pursuing entrepreneurial opportunities tends to be a resource-intensive process with uncertain, often long-term benefits (Covin and Slevin, 1991; Romanelli, 1987). Additionally, in many cases this process requires the same resources as advantage-seeking behaviors (McGrath and MacMillan, 2000). In contrast, the entrepreneurial leader in a small entrepreneurial venture may need to adjust the allocations of the venture's resources so the culture will support advantage-seeking behaviors in a setting in which opportunity-seeking behaviors are typically dominant.

To enhance the firm's ability to properly emphasize different resources, entrepreneurial leaders must provide vision, knowledge assets, financial resources, and trust to assist in forming an entrepreneurial culture, increasing the value of the firm's internal social capital while doing so (Chandler, Keller and Lyon, 2000; Covin and Slevin, 1991). A vision enhances a firm's efforts by motivating individuals and honing their actions on common, distinct opportunities. An opportunity register can expand the entrepreneurial leader's bounded rationality, thereby enabling the design of a more compelling vision (McGrath and MacMillan, 2000). In addition, a firm's highly talented human capital must be reassigned from advantage-seeking behaviors to opportunity-seeking behaviors in order to fully explore potential opportunities and to signal the importance of opportunity-seeking behaviors to all parts of the firm's stock of human capital (McGrath and MacMillan, 2000). These individuals must also have the support of other human resources, information, and materials because a lack of resources can decrease the perceived value of projects and consequently lead to a reduction in commitment (Chandler et al., 2000). Likewise, financial resources are necessary to sustain the simultaneous exploration of some opportunities and exploitation of others, and they are an important resource for funding incentive rewards for creative and innovative behaviors (Chandler, 1993;

Chandler et al., 2000; McGrath and MacMillan, 2000). Trust is derived from a longer-term effect. It is formed by consistent actions and constant communication from the entrepreneurial leader (Leana and Van Buren, 1999), aiding to overcome uncertainty in the vision of the firm and in the external environment. Over time, trust facilitates efforts to form an entrepreneurial culture, one that supports the risk-taking, proactive, autonomous, innovative behaviors required by an entrepreneurial orientation.

Managing Resources Strategically for Competitive Advantage in Emerging Economies

Both large established organizations and small entrepreneurial ventures encounter difficulties in managing resources. These difficulties surface in large firms from the inability to acquire and bundle resources quickly and effectively as well as from their large resource endowments. An entrepreneurial orientation facilitates the large firm's efforts to identify opportunities. However, the inertia that can be associated with a larger, established firm's resources and the subsequent competitive advantages might stifle or hinder exploration efforts. Secondary to creating an entrepreneurial orientation that enables a firm to react effectively, large firms need to evaluate and bundle resources in an efficient manner. For the large firm, this implies decreasing core rigidities and increasing strategic transparency (Mosakowski, 2002), thereby creating more flexibility and agility so the large firm can take advantage of changes in dynamic, uncertain environments such as those epitomized by non-domestic, emerging economies.

Smaller entrepreneurial ventures or firms possess many of the structural characteristics that facilitate an entrepreneurial orientation. Because of their smaller size, for example, communication within these firms is more rapid, enabling them to be proactive and aggressive by allowing a quicker mobilization of resources. The small entrepreneurial firm's flatter hierarchy provides autonomy to both individuals and work teams, increasing their tendency for risk-taking behavior and propensity for innovativeness. On the other hand, entrepreneurial ventures or firms commonly lack the resources necessary to compete (Calof, 1993), possibly due to liabilities of newness or adolescence (Freeman et al., 1983; Hannan and Freeman, 1984; Levinthal and Fichman, 1988; Stinchcombe, 1965). Therefore, to improve their competitiveness, entrepreneurial organizations must emphasize the efficiency of using resources in order to develop competitive advantages required to pursue what may be a large set of identified opportunities.

Managing resources is a process of three simultaneous, continual activities – structuring the resource portfolio, bundling resources and capabilities, and leveraging these resources and capabilities to exploit opportunities (Sirmon and Hitt, 2003; Sirmon et al., 2004). The entrepreneurial leader and the firm's internal social capital are major factors in the success of the resource management activities. For both large and smaller entrepreneurial firms, taking entrepreneurial actions in dynamic, uncertain environments such as emerging economies can be stressful, and many resource management activities create substantial changes to the firm, adding to this stress.

The ability of the entrepreneurial leader to create a vision that is shared within the entirety of an organization's entrepreneurial culture greatly enhances the firm's ability to create value through managing resources.

Structuring resources

The activity of structuring the resource portfolio can be further broken down into the acquisition (Barney, 1986; Denrell, Fang and Winter, 2003; Makadok, 2001), accumulation (Dierickx and Cool, 1989; Thomke and Kuemmerle, 2002), and divestiture of resources (Sirmon et al., 2004). Each of these actions is a viable option for competing under environmental uncertainty, and the choice should be driven by knowledge gathered in the exploration phase. Resource structuring in the large firm should be focused on streamlining competencies to take advantage of arising entrepreneurial opportunities. On the other hand, in the smaller, entrepreneurial firm, the lack of necessary resources to compete requires an efficient search for and integration of additional resources. These actions are facilitated in both firms by an understanding of the symbiotic relationships between a firm's knowledge assets and its financial capital. A firm is limited by its absorptive capacity in the amount and type of knowledge it can absorb and integrate with existing knowledge stocks (Cohen and Levinthal, 1990). In addition, because of bounded rationality, firms with ample absorptive capacity can only integrate so much knowledge due to time constraints, meaning that entrepreneurial leaders must use heuristics as templates to construct decisions (Dequech, 2001). Firms should only acquire and accumulate those resources that can be integrated and that can complement existing knowledge stocks and financial capital in the pursuit of an entrepreneurial opportunity. Because emerging economies are dynamic and unstable, firms should focus on acquiring knowledge of the highest quality and lowest quantity, thereby enhancing the firm's strategic flexibility.

More likely in the large firm is the necessity to divest non-performing, excess assets. Large firms have a tendency to be plagued by core rigidities, impeding their ability to mobilize resources quickly and effectively. Core rigidities result from routines in the firm derived from past successes and the assets leading to those successes (Leonard-Barton, 1992; Mosakowski, 2002). Although transitions occur in the external environment, firms are often unwilling to pull assets from the activities supporting successful advantage-seeking behaviors in order to reallocate them to support uncertain, opportunity-seeking behaviors. This reluctance eventually leads to competitive disadvantage.

A lack of strategic transparency also hinders value-creating activities in larger, established organizations. As with core rigidities, this stems from the firm's larger resource endowments, although the resources creating strategic transparency may in some instances be valuable to the firm's current strategy (Mosakowski, 2002). While these resources guide the firm in its advantage-seeking behaviors, they also enhance the ability of competitors to predict and disrupt its future behaviors. To minimize the disadvantages associated with large resource endowments, large firms should divest any asset stock not pertinent to sustaining their *future* competitive advantage. This process should both decrease the strategic transparency of the firm and provide it with greater amounts of slack and flexibility to cope with environmental changes in the emerging economy (Sirmon et al., 2004; Sirmon and Hitt, 2003); however, without appropriate communication and an effective entrepreneurial culture, these actions can lead to uncertainty and a lack of trust, decreasing the value of the firm's internal social capital (Leana and Van Buren, 1999).

Bundling resources and capabilities

After the firm has identified an appropriate resource structure, it must integrate its resources in a process of resource bundling for the purpose of performing one or more activities. Stabilizing, enriching, and pioneering are the three initiatives in this process. Stabilizing involves incrementally combining new knowledge assets with current capabilities (Sirmon et al., 2004). This option is favorable for emerging economies experiencing slower transitions, as the firm makes only minor investments in current resources bundles with the intent of exploiting extensions of a current strategy while providing the resource flexibility to simultaneously explore other entrepreneurial opportunities. Enriching involves a heavier resource investment than stabilizing for combining knowledge and skills with current capabilities. This can be undertaken by bolstering the firm's human capital internally or through tapping external social networks. Because individual firms, large and small alike, do not possess the resource scope to explore and exploit every entrepreneurial opportunity alone, alliances and other external ties can provide firms with the necessary pipeline of knowledge and skills for competing in dynamic, uncertain environments (George et al., 2001), which can then be used to enrich current capabilities to accommodate potential transitions. Whereas stabilizing and enriching are more appropriate for dealing with incremental innovations, pioneering is the more suitable resource bundling process for handling radical innovations. In this context, pioneering finds firms forming completely new resources and capabilities to exploit opportunities entirely isolated from the firm's current strategy (Sirmon et al., 2004). Although the risks inherent to pioneering can be mediated by using real options, the entrepreneurial leader must maintain a shared vision and entrepreneurial culture while simultaneously avoiding an escalation of commitment should trends change in the emerging economy.

A firm operating entrepreneurially in an emerging economy where transitions are frequent should simultaneously undertake stabilizing, enriching, and pioneering activities. The simultaneity of these activities places the firm in a favorable position to continuously renew current competencies as well as to quickly take advantage of arising opportunities. Firms capable of doing this have learned how to balance the allocation and use of their resources to promote the firm's effectiveness and efficiency as it engages in competitive contests.

Leveraging resource and capability bundles

The process of leveraging resources consists of two primary activities: coordinating and deploying. Coordination is concerned with the activities taken to integrate resource and capability bundles while deployment entails the physical use of these integrated bundles to exploit an opportunity.

Large firms have two distinct advantages over younger, new ventures in the leveraging process. Large firms have developed routines enabling them to effectively and efficiently coordinate resource and capability bundles (Alvarez and Barney, 2002; Sirmon et al., 2004). In addition, because of constrained resource stocks, smaller, new ventures lack the flexibility allowed by slack resources to experiment in coordination and deployment. This is especially true in an uncertain, dynamic environment epitomized by emerging economies where experimentation may not always lend knowledge for future successful actions because of continuous environmental changes. Therefore, for smaller firms to gain competitive advantage in pursuing entrepreneurial opportunities in emerging economies, they must enhance their skills that permit the efficient use of resource bundles.

A resource-efficient approach to leveraging resource and capability bundles entails the small, new venture taking actions necessary to imitate the large firm's routines. Because these routines more than likely stem from tacit, contextual knowledge, the necessary capabilities may not be readily obtainable through internal investments in intellectual capital, and may be a product of experience only (Nonaka, 1994). Emerging economies are characterized by constantly changing conditions; therefore, the small, new venture probably does not have the time to develop this experiential knowledge and must tap external ties in order to capture the knowledge needed to leverage resources and capabilities. External social capital can provide the small, entrepreneurial venture with access to the knowledge of multiple, different experiences valuable to coordinating and deploying resources and capabilities (Hitt et al., 1999). Consequently, the small firm will be able to focus on leveraging resources and capabilities in an appropriate (that is, efficient) manner rather than haphazardly experimenting with coordination and deployment processes.

The development of internal social capital and structural human capital elements can facilitate the communication and understanding of this experiential knowledge within the small firm (Hitt and Ireland, 2002; Hunter et al., 2002), enhancing its capacity to create its own routines for leveraging resources and capabilities. An opportunity register is one structural human capital element for providing a shared vision and direction during the exploration phase. As human capital and social capital investments develop, these opportunities should be removed from the opportunity register and re-listed in an advantage register. Whereas the opportunity register facilitates decision making and offers guidance for opportunity-seeking behaviors, the advantage register acts to provide clarity for the direction of advantage-seeking behaviors during the exploitation phase. Beneficial to any firm, an advantage register is especially vital to the entrepreneurial venture competing in emerging economies where environmental transitions are frequent. The advantage register is a structural human capital component evolving from promising investments within the opportunity register. By delineating a specific target and the necessary resource structuring and leveraging actions that will be needed to take advantage of this target to all employees, a common vision can be formed. The entrepreneurial leader must convey this vision with constant, consistent communication as well. Consequently, this shared vision can facilitate greater agility and flexibility in structuring and mobilizing resources efficiently.

Conclusions

Our arguments offer a perspective for large established firms as well as smaller entrepreneurial ventures. Firms should consider these arguments when considering how to use entrepreneurial actions to successfully compete in emerging economies. We have described the roles of financial capital, human capital, and social capital in exploring for and exploiting entrepreneurial opportunities. While certain resource bundles are necessary to flexibly accommodate the identification of entrepreneurial opportunities in the dynamic uncertainty associated with emerging economies, other resource bundles are more appropriate for undertaking entrepreneurial efforts in an international context. Through their existing resource bundles, large and small firms have developed different competencies that enhance their competitive advantage in different phases of international entrepreneurship efforts. Large firms, for example, own ample financial resources and have a wealth of experiential knowledge with established routines – characteristics that are vital to exploiting opportunities. On the other hand, because of their size, smaller, entrepreneurial ventures can more quickly and flexibly identify opportunities while engaging in exploration activities. These firms must complement their respective resource bundles and resulting skills with the resources needed to overcome their inherent disadvantage with respect to either exploration or exploitation. To efficiently and effectively manage resources, both the larger, established firm and the smaller, entrepreneurial venture must have an understanding of the symbiotic relationships existing among financial capital, human capital, and social capital. The strategic challenge is to balance the allocation of either the larger, established organization's or the entrepreneurial venture's resource bundles (as noted by its financial capital, human capital, and social capital) in ways that support an appropriate, simultaneous, and consistent emphasis on opportunity-seeking and advantage-seeking behaviors.

References

Adler, P., and Kwon, S-W. 2002. Social capital: Prospects for a new concept. *Academy of Management Review*, 27: 17–40.

Alvarez, S. A., and Barney, J. B. 2002. Resource-based theory and the entrepreneurial firm. In M. A. Hitt, R. D. Ireland, S. M. Camp, and D. L. Sexton (Eds.), *Strategic Entrepreneurship: Creating a New Mindset*. Oxford: Blackwell, 89–105.

Anand, V. 2002. Thriving on the knowledge of outsiders: Tapping organizational social capital. *Academy of Management Executive*, 16(1): 87–101.

Augier, M., Shariq, S. Z., and Vendelo, M. T. 2001. Understanding context: Its emergence, transformation and role in tacit knowledge sharing. *Journal of Knowledge Management*, 5: 125–36.

Autio, E., Sapienza, H. J., and Almeida, J. G. 2000. Effects of age at entry, knowledge intensity, and imitability on international growth. *Academy of Management Journal*, 43: 909–24.

Barney, J. B. 1986. Strategic factor markets: Expectations, luck, and business strategy. *Management Science*, 32: 1231–41.

Barney, J. B. 1991. Firm resources and sustained competitive advantage. *Journal of Management*, 17: 99–120.

Bergh, D. D. 2001. Diversification strategy research at a crossroads: Established, emerging and anticipated paths. In M. A. Hitt, R. E. Freeman, and J. S. Harrison (Eds.), *Blackwell Handbook of Strategic Management*. Oxford: Blackwell, 362–83.

Bergmann-Lichtenstein, B. M., and Brush, C. G. 2001. How do "resource bundles" develop and change in new ventures? A dynamic model and longitudinal exploration. *Entrepreneurship Theory and Practice*, 25(3): 37–58.

Birkinshaw, J. 1997. Entrepreneurship in multinational corporations: The characteristics of subsidiary initiatives. *Strategic Management Journal*, 18: 207–29.

Bloodgood, J. M., Sapienza, H. J., and Almeida, J. G. 1996. The internationalization of new high-potential U.S. ventures: Antecedents and outcomes. *Entrepreneurship Theory and Practice*, 20(4): 61–76.

Burgelman, R. 1983. Corporate entrepreneurship and strategic management: Insights from a process study. *Management Science*, 29: 1349–63.

Calof, J. G. 1993. The impact of size on internationalization. *Journal of Small Business Management*, 3(4): 60–9.

Chandler, G. N. 1993. Reward perceptions and the performance of emerging technology dependent and non-technology dependent manufacturing firms. *Journal of High Technology Management Research*, 4(1): 63–76.

Chandler, G. N., and Hanks, S. H. 1998. An examination of the substitutability of founders human and financial capital in emerging business ventures. *Journal of Business Venturing*, 13: 353–69.

Chandler, G. N., Keller, C., and Lyon, D. W. 2000. Unraveling the determinants and consequences of an innovative-supportive organizational culture. *Entrepreneurship Theory and Practice*, 25(1): 59–76.

Cohen, W., and Levinthal, D. 1990. Absorptive capacity: A new perspective on learning and innovation. *Administrative Science Quarterly*, 35: 128–52.

Covin, J. G., and Slevin, D. P. 1989. The strategic management of small firms in hostile and benign environments. *Strategic Management Journal*, 10: 75–87.

Covin, J. G., and Slevin, D. P. 1991. A conceptual model of entrepreneurship as firm behavior. *Entrepreneurship Theory and Practice*, 16(1): 7–25.

Covin, J. G., and Slevin, D. P. 2002. Entrepreneurial imperatives of leadership. In M. A. Hitt, R. D. Ireland, S. M. Camp and D. L. Sexton (Eds.). *Strategic Entrepreneurship: Creating a New Mindset*. Oxford: Blackwell, 309–42.

Davidson, W., and Dutia, D. 1991. Debt, liquidity, and profitability problems in small firms. *Entrepreneurship Theory and Practice*, 16(1): 53–64.

Davidsson, P., and Honig, B. 2003. The role of social and human capital among nascent entrepreneurs. *Journal of Business Venturing*, 18: 301–31.

Denrell, J., Fang, C., and Winter, S. G. 2003. The economics of strategic opportunity. *Strategic Management Journal*, 24: 977–90.

Dequech, D. 2001. Bounded rationality, institutions, and uncertainty. *Journal of Economic Issues*, 35: 911–29.

Dess, G. G., and Picken, J. C. 1999. *Beyond Productivity: How Leading Companies Achieve Superior Performance by Leveraging their Human Capital*. New York: AMACOM.

Dierickx, I., and Cool, K. 1989. Asset stock accumulation and sustainability of competitive advantage. *Management Science*, 35: 1504–13.

Dimitratos, P., and Plakoyiannaki, E. 2003. Theoretical foundations of an international entrepreneurial culture. *Journal of International Entrepreneurship*, 1: 187–215.

Dougherty, D. 1990. Understanding new markets for new products. *Strategic Management Journal*, 11: 59–78.

Dougherty, D., and Hardy, C. 1996. Sustained product innovation in large, mature organizations: Overcoming innovation-to-organization problems. *Academy of Management Journal*, 39: 1120–53.

Evans, D. S., and Leighton, L. S. 1989. Some empirical aspects of entrepreneurship. *American Economic Review*, 79: 519–35.

Franko, L. G. 1989. Global corporate competition: Who's winning, who's losing and the R&D factor as one reason why. *Strategic Management Journal*, 10: 449–74.

Freeman, J., Carroll, G. R., and Hannan, M. T. 1983. The liability of newness: Age dependence in organizational death rates. *American Sociological Review*, 48: 692–710.

George, G., Zahra, S. A., Wheatley, K. K., and Khan, R. 2001. The effects of alliance portfolio characteristics and absorptive capacity on performance: A study of biotechnology firms. *Journal of High Technology Management Research*, 12: 205–26.

Grant, R. M. 1996. Knowledge, strategy, and the theory of the firm. *Strategic Management Journal*, 17: 109–22.

Hannan, M. T., and Freeman, J. 1984. Structural inertia and organizational change. *American Sociological Review*, 49: 149–64.

Hitt, M. A., Bierman, L., Shimizu, K., and Kochhar, R. 2001. Direct and moderating effects of human capital on strategy and performance in professional service firms: A resource-based perspective. *Academy of Management Journal*, 44: 13–28.

Hitt, M. A., and Ireland, R. D. 2002. The essence of strategic leadership: Managing human and social capital. *Journal of Leadership and Organizational Studies*, 9(1): 3–14.

Hitt, M. A., Keats, B. W., and DeMarie, S. 1998. Navigating in the new competitive landscape: Building strategic flexibility and competitive advantage in the 21st century. *Academy of Management Executive*, 12(4): 22–42.

Hitt, M. A., Nixon, R. D., Hoskisson, R. E., and Kochhar, R. 1999. Corporate entrepreneurship and cross-functional fertilization: Activation, process and disintegration of a new product design team. *Entrepreneurship Theory and Practice*, 23(3): 145–67.

Hitt, M. A., and Reed, T. 2000. Entrepreneurship in the new competitive landscape. In G. D. Meyer and K. Heppard (Eds.), *Entrepreneurship as Strategy: Competing on the Entrepreneurial Edge*. Thousand Oaks, CA: Sage, 23–48.

Hlavacek, J., and Thompson, V. 1973. Bureaucracy and new product innovation. *Academy of Management Journal*, 16: 361–72.

Hunter, L., Beaumont, P., and Matthew, L. 2002. Knowledge management practice in Scottish law firms. *Human Resource Management Journal*, 23(2): 4–21.

Ibeh, K. I. N., and Young, S. 2001. Exporting as an entrepreneurial act: An empirical study of Nigerian firms. *European Journal of Marketing*, 35: 566–86.

Ireland, R. D., Hitt, M. A., and Sirmon, D. G. 2003. A model of strategic entrepreneurship: The construct and its dimensions. *Journal of Management*, 29: 1–26.

Ireland, R. D., Hitt, M. A., and Vaidyanath, D. 2002. Alliance management as a source of competitive advantage. *Journal of Management*, 28: 413–46.

Ireland, R. D., Hitt, M. A., Camp, S. M., and Sexton, D. L. 2001. Integrating entrepreneurship and strategic management action to create firm wealth. *Academy of Management Executive*, 15(1): 49–63.

Johanson, J., and Vahlne, J-E. 1977. The internationalization process of the firm: A model of knowledge development and increasing foreign market commitments. *Journal of International Business Studies*, 8: 23–32.

Kazanjian, R. K., Drazin, R., and Glynn, M. A. 2002. Implementing strategies for corporate entrepreneurship: A knowledge-based perspective. In M. A. Hitt, R. D. Ireland, S. M. Camp, and D. L. Sexton (Eds.). *Strategic Entrepreneurship: Creating a New Mindset.* Oxford: Blackwell, 173–99.

Kirzner, I. 1997. *How Markets Work: Disequilibrium, Entrepreneurship and Discovery.* Great Britain: The Institute of Economic Affairs.

Knoke, D. 1999. Organizational networks and corporate social capital. In R. Th. A. J. Leenders and S. M. Gabbay (Eds.), *Corporate Social Capital and Liability.* Boston: Kluwer Academic, 1–14.

Koestler, A. 1964. *The Act of Creation.* New York: Dell.

Leana, C. R., and Van Buren, H. J. 1999. Organizational social capital and employment practices. *Academy of Management Review*, 24: 538–55.

Leonard-Barton, D. 1992. Core capabilities and core rigidities: A paradox in managing new product development. *Strategic Management Journal*, 13: 111–25.

Levinthal, D. A., and Fichman, D. 1988. Dynamics of interorganizational attachments: Auditor-client relationships. *Administrative Science Quarterly*, 33: 345–69.

Liao, J., and Welsch, H. 2003. Social capital and entrepreneurial growth aspiration: A comparison of technology- and non-technology-based nascent entrepreneurs. *Journal of High Technology Management Research*, 14: 149–70.

Loch, C., Stein, L., and Terwiesch, C. 1996. Measuring development performance in the electronics industry. *Journal of Product Innovation Management*, 13(1): 3–20.

Lu, J. W., and Beamish, P. W. 2001. The internationalization and performance of SMEs. *Strategic Management Journal*, 22: 565–86.

Lumpkin, G. T., and Dess, G. G. 1996. Clarifying the entrepreneurial orientation construct and linking it to performance. *Academy of Management Review*, 21: 135–72.

Luo, Y., and Peng, M. W. 1999. Learning to compete in a transition economy: Experience, environment, and performance. *Journal of International Business Studies*, 30: 269–95.

Luthans, F., Stajkovic, A. D., and Ibrayeva, E. 2000. Environmental and psychological challenges facing entrepreneurial development in transitional economies. *Journal of World Business*, 35: 95–110.

Makadok, R. 2001. Towards a synthesis of the resource-based and dynamic-capabilities view of rent creation. *Strategic Management Journal*, 22: 387–401.

Makino, S., and Delios, A. 1996. Local knowledge transfer and performance: Implications for alliance formation in Asia. *Journal of International Business Studies*, 27: 905–28.

March, J. G. 1991. Exploration and exploitation in organizational learning. *Organization Science*, 2: 71–87.

McDougall, P. P., and Oviatt, B. M. 2000. International entrepreneurship: The intersection of two research paths. *Academy of Management Journal*, 43: 902–8.

McGrath, R. G., and MacMillan, I. 2000. *The Entrepreneurial Mindset.* Boston: Harvard Business School Press.

Mitchell, W., Shaver, J. M., and Yeung, B. 1992. Getting there in a global industry: Impacts on performance of changing international presence. *Strategic Management Journal*, 13: 419–32.

Mosakowski, E. 2002. Overcoming resource disadvantages in entrepreneurial firms: When less is more. In M. A. Hitt, R. D. Ireland, S. M. Camp, and D. L. Sexton (eds.). *Strategic Entrepreneurship: Creating a New Mindset.* Oxford: Blackwell, 106–26.

Mueller, S. L., and Goic, S. 2002. Entrepreneurial potential in transition economies: A view from tomorrow's leaders. *Journal of Developmental Entrepreneurship*, 7(4): 399–414.

Newman, K. 2000. Organizational transformation during institutional upheaval. *Academy of Management Review*, 25: 602–19.

Nohria, N., and Gulati, R. 1996. Is slack good or bad for innovation? *Academy of Management Journal*, 39: 1245–64.

Nonaka, I. 1994. A dynamic theory of organizational knowledge creation. *Organization Science*, 5: 14–37.

Oviatt, B. M., and McDougall, P. P. 1997. Challenges for internationalization process theory: The case of international new ventures. *Management International Review*, 37(2): 85–99.

Paradine, T. 1996. Venturing abroad: The challenges of emerging economies. *Risk Management*, 43(7): 73–5.

Peng, M. W. 2001a. How entrepreneurs create wealth in transition economies. *Academy of Management Executive*, 15(1): 95–108.

Peng, M. W. 2001b. The resource-based view and international business. *Journal of Management*, 27: 803–29.

Peng, M. W., and Heath, P. S. 1996. The growth of the firm in planned economies in transition: Institutions, organizations, and strategic choice. *Academy of Management Review*, 21: 492–528.

Rhee, J. H. 2002. An exploratory examination of propensity and performance in new venture internationalization. *New England Journal of Entrepreneurship*, 5(1): 51–66.

Romanelli, E. 1987. New venture strategies in the microcomputer industry. *California Management Review*, 30(1): 160–75.

Shane, S., and Venkataraman, S. 2000. The promise of entrepreneurship as a field of research. *Academy of Management Review*, 25: 217–36.

Sharfman, M. P., Wolf, G., Chase, R. B., and Tansik, D. A. 1988. Antecedents of organizational slack. *Academy of Management Review*, 13: 601–14.

Sharma, P., and Chrisman, J. J. 1999. Toward a reconciliation of the definitional issues in the field of corporate entrepreneurship. *Entrepreneurship Theory and Practice*, 23(3): 11–27.

Simon, H. A. 1982a. *Models of Bounded Rationality*, Volume 1. Cambridge, MA: MIT Press.

Simon, H. A. 1982b. *Models of Bounded Rationality*, Volume 2. Cambridge, MA: MIT Press.

Sirmon, D. G., and Hitt, M. A. 2003. Managing resources: Linking unique resources, management, and wealth creation in family firms. *Entrepreneurship Theory and Practice*, 27(4): 339–58.

Sirmon, D. G., Hitt, M. A., and Ireland, R. D. 2004. Dynamically managing firm resources for value creation. Working Paper, Arizona State University.

Smith, K. G., and Di Gregorio, D. 2002. Bisociation, discovery, and the role of entrepreneurial action. In M. A. Hitt, R. D. Ireland, S. M. Camp, and D. L. Sexton (Eds.). *Strategic Entrepreneurship: Creating a New Mindset*. Oxford: Blackwell, 129–50.

Stinchcombe, A. L. 1965. Social structure and organizations. In J. G. March (Ed.), *Handbook of Organizations*. Chicago: Rand-McNally, 142–93.

Tallman, S., and Li, J. 1996. Effects of international diversity and product diversity on the performance of multinational firms. *Academy of Management Journal*, 39: 179–96.

Thomke, S., and Kuemmerle, W. 2002. Asset accumulation, interdependence and technological change: Evidence from pharmaceutical discovery. *Strategic Management Journal*, 23: 619–35.

Tsai, W. 2001. Knowledge transfer in intraorganizational networks: Effects of network position and absorptive capacity on business unit innovation and performance. *Academy of Management Journal*, 44: 996–1004.

Webb, J., Ireland, R. D., and Coombs, J. E. 2004. Resource efficiency of start-up ventures: The link to effectiveness in terms of the creative destruction process. Paper presented during the Babson/Kauffman Research Conference.

Zaheer, S. 1995. Overcoming the liability of foreignness. *Academy of Management Journal*, 38: 341–63.

Zaheer, S., and Mosakowski, E. 1997. The dynamics of the liability of foreignness: A global study of survival in financial services. *Strategic Management Journal*, 18: 439–64.

Zahra, S. A., and Garvis, D. M. 2000. International corporate entrepreneurship and company performance: The moderating effect of international environmental hostility. *Journal of Business Venturing*, 15(5): 469–92.

Zahra, S. A., and George, G. 2002a. Absorptive capacity: A review, reconceptualization, and extension. *Academy of Management Review*, 27: 185–203.

Zahra, S. A., and George, G. 2002b. International entrepreneurship: The current status of the field and future research agenda. In M. A. Hitt, R. D. Ireland, S. M. Camp, and D. L. Sexton (Eds.), *Strategic Entrepreneurship: Creating a New Mindset*. Oxford: Blackwell, 225–88.

Zahra, S. A., Ireland, R. D., Gutierrez, I., and Hitt, M. A. 2000a. Privatization and entrepreneurial transformation: Emerging issues and a future research agenda. *Academy of Management Review*, 25: 509–24.

Zahra, S. A., Ireland, R. D., and Hitt, M. A. 2000b. International expansion by new venture firms: International diversity, mode of market entry, technological learning, and performance. *Academy of Management Journal*, 43: 925–50.

Zahra, S. A., Matherne, B. P., and Carleton, J. M. 2003. Technological resource leveraging and the internationalisation of new ventures. *Journal of International Entrepreneurship*, 1: 163–86.

Zirger, B. J., and Maidique, M. A. 1990. A model of new product development: An empirical test. *Management Science*, 36: 867–83.

National Context and New Enterprises

CHAPTER FIVE

Entrepreneurship in Developing Countries

Arnold C. Cooper and Xiaoli Yin

Introduction

This chapter examines influences upon the creation of entrepreneurial ventures, particularly those leading to innovative and growth-oriented firms. Our focus will be upon entrepreneurship in developing countries. Although much of the academic literature involves studies in developed countries, many of the findings appear to have implications for developing countries. We shall draw heavily upon the Global Entrepreneurship Monitor (GEM) studies, which provide relevant data on rates of entrepreneurial activity and factors influencing entrepreneurship across countries.

We shall consider advantages and disadvantages of smaller firms seeking to engage in innovation. Established organizations can be sources of innovation and new business activity, so we shall also examine some of the factors influencing entrepreneurship in established organizations.

In this chapter we shall consider the following:

- rates of entrepreneurial activity across countries;
- different kinds of entrepreneurship;
- factors influencing differences in entrepreneurial activity across countries;
- influences upon new firm performance;
- innovation in new and small firms;
- innovation in established organizations.

Rates of Entrepreneurial Activity across Countries

There appear to be wide differences in entrepreneurial activity across countries according to the Global Entrepreneurship Monitor (GEM) series, which has been gathering cross-country data since 1999 (Reynolds et al., 1999; 2000; 2001; 2002; 2003). Counting total entrepreneurial activity (TEA) as the sum of those people involved in efforts to start firms and those people involved in managing new businesses, they find wide differences across countries. For instance, the 2003 Executive Report finds rates of TEA varying from more than 25 per 100 people in Uganda and Venezuela; between 15 and 25 in Argentina, and Chile; and less than 5 per 100 people in a number of countries, including France, Croatia, Japan, Italy, Hong Kong, and the Netherlands (Reynolds et al., 2003, p. 6).

Note that it is not the case that developing countries were laggards in regard to entrepreneurial activity; many of the most active countries reported in the 2003 report are in Latin America.

Kinds of Entrepreneurship

We should recognize that entrepreneurs may be motivated for different reasons and that new firms differ widely in their prospects.

The GEM series of studies has drawn distinctions between necessity-based and opportunity-based entrepreneurship (Reynolds et al., 2000, pp. 8–9). The former involve entrepreneurs reporting "no better choices for work." Many of those driven to start firms for this reason are in developing countries, including India, Mexico, and Brazil. Their entrepreneurial activities presumably reflect a lack of employment opportunities. They are also more likely to be from low income households (Reynolds et al., 2001, pp. 9 and 41). Opportunity-based entrepreneurship in these studies was defined as "pursuing a business opportunity for personal interest" (Reynolds et al., 2000, p. 8). This involved 54 percent of the approximately 7,400 entrepreneurs in 29 countries reported on in 2001. Many of these opportunities were pursued while the entrepreneur continued to hold other jobs and thus were often part-time ventures. Since these people appeared to have other opportunities, they probably had greater human capital (education and experience) and greater social capital (networks of contacts). This may have made it possible for them to establish and build more substantial businesses. However, since many of their ventures were part-time at the time of the survey, their full economic impact was not yet evident.

One study reported upon three main types of entrepreneurship in China. The first type is called *getihu*, which occurred throughout the 1980s and consisted of very small-scale business activities in retail and services such as street vendors. This type of entrepreneurship is necessity-based as those involved are of low social status and with little education. They start out on their own mostly because they are excluded from the state system. For them, business is a means of subsistence. The second type of entrepreneurship in China is called *siying qiye*, which operates in all sectors. It emerged in the late 1980s and involved mostly highly educated individuals such as engineers or managers of state-owned enterprises. Their businesses operate on a larger scale and are mostly opportunity based. The third type is the new venture initiated by the foreign-educated or trained Chinese returning to China. It is also opportunity based and is a prominent phenomenon in the Internet sector (Liao and Sohmen, 2001).

Previous studies have also found that there are many similarities in the value sets between entrepreneurs of developed and developing countries, even though entrepreneurs in developing countries also have their own unique attributes. Holt (1997) studied the differences and similarities in work-related values between Chinese entre-preneurs, Chinese managers, and US entrepreneurs. The study found that the respon-dent Chinese managers and entrepreneurs differed sharply on many crucial value dimensions. The Chinese entrepreneurs demonstrate a high degree of independence and self-determination, are more likely to accept uncertainty and question authority. The findings suggest that entrepreneurial values associated with individualism and self-determination can prevail in a society like China that is collectivist and con-formist. The study also revealed many similarities between the responses of Chinese and US entrepreneurs, which suggests that fundamental characteristics of entrepre-neurship may transcend national boundaries. The study also found important differ-ences between the two groups. Specifically, Chinese entrepreneurs are more likely than their US counterparts to value family security, to avoid conspicuous wealth, and to refrain from external recognition of achievements.

Start-up ventures can be distinguished not only by the motives of the entrepre-neur, but also by the expected growth of the new firm. One measure is expected job creation. The GEM study in 2003 involving respondents in 41 countries reported that 8 percent never expected to provide any jobs, 35 percent expected to provide 5–9 jobs, 18 percent expected to provide 10–19 jobs, and 21 percent expected to provide 20 or more jobs (Reynolds et al., 2003, p. 23). There were wide differences across countries, with the average business expected to generate just under 10 jobs. The entrepreneurs in Uganda, Venezuela, and Thailand anticipated having the great-est impact in job creation and those in Belgium, Croatia, and Hong Kong expected to have the least impact (Reynolds et al., 2003, p. 24). Overall, it is clear that indi-vidual ventures appear to vary widely in their expected growth and economic impact. Many of the entrepreneurs in developing countries had high expectations in regard to job creation. Entrepreneurs tend to be optimistic and these estimates may differ in their realism. In fact, most new firms generate only one or two jobs (Reynolds et al., 2003, p. 69).

The differences across firms reflected in these estimates are consistent with the find-ings of Birch (1987) who reported upon job creation over time in the United States. He found that a small percentage of growth-oriented firms, which he labeled "gazelles," accounted for much of the job creation in the United States.

New firms may also vary in whether they are likely to be innovative. The GEM 2003 study reported most entrepreneurs did not expect to engage in much innova-tion. Technically oriented new firms emphasizing innovation as their primary way of trying to achieve a competitive advantage represent only a small percentage of all new firms, maybe only about 3 percent of all start-ups (Reynolds et al., 2003, pp. 24–5). These innovative firms were more likely to have multiple owners and larger numbers of employees when surveyed (Reynolds et al., 2003, pp. 26–7). They were also more likely to be started because of a perceived opportunity, rather than because the founder had no better alternatives. Although small in number, these innovative firms can have a substantial impact on the innovativeness of the countries where they are located.

Although entrepreneurial activity appears to vary widely across countries, it seems clear that in every country many of the start-ups are small; many are part-time; and most are not very innovative. However, most hope to generate jobs in the years after founding. These patterns appear to apply in both developing and more developed countries.

Factors Influencing Entrepreneurship

The GEM studies have examined a wide range of factors which may impact entrepreneurial activity. Many of these influences seem to vary substantially across countries.

In regard to demographics, entrepreneurial activity is not equally distributed across different groups in any country. For instance, age and gender seem to make a difference. In general, 25–44 year-olds represent the most active age group (Reynolds et al., 2001, p. 15). Across all countries surveyed, they represent 55 percent of entrepreneurs. Those who are younger account for 22 percent of entrepreneurial activity. They may be strongly motivated, but often lack the financial, human, and social capital to get started. However, this younger group has the highest percentage pursuing necessity-based entrepreneurship (particularly in developing countries). This presumably reflects conditions where they cannot find acceptable jobs (Reynolds et al., 2001, p. 14). Those who are 45 or older account for 22 percent of entrepreneurial activity. They usually have more relevant resources to bring to the start-up process, but they may hesitate to risk what they have.

In regard to gender, men are more than twice as active in entrepreneurship as women across the countries surveyed. The rate of entrepreneurial activity for women varies widely across countries. The ratio of male to female entrepreneurs varies from 3.4 in Israel and 2.8 in Slovenia and Croatia to 1.1 in China, Venezuela, and Thailand (Reynolds et al., 2003, p. 37). There are differences between male and female entrepreneurs in their motivations and in the kinds of firms started, with males more likely to start necessity-based firms and also more likely to expect their firms to grow and have an economic impact. In regard to innovative businesses expected to grow, men were about 10 times as likely to start such firms (Reynolds et al., 2003, p. 36).

Countries with aging populations and those which discourage women from entrepreneurship are less likely to experience high rates of new venture formation. Many developing countries have large populations of young people, a potential pool of entrepreneurs. According to the GEM studies, many are in the intermediate to low range in regard to the ratio of male to female entrepreneurs. These ratios were 2.02 for India, 1.92 for Argentina, 1.81 for Mexico, 1.56 for Chile, 1.55 for Uganda, 1.50 for Brazil and 1.13 for Venezuela. For the 41 countries surveyed for the 2003 report, the median ratio was 1.93 (Reynolds et al., 2003, p. 37). Thus, many developing countries seem to be relatively favorably situated in regard to these demographic variables influencing entrepreneurship.

Previous research has studied different factors that might affect female entrepreneurs in developing countries. Shabbir and Gregorio (1996) examined how the relationship between women's personal goals and structural factors affects their decision to start a business. Data were gathered through in-depth interviews of 33 participants of an entrepreneurship development program in Pakistan. The study found that previous work experience/special qualifications and the extent to which their family was supportive are two key factors that had a major impact on women's ability to start a business. However, the ability of women to start a business needs to be balanced against the strength of their will to do so.

Societal attitudes toward entrepreneurship may exert an important influence. The first GEM study (1999) asked, "Do you think starting a new business is a respected occupation in your country?" Answers varied from 8 percent for Japan to 38 percent for the United Kingdom to 91 percent for the United States (Reynolds et al., 1999, p. 30). In 2000, the GEM survey examined social legitimacy through asking whether the respondent had recently known any entrepreneurs, the degree of perceived respect for entrepreneurship in the community, the extent to which fear of failure might deter entrepreneurs, and the perceived attitudes relating to whether society resented successful, wealthy entrepreneurs. There was little gap between countries with high and medium levels of entrepreneurship, but countries with low levels of entrepreneurship showed lower values for all of these measures of social legitimacy (Reynolds et al., 2000, p. 26). The 2003 GEM report, which included data on many developing countries, noted that those who knew someone who started a business in the previous six months were two to three times as likely to become entrepreneurs. Furthermore, in regard to cultural support, those who perceive that entrepreneurs are following a desirable career choice; those who perceive that starting a new business leads to high respect; and those who report seeing stories about successful new businesses in the media are much more likely to engage in entrepreneurship (Reynolds et al., 2003, pp. 43–5).

Cultures of particular countries or groups within countries may influence entrepreneurship. The extent to which people are achievement oriented, or feel they can influence what happens to them, or are able to perceive opportunities can vary across groups. Thus, McClelland (1961) developed the concept of need for achievement and reported that those who tend to set goals and measure themselves according to whether they meet those goals are also people who act in entrepreneurial ways. He found considerable differences across countries in this tendency. A study of Chinese business owners found that those with high need for achievement were more likely to plan to expand (Lau and Busenitz, 2001).

Locus of control is a psychological attribute indicating the extent to which individuals feel that they can influence what happens to them. Several studies have reported that entrepreneurs tend to have higher internal locus of control scores, meaning that they believe they can influence outcomes in their lives (Perry, 1990; Shapero, 1975). A study of Russian entrepreneurs and students, conducted after the collapse of the Soviet Union, reported that Russian entrepreneurs reported relatively high internal locus of control scores. Contrary to what was expected, the Russian entrepreneurs had lower internal scores than the Russian students. Interestingly, Russian entrepreneurs and students both reported lower internal scores than their counterparts in most other countries. The authors attributed this to the Russians' experience of living in a country in which individuals had had limited rights (Kaufmann et al., 1995).

Entrepreneurs have been described as those who are alert to market opportunities (Kirzner, 1979). They also have the ability and willingness to exploit those opportunities (Shane and Venkataraman, 2000). An explanatory study of entrepreneurial activities in a remote sub-arctic community found that the native Eskimos had a lower tendency than the non-native residents to become entrepreneurs. Furthermore, the native Eskimos tended not to be opportunity seekers, but rather were reactive and engaged in traditional activities, such as herding (Dana, 1995). The author attributes this in part to the traditional values of these people, including their inclination to work collectively.

Availability of capital influences new firm formation. Most entrepreneurs appear to rely upon personal savings and friends and relatives as important sources of start-up capital (Cooper et al., 1990, p. 29). The extent to which individuals can save enough to get started obviously depends upon income levels and taxation rates. Informal investment, in which individuals privately invest in particular ventures, is extremely important in many countries. The GEM survey of 2001 estimated that informal investment in start-up and growing businesses was 1.1 percent of the combined GDP for the 29 countries surveyed. Furthermore, in all countries surveyed the estimated pool of informal venture capital exceeded that from classic venture capital. In 2003, the percentage of the adult population making such investments ranged from a high of over 12 percent in Uganda and over 6 percent in Ireland to less than 2 percent in Belgium, the Netherlands, and Brazil (Reynolds et al., 2003, p. 59). The 2003 study showed a diverse pattern of informal investing across the developing countries surveyed, with some, such as Uganda, China, and Mexico, showing high rates, and others, such as India and Brazil, reporting low rates.

Classic venture capital, coming from firms which are in the business of raising capital and investing it in new and growing firms, is very important for a small number of growth-oriented firms. The GEM studies estimated that fewer than 20,000 businesses in the 29 countries examined received venture capital from this source in 2000. Furthermore, most of these were in a small number of countries, with the United States accounting for more than 5,000 and Germany, Japan, and France accounting for more than 2,000 each (Reynolds et al., 2001, pp. 24–6). However, the small number of ventures backed by venture capital firms often grew substantially and, according to the GEM estimates, accounted for 3.3 percent of the total jobs and 7.4 percent of the GDP in the United States (Reynolds et al., 2001, p. 24). Relatively little of this venture capital goes to start-up firms. Most goes to support the growth of promising firms already established.

The growth-oriented firms which attract venture capital investment often are leaders in innovation. Many of the most innovative and rapidly growing industries, such as biotechnology and information technology, have attracted large quantities of venture capital. There is limited data about classic venture capital in developing countries. We know there are some venture capital firms in such countries, but they are often limited in how much they have available to invest. Capital markets are often less advanced in developing countries. One result is that very diversified companies, such as the Tata Group in India and Sime Darby in Malaysia have served as sources of venture capital through financing internally entry into promising markets and technologies.

Developing countries would appear to be at a disadvantage in not being able to provide the informal venture capital or classic venture capital needed to support entrepreneurship. However, many promising ventures, even in the United States, start with modest amounts of capital. For instance, the INC 500 lists the fastest growing private firms; in 2000, 58 percent of these firms had started with less than $20,000 (INC, 2000, p. 65).

In China, availability of capital is one of the major challenges faced by new ventures. The commercial banks in China have much higher levels of regulations than do banks in other countries. For example, only 0.03 percent of loans were granted to the private enterprises by state-owned banks in 1998 (*Chinese Financial Yearbook*, 1989–99). Venture capital is fairly new in China and is not sufficient to provide enough funding to most start-ups (Liao and Sohmen, 2001). The private sector also hardly uses the stock market to finance its businesses. Therefore, rather than relying on banks or government, entrepreneurs in China typically raise capital through informal borrowing from friends, relatives, firms, institutions, or investors from abroad.

One study of existing small business owners in China indicated that those perceiving difficulties in bank borrowing and those firms which were larger were more likely to pursue cooperative arrangements with other firms (Lau and Busenitz, 2001).

Access to funding and capital remains a major challenge for entrepreneurs in China. One exception is a small group of successful Internet entrepreneurs, such as Sina.com, Netease.com, and Sohu.com. The Chinese government has been encouraging high-tech entrepreneurship by establishing many high-tech parks throughout the country. Many high-tech ventures are foreign-funded or are seeking foreign funding. As a result, many of these high-tech ventures are started by foreign-educated Chinese and controlled by foreign venture capital funds (Liao and Sohmen, 2001). For example, some of the major portals, such as Sina.com and Sohu.com, are foreign controlled through venture capital funds from the United States. While funding might be less of an issue for Internet entrepreneurs, access to labor is still a major challenge. Lack of skilled labor is one of the common issues faced by entrepreneurs in developing countries. This also places a constraint on the technological level of the private enterprises (Liao and Sohmen, 2001).

Availability of capital may also present a major obstacle for small start-ups, female entrepreneurs and immigrants. Anecdotal evidence suggests that small businesses and women entrepreneurs might have more difficulty accessing start-up capital than larger corporations and male entrepreneurs. Empirical evidence, however, failed to support allegations of bias against small businesses and women entrepreneurs in business funding decisions. Churchill and Lewis (1986) studied whether possible different lending policies and account profitability exist for different size companies under $50 million in sales. The research examined 116 individual account relationships representing both large and small borrowers. The study found that loan relationships were profitable for small companies of all sizes. It paints a very encouraging picture for the future availability of credit to small and growing businesses. For example, except for very young businesses (primarily those just starting out) banks treat small companies in a rather even-handed manner and do not seem to discriminate with respect to size. Meanwhile, bank relationships with small companies of any size are more profitable than relationships with large companies. Deposits kept by small businesses are the key to this greater profitability. It conveys the message that banks can view small business as a very attractive source of profit. Buttner and Rosen (1989) examined whether women entrepreneurs may have more difficulty obtaining financial support than men. Based on a loan decision simulation, the study found that there was no evidence that sex stereotypes influenced business funding decisions. However, the results also suggest that using students as proxies for bank loan officers has very limited generalizability. These findings suggest that small business owners can continue receiving bank financing as long as profit continues to be a motivator for banks. Meanwhile, female entrepreneurs should seek opportunities to meet with loan officers and present their business proposals in order to obtain start-up capital.

While obtaining loan capital might be an obstacle for all small business ventures, the problem is particularly severe for immigrants or ethnic minority entrepreneurs (Light et al., 1990). Bates (1997) examined how self-employment entry was financed by Chinese and Korean immigrants who started businesses between 1979 and 1987 as compared with cohort non-minorities and Asian Americans who are not immigrants. Conventional wisdom claims that Asian immigrant entrepreneurs benefit from the operation of rotating credit associations (RCA) and supportive social networks. RCA "typifies the process through which peer and community subgroups assist in the creation and operation of firms by providing social capital in the form of loans" (Bates, 1997, p. 109). The study found that the majority of start-up capital that financed small business formation came from family wealth (equity) and financial institution loans (debt) for both immigrant owned firms and firms owned by non-minorities and Asian Americans who are not immigrants. Korean/Chinese immigrant-owned firms have high levels of start-up capital, due to their heavy reliance upon family wealth to finance small business creation. Nontraditional credit sources (such as family, friends, and RCAs) are of secondary importance and they are utilized more by the weaker start-ups. Immigrant Korean/Chinese firms typically face reluctant banks and tight-fisted family and friends. They had less success than any other group in leveraging their equity. Friends and family provide even less leverage than financial institutions. Different from conventional wisdom, immigrant Korean/Chinese firms stand out as well capitalized because of their large owner equity investment based on household wealth (Bates, 1997).

In developing nations, microfinancing programs, where aid groups make small loans to poor entrepreneurs who are not eligible for conventional loans, have been proven to be very effective. In countries such as Bolivia, Indonesia, Uganda, and Bangladesh, microlending programs are proving that small sums can dramatically help boost small business start-ups and lift living standards (Engardio, 2003). One estimate indicates that the number of microcredit banks has tripled to 2,200 and have reached 52 million people worldwide in the past five years (Engardio, 2003). Typically, a microcredit bank lends about $100 for four months and also provides business and bookkeeping expertise to ensure repayment. Upon repayment, the young entrepreneurs get fresh loans. In Bangladesh, microcredit was pioneered in the 1970s. Since then hundreds of thousands of small enterprises were started with microloans, which have helped generate 5 percent per year economic growth for the past decade. Countries in Africa experienced similar success. In Uganda, for example, 245,000 families have borrowed from village banks run by international and local agencies. The small loans have been used to start businesses from rabbit farms to grocery stores (Engardio, 2003). Microlending programs have been proven to be a very effective method to fund small business start-ups in developing nations.

Do differences in infrastructure lead to some countries becoming more entrepreneurial than others? GEM surveyed key informants in different countries in regard to perceived characteristics of the infrastructure. A number of infrastructure factors were perceived *not* to differ across countries with low, medium, and high levels of entrepreneurial activity. These include the availability of loan subsidies, satisfactory legal, accounting, and banking services, government policies and procurement practices, complexity of taxes, licensing, and government regulations, and internal market openness. Interestingly, government programs intended to help new and small firms were perceived to be of little value in all countries. However, there were differences in the perception of whether private individuals have provided financial support for new and growing firms. Countries with high rates of entrepreneurial activity reported more availability of capital from private individuals. They were also perceived to have more flexible labor markets and to provide settings in which new and growing firms had access to new research and technology (Reynolds et al., 1999, pp. 22–3). Barriers to entrepreneurship (including the registration processes) appear to reduce entrepreneurship in wealthy countries, but not in poorer countries, where large-scale informal or unregistered entrepreneurship occurs (Reynolds et al., 2003, p. 79).

The above findings represented averages across the range of countries surveyed. However, entrepreneurs may face particular challenges in certain countries. Tsang (1994) conducted a comprehensive analysis of the environment experienced by private businesses in China through examining their relationships with the major stakeholders, such as government, suppliers, employees, customers, and competitors. He found that close connections with local governments are critical for the survival of private businesses, as these ensure access to crucial raw materials and access to credit through state banks.

Another study, focusing upon six high-technology entrepreneurial firms in China, proposed that successful firms would seek alliance with individuals or organizations who could help them and that furthermore they would tend to locate in areas where they already had established relationships (Ahlstrom and Bruton, 2002). Since economic reform occurred, it is easier for private firms to secure raw materials and employ unskilled workers. However, competition is becoming much keener as state-owned enterprises are becoming more efficient and large multinational corporations are rushing in. In addition, private entrepreneurs are also competing fiercely among themselves. For example, large private enterprises have to compete with state, collective, and foreign enterprises for managerial staff who are in short supply. Meanwhile, under the current socialist ideology in China, the private sector is assigned a supplementary role in the economy. The unique environment of the Chinese economy presents both opportunities and threats to the private sector. The Chinese experience of liberalizing the private sector offers useful insights to governments of other developing countries in promoting private business development.

The tendency to engage in entrepreneurship does not seem to be greatly affected by educational level. However, the primary motivations of the entrepreneurs do vary according to educational background. Those with little educational background are much more likely to be "necessity entrepreneurs," starting a firm because it is the best alternative available. Those with more education are more likely to be "opportunity entrepreneurs," starting a business to pursue a particular opportunity. Those who start firms which are expected to have an impact on the market and which are likely to grow, are much more likely to have more education, often with post-secondary or graduate education (Reynolds et al., 2003, pp. 40–1). In developing countries, rates of entrepreneurship are sometimes quite high. However, the rate of formation of high growth potential firms is much lower, reflecting, in part, the lower levels of human capital in the pool of potential entrepreneurs.

A striking feature of entrepreneurship all over the world is the large number of start-ups which are formed while the entrepreneurs still have jobs. GEM reported that 80 percent implement a start-up while still employed (Reynolds et al., 2003, p. 41). There are, of course, benefits to starting in this way. The entrepreneur can test the market, gradually establish networks of contacts, and assemble resources over time. Of course many die out before becoming larger and many stay as part-time businesses. In the United States, numerous new firms are closely related to what the entrepreneur did before. According to a number of studies, about 60–70 percent of new full-time businesses and about 85 percent of technically oriented firms serve similar markets or utilize similar technologies as the organizations which the entrepreneurs had left (Cooper, 1985, p. 77). This, of course, has important implications for the kinds of new businesses which entrepreneurs can start. If the entrepreneur had previously been working in an innovative organization, one positioned in a growing market and utilizing promising technology, then the entrepreneur will have learned things which can be used to start an innovative business. Entrepreneurs usually do not move when they start firms. Thus, innovative businesses are likely to be established near other innovative firms.

Consistent with the comments above, we should note that entrepreneurship is not equally distributed within countries. Studies in the United States examining rates of entrepreneurship by labor market area showed that start-ups were highest in areas characterized by economic diversity and greater personal wealth; the presence of volatile industries and a workforce with promising age, education, and experience characteristics (Reynolds et al., 1995). Job creation, which often is tied to entrepreneurship, has been found to be highest in the "collar counties," those located around metropolitan areas (Birch, 1987). There also has been considerable research showing that clusters of similar firms develop in the same area. Firms located there can benefit from specialized suppliers and workers and from knowledge transfer across firms. However, there can be loss of proprietary knowledge across firms and costs of doing business can be driven up if there is congestion. Nevertheless, entrepreneurs usually start firms where they are already living and working and they often start firms related to what they did before. Thus, clusters of firms in particular industries are likely to spin off new firms in those industries. Why doesn't the process continue indefinitely? The life cycles of the industries within a cluster will have an important influence. As industries mature and offer fewer entrepreneurial opportunities, then clusters of firms will experience less entrepreneurship.

Developing countries are most likely to see innovative, growth-oriented firms established in areas where there are already some established organizations of that type. These can function as the "incubators" where the pool of potential entrepreneurs can learn industry practices, identify market opportunities, accumulate capital, and form contacts.

Influences upon New Firm Performance

Many of the studies of predictors of new firm performance have been conducted in developed countries. However, the findings may have implications for developing countries as well.

The background of the entrepreneur seems to make a difference. Entrepreneurs with more education are more likely to survive and also more likely to grow (Cooper et al., 1994). Education presumably adds to the problem-solving abilities of the entrepreneur. More education may also add to the credibility of the entrepreneur and be a reflection of an ability to meet personal goals. Technically-oriented firms are often started by entrepreneurs with substantial education, often a Master's degree. However, based upon studies of spin-offs from MIT, there appears to be somewhat of an "inverted U" relation between company performance and education level, with those with Master's degrees doing best (Roberts, 1991).

Industry experience is associated with greater likelihood of survival and also of growth (Cooper et al., 1994; Cooper and Bruno, 1977). Those who start businesses in fields they already know may be more aware of market opportunities. They also have contacts, which help them in gathering relevant information and make it more likely that suppliers and customers will trust them and provide assistance. By contrast, those lacking industry experience don't know what they don't know; they have to learn how to manage in a particular industry while they are getting started.

Managerial experience also benefits the new firm (Cooper et al., 1994). Those who have already managed have less to learn and may make fewer mistakes. They are more likely to have contacts with bankers, customers, and suppliers and they have been in a better position to identify market opportunities and promising strategies.

New firms started by teams are more likely to grow (Cooper and Bruno, 1977). The complementary knowledge, skills and contacts of teams add to the human and social capital of the new venture. Those who had previously worked together in the same organization were more likely to grow, presumably because they could assess their mutual compatibility better before starting and because they had already developed ways of working together (Eisenhardt and Schoonhoven, 1990). Teams which were "more complete," in the sense of having members who had experience in each functional area, and teams which had worked together previously did better (Roure and Maidique, 1986). Interestingly, one study found that firms started by teams were more likely to grow, but not more likely to survive. The authors speculated that, although team-based ventures had more human and social capital to build upon, they were also subject to breakups due to conflict within the team; this adversely affected survival rates (Cooper et al., 1994). In general, innovative high-technology firms are much more likely to be started by teams. The potential of these firms makes it more likely that they can attract and support the members of a team.

It is not surprising that a number of studies show that firms with more initial capital are more likely to survive or more likely to grow (Cooper et al., 1994). More capital enables an entrepreneur to support operations while overcoming problems or absorbing environmental shocks. Product development may take longer than expected or a local market may be temporarily depressed. New venture creation often involves learning while the entrepreneur works to find the right suppliers, the right employees, and the right market segments to serve. Greater financial resources make it more likely that the new firm can survive during such precarious times. The amount of initial capital also influences the strategy of the new firm. For a retail firm, more capital permits the new firm to choose a better location, to stock a broader inventory, and to invest more in advertising. For a technically oriented firm, more capital can support more ambitious product development, more market tests, and the hiring of a larger and better qualified staff.

Previous research found that resource access, including access to financial capital, is important in the survival and performance of new ventures in developing countries. Thakur (1998) examined the interplay of resources, opportunities, and capabilities in new venture growth, based on nearly 50 case studies carried out in North India. The findings suggest that resource access itself limits the range of opportunity choice and growth potential. Contrary to conventional wisdom, the study suggests that opportunity choice, such as pursuing demand and supply gaps, innovation, or technological substitution, is itself constrained by resource access barriers. Resource access and opportunity choice together define the growth potential of the firm. Within these constraints, managerial capabilities become crucial to the entire process of creation, survival, and growth of the new firms.

The network contacts of the entrepreneur also bear upon prospects for success. If the entrepreneur has embedded relationships, suppliers may be more willing to give preferred treatment, supply detailed information, or work to solve problems jointly (Uzzi, 1997). Relationships can also decrease the need for capital, as the entrepreneur borrows space or begs for the use of excess resources (Starr and MacMillan, 1990). If the young company can establish affiliations with well-respected, established firms, it benefits from their reputation (Stuart et al., 1999). If the new venture's professional advisers, or investors, or first customers are well known, then the new business acquires legitimacy. Others will assume that the new firm is promising.

In interpreting studies which use survival as a measure of performance, it should be recognized that many young firms experience marginal performance. The decision about whether to continue or close the business will be a conscious decision of the entrepreneur, reflecting the required "threshold level of performance." The threshold is a function of switching costs, opportunity costs, and non-economic benefits (Gimeno et al., 1997). Thus, entrepreneurs who realize substantial psychic income from a venture, who perceive few attractive alternatives, and who think it would be difficult to find another job will keep a marginal business going.

Most of the research to date on predictors of performance has been conducted in developed countries. What would be different in developing countries? The necessity-based entrepreneurs who are so prevalent in developing countries probably have less human, financial, and social capital to bring to their new ventures. Many probably have a low required threshold level of performance because they perceive few alternatives; this would lead to their continuing to operate marginal ventures. However, we might expect that most of these businesses would not be very innovative and would not grow much. The opportunity-based ventures started by entrepreneurs who typically already have jobs are usually more promising. Their entrepreneurs usually would have more human, financial, and social capital to draw upon. However, whether innovative, growing firms can be developed will depend upon whether those entrepreneurs have experience in promising industries, whether they have previously learned to manage in innovative firms, and whether they have accumulated enough financial capital and contacts to get started. These firms are less likely to be unregistered, so that the complexity and cost of taxes and government regulations are likely to bear upon their prospects.

A few research studies have been conducted to compare different success factors of entrepreneurs between developed and developing countries. Learner et al. (1997) examined individual factors influencing performance of 200 Israeli women-owned businesses. The study applied five theoretical perspectives, derived from studies in OECD countries in a non-OECD context. The study supports previous research from the United States and Europe on women entrepreneurs, which found that perform-ance is related to previous industry experience, business skills, and achievement moti-vation. Further, achievement motivation and having a single strong affiliation with a women's organization are also important to improving performance. However, con-trary to previous research, the study found that education level, area of study, and previous entrepreneurial experience had no effect on performance. Overall, the study suggests that theories regarding entrepreneurship derived from studies in OECD countries need to be carefully examined and tested before being used in non-OECD and developing countries. Different social structures affect the explanatory power of previous theories in predicting the performance of entrepreneurs.

A related study examined the performance of 215 informal microentrepreneurs in Jamaica and studied the influence of human capital, social capital, and financial capital of the owners on their business profitability (Honig, 1998). The study found that different organizational settings (e.g., firms with employees vs. without employees and firms of different technological sophistication) may alter the rates of return to human, social, and financial capital. Vocational training, mother's high occupational status (a proxy for socioeconomic status) and years of experience in the business are consistently positive and strongly associated with increasing profits. However, while additional starting capital and obtaining a small business loan play an important role for both the businesses with and without employees, increasing amounts fail to dif-ferentiate the success of those firms that were already in the higher technological sector. Marital status, a form of social capital, is positively associated with income in all settings. Frequent church attendance, another form of social capital, is negatively associated with income in the higher technological tier.

Innovation in New and Small Firms

Smaller companies have made "a disproportionately large contribution to innovation in the United States" (US Department of Commerce, 1979, p. 258). According to a National Science Foundation study "Firms with 100 or fewer employees produced 24% of the (most significant) innovations. In addition, the cost of innovation in a small firm was found to be less than in a large firm since small firms produced 24 times more major innovations per research and development dollar" (US Depart-ment of Commerce, 1979, p. 259). There is evidence that in some industries, large firms have higher rates of innovation, while in other industries, smaller firms are more innovative (Acs and Audretsch, 1990, p. 22). However, many of the industries characterized by rapid technological advance (such as biotechnology and information technology) are in industries characterized by many smaller firms.

Smaller companies clearly have some disadvantages as they seek to develop and commercialize new technology. With limited resources, they usually have smaller staffs, so that they cannot support the same number of people on projects as their large firm counterparts. This may mean that their scientists and engineers have to develop broader skill sets. It often means that the firms have to select projects carefully, those which they have the resources to complete and those which they can commercialize or license.

Smaller companies have to finance their development from their cash flow (often limited) or the capital markets, where the cost and availability of funds can vary widely over time. Often smaller firms lack the complementary assets, such as manufacturing or distribution strengths, needed to commercialize promising technology. New firms also lack the credibility that would help persuade customers, suppliers, or developers of complementary technologies to take a chance on the new technology.

Patents can be very important in protecting the new technology developed by pioneering small firms. However, it takes money to protect patent positions in the courts.

With all of these disadvantages, how does it happen that new and small firms often lead the way in developing new technologies, particularly major innovations? (We should note that established firms are often very experienced in improving their existing products and in extending their existing product lines. However, they are often less successful in developing completely new products.)

New and small firms can move quickly. There are few decision-makers to convince. If the top management is committed, the company can move ahead on the basis of "gut feel," rather than have to do elaborate analyses. Such companies may have greater incentive to commit to major innovations. They have less of a stake in the status quo; if they revolutionize an industry they usually do not have to worry about cannibalizing existing sales. The potential market for major innovations is often highly uncertain. In the early stages of development, when costs are high and technical performance is limited, it may be that only a limited segment of the market will find that the new technology meets their needs. Larger firms typically find such limited sales to be too small to be of interest. However, a smaller firm may find an initially small market to be profitable and well matched with its limited resources.

New and small firms may be able to attract unusually talented and dedicated engineers and managers. They can offer stock ownership and a chance to shape a firm's destiny – to be a major part of a team which shares a dream. There is some evidence that smaller firms are more efficient in product development, with one study finding that larger companies spent about seven times as much as smaller firms to develop particular major innovations (Cooper, 1964). Smaller companies benefit from highly dedicated engineers, quick decision-making, a willingness to develop a product satisfactory for some market segment (even if small), and a commitment to economize, to borrow, to do anything that will keep costs down (Starr and MacMillan, 1990).

We might expect new and small firms in developing countries to operate with the same disadvantages and advantages as their counterparts in developed countries.

The entrepreneurs in developing countries clearly can benefit from being able to identify market opportunities in their home countries and from lower factor costs, such as labor. Inventive people can be found in every county. However, in many developing countries such creative people may find it more difficult to develop state-of-the-art knowledge of current technology through education or work experience. Much may depend upon the specific educational institutions, branches of multinational firms, and innovative local firms that are located there. We do know that in some countries, such as India, many young software engineers are among the best in the world and have become the nucleus of successful, innovative new firms.

In China, for example, one of the key barriers for smaller new ventures to engage in technological innovation is lack of technical and managerial personnel. Many small businesses, known as *getihu*, are initiated by people who have little education. More formal private enterprises, known as *siying qiye*, operate in different industries, ranging from restaurants to transportation to manufacturing. These enterprises tend to be established by those with prior working experience and technical and managerial background. However, it remains a major challenge to attract other experienced personnel to work for these ventures (Liao and Sohmen, 2001). Most university graduates lack work experience and tend to move easily to better opportunities once they gain experience. Even the popular high-tech ventures have difficulty attracting employees with technical and managerial expertise. Many successful high-tech ventures are established by foreign-educated or trained Chinese returning to their home country. However, most of these returning Chinese entrepreneurs have "back-up plans" and thus are less committed to their ventures in the long term as compared to other types of entrepreneurs.

Innovation in Established Organizations

Established, larger organizations are often very good at applying their considerable resources to improving existing products and processes and to extending existing product lines. However, for reasons noted above, they often face challenges in trying to develop major innovations.

There are a number of approaches which established firms can adopt in attempting to become more innovative or in seeking to participate in successful innovative ventures. The approach most separated from current operations would be to make venture capital investments in small firms with promising technologies. In 2000, corporate venture capital investments totaled about $16 billion (*Venture Economics*, 2001). This approach permits an established firm to avoid structural changes. These investments can be made primarily for strategic reasons to provide a "window on new technology" or to help support the development of markets of interest to the investing firm. For instance, in 2004 Intel listed 228 firms in its investment portfolio. If successful, these companies would increase the demand for Intel's products. Alternatively, the primary motivation can be financial, as the operating firm seeks to be a successful venture capitalist. In general, corporate venture groups seem to do better if they have considerable autonomy and if the established corporation is relatively patient.

Another approach, particularly prominent in the pharmaceutical industry, is to engage in alliances, such as agreements with innovative small firms to support their research, with the larger firm to become a licensee for certain applications of the new technology developed. Alternatively, the established firm can invest in joint ventures which draw upon the resources of the parent firms to exploit particular technologies or geographic markets. In both instances, the established firm is taking advantage of the ability of a new firm to develop new technology, to form strategy attuned to a particular market, or to attract needed stakeholders whose resources are needed to make the venture viable.

These approaches, investing as a venture capitalist or participating in a joint venture or alliance, enable an established firm to realize some of the benefits of entrepreneurial ventures without having to change the established organization very much. An approach which does involve internal changes is to create a new venture department or division. New venture departments are charged with trying to develop or grow new businesses inside the established organization. They vary from "macro venture divisions" which have their own engineering, manufacturing, and sales capabilities to "micro venture divisions" which borrow needed resources from operating divisions (Fast, 1977). New venture departments may develop quick moving flexible teams like their counterparts in independent firms. They may be exempt from many corporate policies which would require staff approval and their performance may be appraised in a more flexible, long-term way than for operating divisions. If successful new businesses are grown, they may be taken over by operating divisions; they may become independent divisions within the corporation; or they may be spun off as independent firms. In managing new venture departments, one question is the extent to which the rewards and risks for corporate entrepreneurs are similar to those for independent entrepreneurs. Can corporate entrepreneurs become wealthy or alternatively lose everything? Are the benefits and costs moderated by their being inside an established corporation? (A study of 42 corporate ventures reported that 69 percent did not compensate venture managers differently and, even when they did, the incentive payments were not very significant: Block and Ornati, 1987.)

Established organizations often have research and development departments intended to improve existing products and processes and extend existing product lines. Sometimes these R&D units play major roles in developing new businesses within existing corporations. The processes by which this can occur involve many challenges. These include securing needed resources for projects which do not fit existing strategies, dealing with measurement and reward issues when payoffs may be years in the future, and adapting to oscillations in corporate strategy (Burgelman, 1984).

A more general approach is to seek to change the structure and culture of an organization – to make it more flexible, more innovative, and more accepting of risk-taking and of failure. Such approaches often involve entrepreneurial leadership, changes in traditional patterns of decision making, training to help lower level managers develop the needed skills and confidence, and reward programs which encourage managers to innovate (Kanter and Richardson, 1991; Gupta et al., 2004).

It should not be assumed that more innovative organizations will always be more successful. Some research suggests that small firms which are innovative do better in hostile environments. Less entrepreneurial organizations seem to do better in more benign environments (Covin and Slevin, 1989). Another study found that proactiveness (seizing initiatives in the marketplace) led to higher performance when the industry was in the early stages of development (Lumpkin and Dess, 2001). This research stream suggests that under some circumstances companies should emphasize innovation and under other circumstances companies should probably minimize efforts at innovation.

There has not been much formal research on innovation in established organizations in developing countries. In many less wealthy countries, large corporations have diversified extensively. They have entered new businesses, while drawing upon their financial resources, their contacts, and their management expertise. Corporate entrepreneurship in developing countries might also take different forms. Entrepreneurship in many developing countries, such as the former Soviet Union (USSR) and China, may develop either through establishing new ventures or through privatizing the previous state-owned enterprises (Ners, 1995). Filatotchev et al. (1999) examined the development of corporate entrepreneurship in privatized firms in Russia, Belarus, and Ukraine. Using large-scale surveys of newly privatized companies, the paper shows that there are differences in the nature and extent of entrepreneurship in established businesses in the three countries. The study found that Russian privatized firms have lower insider stakes, greater outside ownership, less employee voice, and greater managerial power within the firm than is the case in Belarus and Ukraine. The differences are attributed to the fact that the active monitoring of managers by outsiders in Russia helps transform Russian firms to more efficient and commercially viable entities. In Ukraine and Belarus, a lack of outside involvement in corporate governance may lead to managerial opportunism and low incentives to attract outside strategic investors, including foreign partners, which will subsequently affect the effectiveness of corporate entrepreneurship. Meanwhile, the study also found that in Russia, entrepreneurial priorities and actions are mainly focused on controlling cash flow, seeking new markets, and redefining businesses through retrenchment and restructuring. The study identified a divergence in entrepreneurial development across the three countries. It suggests that corporate entrepreneurship behavior seems to be affected by the prevailing conditions of a specific country. Lower employee and higher outside ownership and control (as in the case of Russia) seem to be associated with a greater incidence of turnover among the senior management team and more realistic managerial decisions and priorities by focusing on retrenchment.

A related study investigates the issue of corporate entrepreneurship in a cross-national study. Antoncic and Hisrich (2001) studied entrepreneurship within existing organizations (sometimes called intrapreneurship) from two contrasting economies, that is, Slovenia and the United States. Specifically, the study integrated previous classifications and measures of intrapreneurship. It also examined the predictors (organizational and environmental characteristics) and consequences (growth and profitability) of intrapreneurship. The study showed strong support for the positive impact of organizational and environmental characteristics on intrapreneurship. The paper found that intrapreneurship is an important predictor of firm growth for both Slovenia and the United States. There is also a relatively stronger effect of intrapreneurship on growth than on profitability in both countries. Firms that nurture organizational structures and values conducive to intrapreneurial activities are more likely to grow than organizations that are low in such characteristics. Open and quality communication, existence of formal controls, intensive environmental scanning, management support, organizational support, and values all help an organization become more intrapreneurial. The study also found that the intrapreneurship antecedents and consequences differ across countries. For example, environmental characteristics are relatively less important for intrapreneurship than is the organization in Slovenia. The situation in the United States is the opposite, with the impact of the environment on intrapreneurship being significantly higher in the United States than in Slovenia. Meanwhile, the impact on profitability was not found in the United States. One implication of the study is that in developing countries and transitional economies, intrapreneurship is very important for the growth and profitability of existing organizations.

Several studies have examined whether such characteristics of national culture as uncertainty avoidance or power distance are related to the entry mode chosen by corporations, such as acquisition or joint venture. For instance, firms in countries characterized by uncertainty avoidance tend to prefer joint ventures. This same stream of work has examined whether particular ways of championing new products are preferred in collectivist or individualistic cultures. Thus, in individualistic countries renegade champions are preferred (Hayton et al., 2002).

Conclusions

Rates of entrepreneurship appear to vary widely across and within countries. The kinds of firms established vary, with many necessity-based ventures in developing countries, where the entrepreneurs may have no better choices for work. In all countries, relatively few growth oriented innovative firms are established.

A number of factors influence rates of entrepreneurship. These include the number of people in the 25–44 year-old group, who constitute the most active pool of entrepreneurs, and the participation of women in entrepreneurship. Other factors include societal attitudes toward entrepreneurship and whether the culture supports such values as acceptance of uncertainty and individualism. The availability of capital, including informal capital, formal venture capital, and corporate sources, are important influences, with the lack of capital being major impediments in many developing countries. Government policies, including registration policies, can be barriers to new firm formation. If clusters of innovative firms can be developed, then these can serve as incubators for new innovative ventures.

Entrepreneurial firms are more likely to grow and be successful if they are started by teams of entrepreneurs with relevant education, industry, and management experience. More initial capital and more extensive network ties also increase the likelihood of success.

If innovative small firms can be established, they are likely to become major contributors to the economies where they are located. Large, established firms may also become more innovative through making venture capital investments, through entering into alliances with innovative small firms, through establishing new venture departments, or through seeking to change the culture and structure of their firms in order to support corporate entrepreneurship.

From the standpoint of public policy, developing countries can seek to elevate the credibility and social attractiveness of entrepreneurship. Programs intended to encourage and support women entrepreneurs can be initiated. Government policies can be reviewed to remove barriers to entrepreneurial action. There is evidence that reducing the scope of government, including privatizing activities, leads to more entrepreneurial opportunities. More extensive social and economic benefit programs are associated with lower levels of entrepreneurship; these lead to higher overhead costs for businesses and remove some of the incentives for potential entrepreneurs. The GEM informants did not consider government support policies, including loan subsidies, to be very effective. However, it seems desirable to explore whether educational and early stage financial support can make a difference in environments where resources are scarce.

It should be recognized that most new ventures will not be very innovative or lead to much growth, regardless of the country setting. The nature of the universities and of the firms already established in an area are likely to be major influences upon whether innovative growth-oriented firms are established. Strong engineering and science programs are likely to result in more young people who have the human capital needed to start innovative new firms.

For prospective entrepreneurs in developing countries, much will depend upon the human and financial capital they can bring to the entrepreneurial process. Many will start necessity-based businesses which can provide a way to make a living. Those who can develop managerial and industry experience in promising industries will be in the best position to accumulate or attract capital and to develop the contacts which can increase their odds for success.

Overall, entrepreneurship has demonstrated that it can be a major force in economic development. As millions of entrepreneurs all over the world start their businesses and try to develop them, countries benefit from their creativity, their energy, and their dreams.

References

Acs, Z. J., and Audretsch, D. B. 1990. *Innovation and Small Firms*. Cambridge, MA: MIT Press.

Ahlstrom, D., and Bruton, G. D. 2002. An institutional perspective on the role of culture in shaping strategic actions by technology-focused entrepreneurial firms in China. *Entrepreneurship Theory and Practice*, 26(4): 53–69.

Antoncic, B., and Hisrich, R. D. 2001. Intrapreneurship: Construct refinement and cross-cultural validation. *Journal of Business Venturing*, 16(5): 495–527.

Bates, T. 1997. Financing small business creation: The case of Chinese and Korean immigrant entrepreneurs. *Journal of Business Venturing*, 12(2): 109–24.

Birch, D. L. 1987. *Job Creation in America*. New York: Free Press.

Block, Z., and Ornati, O. A. 1987. Compensating corporate venture managers. *Journal of Business Venturing*, 2(1): 41–52.

Burgelman, R. A. 1984. Managing the internal corporate venturing department: Some recommendations for practice. *Sloan Management Review*, 25(2): 33–48.

Buttner, E. H., and Rosen, B. 1989. Funding new business ventures: Are decision makers biased against women entrepreneurs? *Journal of Business Venturing*, 4(4): 249–61.

Chinese Financial Yearbook. 1989–99 editions.

Churchill, N. C., and Lewis, V.L. 1986. Bank lending to new and growing enterprises. *Journal of Business Venturing*, 1(2): 193–206.

Cooper, A. C. 1964. R & D is more efficient in small companies. *Harvard Business Review*, 42(3): 75–83.

Cooper, A. C. 1985. The role of incubator organizations in the founding of growth-oriented firms. *Journal of Business Venturing*, 1(1): 75–86.

Cooper, A. C., and Bruno, A. 1977. Success among high-technology firms. *Business Horizons*, 20(2): 16–22.

Cooper, A. C., Dunkelberg, W. C., Woo, C. Y., and Dennis, W. J. Jr. 1990. *New Business in America: The Firms and their Owners.* Washington, DC: The NFIB Foundation.

Cooper, A. C., Gimeno-Gascon, F. J., and Woo, C. 1994. Initial human and financial capital as predictors of new venture performance. *Journal of Business Venturing*, 9(5): 371–95.

Covin, J. G., and Slevin, D. P. 1989. Strategic management of small firms in hostile and benign environments. *Strategic Management Journal*, 10(1): 75–87.

Dana, L. 1995. Entrepreneurship in a remote sub-arctic community. *Entrepreneurship Theory and Practice*, 20(1): 57–72.

Eisenhardt, K. M., and Schoonhoven, C. B. 1990. Organizational growth – Linking founding team strategy, environment, and growth among United States semiconductor ventures, 1978–1988. *Administrative Science Quarterly*, 35(3): 504–29.

Engardio, P. 2003. A way to help Africa help itself. *Business Week*, July 21(3842): 40.

Fast, N. 1977. The evolution of corporate new venture divisions. Graduate School of Business Administration, Harvard University, thesis.

Filatotchev, I., Wright, M., Buck, T., and Zhukov, V. 1999. Corporate entrepreneurs and privatized firms in Russia, Ukraine, and Belarus. *Journal of Business Venturing*, 14(5–6): 475–92.

Gimeno, J., Folta, T., Cooper, A., and Woo, C. 1997. Survival of the fittest? Entrepreneurial human capital and the persistence of underperforming firms. *Administrative Science Quarterly*, 42(4): 750–83.

Gupta, V., MacMillan, I. C., and Surie, G. 2004. Entrepreneurial leadership: Developing and measuring a cross-cultural context. *Journal of Business Venturing*, 19(2): 241–60.

Hayton, J. C., George, G., and Zahra, S. A. 2002. National culture and entrepreneurship: A review of behavioral research. *Entrepreneurship Theory and Practice*, 26(4): 33–52.

Holt, H. 1997. A comparative study of values among Chinese and U.S. entrepreneurs: Pragmatic convergence between contrasting cultures. *Journal of Business Venturing*, 12(6): 483–505.

Honig, B. 1998. What determines success? Examining the human, financial, and social capital of Jamaican microentrepreneurs. *Journal of Business Venturing*, 13(5): 371–94.

INC (2000). The 2000 INC 500 almanac, *INC*, 22(15): 57–65.

Kanter, R. M., and Richardson, L. 1991. Engines of progress: Designing and running entrepreneurial vehicles in established companies – The enter-prize program at Ohio Bell, 1985–1990. *Journal of Business Venturing*, 6(3): 209–29.

Kaufmann, P. J., Welsh, D. H. B., and Bushmarin, N. V. 1995. Locus of control and entrepreneurship in the Russian Republic. *Entrepreneurship Theory and Practice*, 20(1): 43–56.

Kirzner, I. 1979. *Perception, Opportunity, and Profit.* Chicago, IL: University of Chicago Press.

Lau, C. M., and Busenitz, L. W. 2001. Growth intentions of entrepreneurs in a transitional economy: The People's Republic of China. *Entrepreneurship Theory and Practice*, 26(1): 5–20.

Learner, M., Brush, C., and Hisrich, R. 1997. Israeli women entrepreneurs: An examination of factors affecting performance. *Journal of Business Venturing*, 12(4): 315–39.

Liao, D., and Sohmen, P. 2001. The development of modern entrepreneurship in China. *Stanford Journal of East Asian Affairs*, 1(1): 27–33.

Light, I., Kwuon, I., and Zhong, D. 1990. Korean rotating credit associations in Los Angeles. Amerasia, 16(1): 35–54.

Lumpkin, G. T., and Dess, G. G. 2001. Linking two dimensions of entrepreneurial orientation to firm performance: The moderating role of environment and industry life cycle. *Journal of Business Venturing*, 16(5): 429–51.

McClelland, D. C. 1961. *The Achieving Society.* Princeton, NJ: Van Nostrand.

Ners, K. 1995. Privatization (from above, below or mass privatization) versus generic private enterprise building. *Communist Economies and Economic Transformation*, 7(1): 105–16.

Perry, C. 1990. After further sightings of the Heffalump. *Journal of Managerial Psychology*, 5(2): 22–31.

Reynolds, P. D., Miller, B., and Maki, W. R. 1995. Explaining regional variation in business births and deaths – U.S. 1976–88, *Small Business Economics*, 7(5): 389–407.

Reynolds, P. D., Bygrave, W. D., and Autio, E. 2003. *Global Entrepreneurship Monitor, 2003 Executive Report.* Kansas City, MO: Ewing Marion Kauffman Foundation.

Reynolds, P. D., Bygrave, W. D., Autio, E., and Hay, M. 2002. *Global Entrepreneurship Monitor, 2002 Executive Report.* Kansas City, MO: Ewing Marion Kauffman Foundation.

Reynolds, P. D., Camp, S. M., Bygrave, W. D., Autio, E., and Hay, M. 2001. *Global Entrepreneurship Monitor, 2001 Executive Report.* Kansas City, MO: Ewing Marion Kauffman Foundation.

Reynolds, P. D., Hay, M., Bygrave, W. D., Camp, S. M., and Autio, E. 2000. *Global Entrepreneurship Monitor, 2000 Executive Report.* Kansas City, MO: Ewing Marion Kauffman Foundation.

Reynolds, P. D., Hay, M., and Camp, S. M. 1999. *Global Entrepreneurship Monitor, 1999 Executive Report.* Kansas City, MO: Ewing Marion Kauffman Foundation.

Roberts, E. B. 1991. *Entrepreneurs in High Technology: Lessons from MIT and Beyond.* New York: Oxford University Press.

Roure, J. B., and Maidique, M. A. 1986. Linking prefunding factors and high-technology venture success: An exploratory study. *Journal of Business Venturing*, 1(3): 295–306.

Shabbir, A., and Gregorio, S. D. 1996. An examination of the relationship between women's personal goals and structural factors influencing their decision to start a business: The case of Pakistan. *Journal of Business Venturing*, 11(6): 507–29.

Shane, S., and Venkataraman, S. 2000. The promise of entrepreneurship as a field of research. *Academy of Management Review*, 25(1): 217–26.

Shapero, A. 1975. The displaced, uncomfortable entrepreneur. *Psychology Today*, 9(6): 83–8.

Starr, J. A., and MacMillan, I. C. 1990. Resource cooptation via social contracting – Resource acquisition strategies for new ventures. *Strategic Management Journal*, 11 (special issue): 79–92.

Stuart, T. E., Hoang, H., and Hybels, R. C. 1999. Interorganizational endorsements and the performance of entrepreneurial ventures. *Administrative Science Quarterly*, 44(2): 315–49.

Thakur, S. P. 1998. Size of investment, opportunity choice and human resources in new venture growth: Some typologies. *Journal of Business Venturing*, 14(3): 283–309.

Tsang, W. K. 1994. Threats and opportunities faced by private businesses in China. *Journal of Business Venturing*, 9(6): 451–68.

US Department of Commerce. 1979. *Advisory Committee on Industrial Innovation: Final Report*. Washington, DC: US Government Printing Office.

Uzzi, B. 1997. Social structure and competition in interfirm networks: The paradox of embeddedness. *Administrative Science Quarterly*, 42(1): 35–67.

Venture Economics. 2001. http://www.ventureeconomics.com/.

CHAPTER SIX

How Much Does Country Matter?

Luiz A. Brito and Flávio C. Vasconcelos

Introduction

Firms do differ. The sources and significance of differences among firms and industries offer a fertile ground for studies in economics and strategy fields (Nelson, 1991; Carroll, 1993). Firms' performances also vary. Although explaining variation in performance is one of the most enduring themes in the study of organizations, it is not a simple issue and faces many problems (March and Sutton, 1997).

Variance components technique can offer interesting insight on the assessment of the several types of effects that determine performance in a descriptive approach. After the original works of Schmalensee (1985) and Rumelt (1991), several authors studied the structure of performance variance, decomposing it into firm, corporate, industry and year effects (Roquebert et al., 1996; Mauri and Michaels, 1998; Brush et al., 1999; McGahan, 1999; Chang and Singh, 2000; Hawawini et al., 2003; McGahan and Porter, 1997, 2002; McNamara et al., 2003).

The vast majority of these studies indicate firm effects as the dominant component of explained variance. This has fueled the debate between the industrial organization derived approach to strategy and the resource-based view. The importance of corporate effects has had contradictory findings and seems to be sensitive to the sample and period analyzed. Year effects have been found to be very small or non-existent. All the studies previously cited were done on US data and depict the business environment of the US economy. One of the few, perhaps the only paper, published on this subject, analyzing the performance variance of firms outside the US, was done by Claver et al. (2002) and the results, analyzing a set of Spanish firms, have shown a performance variance composition similar to that found in the United States. There is very little evidence to support that it is possible to generalize the findings from US data to the rest of the world. In the globalized economic environment of today, it is unnecessary to stress the importance of this shortcoming.

Since the overwhelming majority of studies were done with US data, location has never been treated as a source of heterogeneity in this type of research. Theories from the fields of Economics and Strategy, however, recognize location as one of the important determinants of firm performance. In the economic research tradition, this aspect can be traced back to the work of classical economist David Ricardo (1817) and the notion of comparative advantages. In the strategy field, Michael Porter's (1990, 1998, 2000) work on the competitive advantage of nations and on clusters, certainly relates performance to location.

This chapter intends to contribute the effort of reducing the above-mentioned shortcomings of current knowledge. The first objective is to detect the country influence in the heterogeneity of performance. Drawing from previous research on variance components, a new type of effect, the country effect, was conceived. The country effect captures the influence of particular countries in all firms belonging to it. It should represent factors in that country economy that influence performance in a positive or negative way like severe recessions or extreme prosperity and growth, specific to that country. In other words, our first objective is to answer the question: does country matter? A significant country effect will mean that these factors do explain part of the total observed variance in performance. The second objective is to answer the logical follow-up question: *how much* does country matter? This will be done by quantifying the magnitude of this effect in different economic sectors.

Country effects, however, may not be independent from other effects. Country related factors may affect only a few industries and be neutral to others. The third objective is thus to expand the findings of the first and second objectives by identifying and quantifying the country–industry interaction with a model that includes this interaction as a variance component.

Finally, this chapter will assess the performance variance composition of firms in 78 different countries. The fourth objective is then to assess the performance variance composition in a truly international environment, expanding what was done by previous studies that used mainly US data. The Compustat global database was used as a source of data. A subset of this database covering results of 12,592 firms during 1997 to 2001, operating in 78 countries, with a total of 60,092 observations was selected.

Having explained what the chapter intends to develop, it is convenient to clarify what it will not cover. The approach of variance components technique is a descriptive rather than a normative one (Rumelt, 1991; McGahan and Porter, 1997). Identifying and quantifying a certain component does not allow one to draw cause and effect conclusions. Further and different research approaches would be necessary to identify which country aspects influence in a positive or negative way the performance. Understanding and mapping the performance distribution is, however, useful. If a large proportion of variance is attributable to a certain factor it is logical that specific aspects encompassed by that factor are worth studying and the opposite is true.

Initially, previous studies on performance variance components are reviewed. The main theoretical streams relating performance and location are then covered. The variance components method, the choice of performance measurement used, and the characteristics of the database are described in the Method and Data section. Results and the discussion follow and a section on conclusions is presented. A final section on directions for future research proposes possible links of this line of strategy research with the new institutional economics and development economics fields.

Reviewing Previous Studies on Variance Components

Schmalensee (1985) published a seminal paper using data from the Federal Trade Commission (FTC), year of 1975, analyzing the results of 1,775 business units. Industry effects accounted for 19–20 percent of total variance. One of the important points of the research resided, however, in what was not found rather than what was unveiled. Recognizing that the model could not explain 80 percent of the variance of business profitability, the author mentions: "While industry differences matter, they are clearly not all that matters" (Schmalensee, 1985, p. 350).

Rumelt (1991) extended the original work of Schmalensee (1985) using the same FTC database, but using four years instead of only one. In total, 6,932 observations were considered. Having four years of results made it possible to identify a part of the total variance associated with the individual business unit, and the variance associated with the year × industry interaction separating fixed and transient industry influences. The model was able to explain 63.33 percent of the variance. Industry membership explained 16.2 percent of total variance, but half of that was associated with transient effects through industry × year interaction, so permanent industry effects were only 8.3 percent. Firm effects, or persistent factors associated with each individual business unit accounted for 46.4 percent of total variance.

Although these two papers provided consistent findings, they have been used to support different views. Schmalensee's (1985) work was used to support the strategic analysis based on industry structure (Montgomery and Porter, 1991) while Rumelt's results were used to question this view since he found a large, significant influence of permanent factors associated with the business unit itself. This emphasized the importance of the resource-based approach (Roquebert et al., 1996).

Roquebert et al. (1996) published a similar research using the Compustat database. The data covered the period of 1985 to 1991, using 16,596 observations. Findings were similar to the two previous studies with one notable exception, the corporate effect. They found a significant corporate effect explaining 17.9 percent of the total variance. The model was able to explain 68.0 percent of total variance leaving 32 percent unexplained.

McGahan and Porter (1997) published a broad work based on Compustat data from 1981 to 1994, with 72,742 observations. While previous studies have used only manufacturing firms, McGahan and Porter (1997) also analyzed other economic sectors besides manufacturing, such as mining and agriculture, retailing, transport, services, lodging and entertainment. When the results of the manufacturing economic sector are compared, the findings were, again, consistent with the previous studies. The largest variance component was associated with the business unit and amounted to 35.45 percent of the total. The industry accounted for 10.81 percent of the variance, and year effects for 2.34 percent. The same manufacturing data was analyzed using Rumelt's (1991) model delivering comparable results.

In other broad economic sectors, such as mining and agriculture, retailing, transport, services, lodging and entertainment, variance composition was significantly different from manufacturing and industry influence was much greater so that when the aggregate results were examined industry accounted for over 17 percent of the variance (McGahan and Porter, 1997).

Table 6.1 Comparative summary of previous studies on variance composition of performance (manufacturing firms), in percent

	Schmalensee	Rumelt	Roquebert et al.	McGahan and Porter, using Rumelt model	McGahan and Porter
Year	n.a.	0	0.5	0.40	2.34
Industrial sector × year	n.a.	7.84	2.3	4.44	n.a.
Industrial sector, fixed	n.a.	8.32	10.2	7.20	10.81
Industrial sector, total	19.59	16.16	12.5	11.64	10.81
Corporation	n.a.	0.80	17.9	2.05	n.a.
Corporation – industry covariance	−0.62	0	n.a.	−1.42	−2.27
Market share	0.62	n.a.	n.a.	n.a.	n.a.
Business unit/ segment	n.a.	46.37	37.1	33.79	35.45
Model	19.59	63.33	68.0	46.46	46.33
Unexplained variance, error	80.41	36.67	32.0	53.54	53.67

Source: McGahan and Porter, 1997; Roquebert et al., 1996; Rumelt, 1991; Schmalensee, 1985.

A comparison of these studies, showing results for manufacturing data only, is presented in Table 6.1. Although there are discrepancies related to corporation effects, there is remarkable coincidence in the other components of the variance given the differences in the data and method used. The largest component of variance has always been the individual business unit characteristics accounting from a third to a half of the total variance. Industry is significant, but its influence is somewhere between 10 and 20 percent of the total variance, and part of that is due to interaction with year.

Other authors also explored the theme using different methodologies and approaches, but reaching conclusions that are consistent with the previous summary. Wernerfelt and Montgomery (1988) used Tobin's q to measure firm performance. Hansen and Wernerfelt (1989) decomposed the profit rates into its economic and organizational components. Powell (1996) used a survey and interview methodology confirming that industry factors could explain around 20 percent of the total. Mauri and Michaels (1998) explored the effects influence on the strategies pursued by the business units. McGahan (1999) explored the use of different performance metrics (Tobin's q, traditional accounting profitability and a hybrid measure, return on replacement value of assets). McGahan and Porter (1999) explored the issue of persistence of the various effects. Hawawini et al. (2003) also explored other financial performance measures and effect of sample composition. McNamara et al. (2003)

used four-year moving windows to observe the changing pattern variance composition using US Compustat data from 1978 to 1997. All these studies used US data. Similar analysis with data from other countries is very limited. Claver et al. (2002) studied Spanish firms finding similar results. All analysis covered only firm, industry, corporate, and year effects. Cross-country studies were never undertaken with this approach. Location was not considered as a factor influencing performance variance.

Location and Performance

Geography has been linked with firms' economic performance since early days of economic thinking. Adam Smith (1776) introduced the idea of absolute advantage by which a region with a lower cost could dominate the market exporting to others. Ricardo (1817) further developed the subject with the notion of comparative advantage. International trade is based on the existence of inequalities in production factors among countries. Countries enjoying abundance of certain production factors can exploit a comparative advantage when producing goods that demand intense use of these factors. Countries where labor cost is low should have a comparative advantage in the production of goods that require high labor intensity in the production process.

Krugman (1994) revisited the effects of external economies related to a particular geographical location on a firm competitive position reaching the conclusion that geography matters, and that the borderless economy has not yet arrived. The increasing degree of integration of modern economy, the reduction of transportation costs, and the increase of information exchange could indicate that we are on the brink of becoming a "borderless" world populated by global, even anational firms. Krugman's (1994) analysis posited that location still matters not only due to the comparative advantages, but also due to the increased competitiveness arising from created advantages. These "created advantages" were advanced by Marshall (1920) and are related to both large-scale clustering of industries in certain areas or nations, and the localization of particular industries in certain specific areas. The advantage arises from labor market pooling, availability at lower cost of specialized inputs and services, and technological externalities or spillovers. Empirical evidence showed that the phenomena can be observed in both high-technology and low-technology industries (*ibid.*).

Kogut (1991) examined the notion of country competitiveness as countries do differ in their prevailing technological and organizational capabilities. These differences influence the performance of firms based in those countries and part of the observed heterogeneity in performance can be attributable to the effects of a firm's country of origin. The persistence of these competitive differences among countries is a function of the relative permeability of country borders versus firms' borders. The slower rate of diffusion of organizational capabilities in relation to technological capabilities is an additional reason for the persistence of these competitive differences.

Michael Porter (1990, 1994, 1998, 2000) developed a whole theory of competition based on clusters. Clusters affect competition in three broad ways: they increase the productivity of constituent firms or industries; they increase their capacity for innovation; and they stimulate new business formation that supports innovation and expands the cluster (Porter, 1998, p. 213). The cluster approach thus offers a dynamic influence of location in competition as opposed to a static one associated with the basic economic analysis. Porter (1990) offered the "diamond" framework to analyze the determinants of a competitive advantage of a nation. The diamond consists of four interrelated sets of attributes linked to location: factor (input) conditions; demand conditions; related and supporting industries; and the context for firm strategy and rivalry.

The above brief, and by no means comprehensive, review indicates that previous research and theory in both economics and strategy fields supports the notion that location affects firms' individual performance. Part of the observed heterogeneity in firms' performance should be attributable to a location determinant. Previous research on variance composition of performance, however, has never considered this type of influence, perhaps because most of it was done using US data only. On the other hand, specific research on clusters and agglomeration of firms and industries looked at specific agglomerations and their effects not putting the analysis in perspective with other factors that affect performance.

The "country effect" proposed in this chapter is related to country specific factors that affect all firms in a given country in a similar way. It captures most of the argument proposed by Kogut (1991), but only part of the influence of clusters as developed by Porter (1994). The influence of the actual cluster is not simple to capture since it involves some firms of a certain industry, not all of them. It also involves some firms of related industries and finally, the geographical definition may not coincide with national borders. Firms located in neighboring countries may be part of a cluster. Some of this "cluster" effect can be captured in the interaction between country and industry, but it must be recognized that this is not the definition of a cluster. The major benefit of the approach is that it looks at the variance as it occurs in the real world and estimates all the components simultaneously allowing the researcher to compare magnitudes and assess one in perspective of the others.

Method and Data

Components of variance

The components of variance technique is widely used in other fields like genetics, but its application to business has been limited (Rumelt, 1991). It attempts to decompose the variance observed in a specific variable into the components (or variances) that represent the contribution of each random effect causing that final variance. Searle et al. (1992) provide a comprehensive treatment of the technique. In the case in study, firm, industry sector, year, and country are taken as random effects, each contributing to the total variance of the observable variable. The basic model, without considering possible interactions is:

$$r_{i,j,k,t} = \mu + \gamma_t + \alpha_i + \beta_j + \phi_k + \varepsilon_{i,j,k,t} \tag{1}$$

where $r_{i,j,k,t}$ is the performance measure of an individual company in the sample. The index t represents the different years considered; i the different industry sectors; j the country where the firm is located; and k the individual firms. The term μ is the average result of all companies taken as one group. The term γ_t is the year effect, α_i is the industry sector effect, β_j accounts for the country effect and, finally, ϕ_k is the individual contribution of the company k to its results, or the firm effect. The error term $\varepsilon_{i,j,k,t}$ is the residual, not explained by the model. This simple model can be extended including the possible interactions of country, industry sector and year by adding another three terms accounting for country-industry, country-year and industry-year interactions.

The variance of the term $r_{i,j,k,t}$ is given by:

$$\sigma_r^2 = \sigma_\gamma^2 + \sigma_\alpha^2 + \sigma_\beta^2 + \sigma_\phi^2 + \sigma_\varepsilon^2 \qquad (2)$$

These variances can be estimated by several methods. This chapter uses MINQUE (Minimum Norm Quadratic Estimation) since it is recognized as unbiased and requires no iteration, reducing the computational power required.

Performance measurement

One important issue in this type of analysis is how to measure firms' performance. Performance has been seen as having a multidimensional nature, relative to the various stakeholders and not representable by a single index (Chakravarthy, 1986; Donaldson and Preston, 1995; Kaplan and Norton, 1996, p. 24). Besides, a true measure of strategic performance should include a futuristic component related to the ability the firm has to face future challenges (Chakravarthy, 1986). Jensen (2001) challenged the multidimensional approach positing that a single value function, incorporating all dimensions should be used to assess firm performance. Financial indicators end up being used since they are available and comparable, but it is necessary to keep in mind that only one and limited dimension of performance is being measured. Most of the previous studies on performance variance composition used the ratio of accounting profit to total firm assets. Some authors, however, explored different financial measures of performance as Tobin's q, economic profit, market value, hybrid measures and even surveys among managers reaching similar conclusions (Wernerfelt and Montgomery, 1988; Powell, 1996; McGahan, 1999; Hawawini et al., 2003). Recognizing all these limitations, as a first approach to measure country effects, this research used return on assets as a measure of performance. The definition of ROA (return on assets) of the Compustat Global Database was used. It is calculated as the income before extraordinary items divided by the average of the most recent two years total assets.

Data

The Compustat Global Database was the data source. This database compiles financial and market data of more than 13,000 companies in over 80 countries around the world. Compustat (Global) data is collected by Standard and Poor's using consistent sets of financial data items that are developed by examining financial statements from a variety of countries and identifying items that are widely reported by companies regardless of their geographic location, business activity, or accounting practices. Data is normalized according to local accounting principles, disclosure methods, and data item definitions. Results for each firm are reported in the country where the firm is incorporated. Multinational companies are often reporting their results in their country of origin rather than the country where the operations are being performed. This study considers country as the country of origin rather than the country where operations are taking place. For the great majority of companies the two country concepts coincide, but not for all. Another limitation is that the Compustat Global database does not provide a breakdown of company activities by business unit. A four-digit SIC (Standard Industry Classification) code is assigned to a company considering its most typical activity. This probably leads to an underestimation of industry effects since results not relating specifically to each industry are pooled together. Data selection for this study started with four basic databases: industrial active, industrial research, financial active, and financial research. Only firms with revenues and total assets of more than US$10 million, and with reported results in at least four of the five years considered (1997–2001), were included. In total, 12,592 firms met these criteria, providing 60,092 observations, covering 78 countries and 448 different four-digit SIC codes. The analysis was done grouping SIC codes by broad economic sector or divisions. Division A included agriculture, forestry and fishing (SIC codes below 1000); division B was mining (SIC codes 1000–1499); division C was construction (SIC codes 1500–1799); division D, the largest one, was manufacturing (SIC codes 2000–3999); division E covered transportation, communications, electric, gas and sanitary service (SIC codes 4000–4971); divisions F and G were analyzed together covering wholesale trade and retail trade (SIC 5000–5999); division H was finance, insurance, and real estate (SIC 6000–6799); division I was services (SIC 7000–8999).

Results and Discussion

The descriptive analysis of the large sample considered, covering 78 countries, offers an interesting perspective of the characteristics of the distribution of performance measured as return on assets. The mean estimate was 1.71 percent and the standard deviation 13.72 percent. This value of standard deviation is comparable to previous studies made on US data only. McGahan and Porter (1997) found a standard deviation of 15.7 percent and Rumelt (1991) 16.7 percent. It is important to note the significance of this dispersion relating it to the interpretation of the result for one individual firm. Being only one standard deviation above the mean results in a quite good performance and a firm situated one standard deviation below is delivering a really poor and troubled performance. Another aspect is the shape of the distribution that can be seen in Figure 6.1. It is a bell-shaped distribution, slightly skewed to the right (skewness coefficient of –7.86) and significantly more "peaked" than the normal distribution. This is a leptokurtic characteristic, indicated by the high kurtosis coefficient of 176.14. Intuitively this distribution represents a situation where the

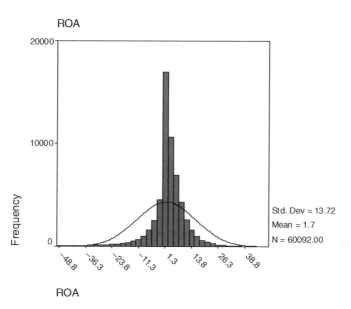

Figure 6.1 Performance distribution

shoulders of the normal curve have been shaved off and this material has been added to the peak and the tails (Spanos, 1999). Firms tend to group their results around the mean closer than one would expect in a normal distribution and, at the same time, show more frequent large deviations (positive and negative) from the mean than would be expected if the distribution were normal. Table 6.2 shows the descriptive results for each economic sector or division.

The analysis of variance components was done for each economic sector and results presented wide variations in variance composition as McGahan and Porter (1997) have found analyzing US data only. Table 6.3 shows the variance composition of each economic sector using a simple model where no interaction in the factors is accounted for.

In most cases, the simple model could explain 40–50 percent of the total variance, which is consistent with previous studies reviewed. Firm effects were the most important class of effects in most economic sectors with the exception of construction and mining where they were the second most influential factor. Industry effects ranged from nil to 15.6 percent in mining. They were surprisingly low in most economic sectors when compared with previous studies. Year effects were always below 3 percent, consistent with all previous studies. Country effects did appear and exhibited a non-systematic variation across the different economic sectors ranging from non-existent in transportation to 20.8 percent in agriculture.

The manufacturing economic sector is the one with the largest number of observations and the one most explored in previous research, so it deserves a more thorough analysis. The standard deviation was 13.16. This figure is not far from the ones found previously: 18.7 percent by Schmalensee (1985); 16.7 percent by Rumelt

Table 6.2 Descriptive analysis of the sample by economic sector

Economic sector	Observations	Firms	Countries	Industry sectors	Mean	Variance	Skewness	Kurtosis
Agriculture, forestry and fishing	400	88	24	5	1.66	83.96	−2.07	8.26
Mining	1594	351	47	11	2.01	237.37	−2.57	15.25
Construction	2446	516	39	8	0.92	84.22	−2.56	102.17
Manufacturing	27928	5940	61	223	2.05	173.11	−9.157	263.98
Transportation	5368	1141	56	37	1.59	180.26	−10.14	203.63
Wholesale and retail	7493	1573	47	63	2.48	91.08	−3.27	30.65
Insurance, finance and real estate	8128	1816	62	40	1.99	85.95	−3.53	97.89
Services	6735	1167	44	61	0.6	509.26	−5.39	56.93
Total	60092	12592	78	448	−1.71	188.18	−7.86	176.14

Source: Analysis by the authors based on the Compustat Global Database.

(1991); and 15.7 percent by McGahan and Porter (1997). Firm effects of 37.2 percent of total variance were also consistent with the 46.37 percent of Rumelt (1991), and the 35.45 percent of McGahan and Porter (1997). Industry effects of only 3.2 percent, however, were lower than the 10.81 percent found by McGahan and Porter (1997). The comparison with the Rumelt (1991) model cannot be properly made since he used a model including year × industry interaction. Rumelt (1991) found a fixed industry effect of 8.32 percent and a transient one (the interaction with year) of 7.84 percent. Since the sample of this study included US and non-US firms, and the previous studies were done with US data only, one of the possibilities was that the variance composition outside the US would be very different. This was checked performing the analysis separately for US and non-US countries, but the results did not show any significant differences for the two sub-samples. Another possible explanation could be the different periods of sample collection and the occurrence of a change in the variance composition with time. McNamara et al. (2003) presented an analysis showing the variance composition in 17 four-year windows from 1978 to 1997, using the Compustat US database. The industry effect showed a clear and steady pattern of reduction since its peak in 1983–6 of 13.1 percent to 3.5 percent for the last time window analyzed, 1994–7. Claver et al. (2002), using a model similar to Rumelt (1991) applied it to Spanish firms during 1994–8, found a fixed industry effect of 2.06 percent and a transient one of 2.78 percent. Under this perspective, the figure of 3.2 percent for the period 1998–2001 seems quite reasonable. Another aspect that could explain the lower percentage of industry effects is that the Compustat Global database assigns the whole company to its most representative SIC code while the US database company's results are split by

Table 6.3 Variance composition, simple model (in percent)

	Agriculture	Mining	Construction	Manufacturing	Transportation	Wholesale and retail	Insurance, finance and real estate	Services
Firm	27.7	14.0	6.5	37.2	49.5	42.6	40.4	43.3
Country	20.8	8.2	16.9	2.0	0.0	5.0	2.9	0.0
Industry	0.0	15.6	0.5	3.2	15.6	0.7	6.8	0.8
Year	0.6	2.9	0.2	1.2	0.4	0.8	0.2	2.5
Error	50.9	59.4	75.8	56.5	34.5	50.8	49.7	53.4
Total	100	100	100	100	100	100	100	100

Source: Analysis by the authors.

significant business lines and reported separately. This leads to a pooling of results that could reduce industry effects in diversified companies. Country effects were found to be 2.0 percent of total variance.

The more complete model, accounting for the interaction of SIC and country (Table 6.4) did not show great differences for manufacturing. In fact, a small negative figure was found for the interaction in this case, so it was set to zero, meaning that the interaction could not be identified in the model. Given the small magnitude of the percentages, they are slightly different in the model with interaction, but the same pattern of small country and industry effects, and large firm effects remains.

Still analyzing the results of the simple model in Table 6.3, country effects were largest in the agriculture and construction economic sectors, accounting for 20.8 percent and 16.9 percent of total variance. They also reached 8.2 percent in mining. This is not surprising since in all these economic sectors geography should have an important effect in production factors economies. Firm effects seem to be less important in mining and construction where they are not the leading factors in explaining the variance composition. McGahan and Porter (1997) grouped the results of all these three economic sectors into one they called "Agriculture, Mining." They found firm effects accounting for 5.02 percent of total variance, industry effects for 29.35 percent and corporate effects accounting for 22.35 percent. The model also found year effects of 2.35 percent and a negative covariance between corporation and industry of –9.45 percent. The model was able to explain 49.52 percent of total variance. Results are not directly comparable given the different grouping of data used. It is clear, however, that firm effects were less important.

The model with interaction, shown in Table 6.4, identified relevant percentages of variance explainable through the country × industry interaction for these three economic sectors. This indicates effects of specific countries in specific industry sectors and could be taken as an imperfect indication of a kind of a "cluster effect." In fact, the definition of a cluster is much stricter since it does not need to include all companies of a given industrial sector in a country, so the fact that part of the variance can be explained through this interaction is highly significant.

The economic sectors of transportation, wholesale and retail, and insurance, finance and real estate have shown a different behavior. In the simple model, firm effects were dominant with over 40 percent of total variance, country effects ranged from nil for transportation to 5.0 percent for wholesale and retail, and industry effects ranged from 0.7 percent for wholesale and retail to 15.6 percent in transportation. This is quite different from what was found by McGahan and Porter (1997) who found a highly significant industry effects and quite small firm effects for transportation and wholesale and retail (the insurance, finance and real estate sector was not analyzed). The same restrictions to a direct comparison previously mentioned apply, given the differences in sample and model, but the results indicate the need for future research in the area. When these economic sectors were analyzed with the model including the country × industry interaction, a surprisingly strong explanatory power due to this interaction could be seen. In transportation the interaction accounted for 45.0 percent of total variance, becoming the dominant effect since firm effects dropped to 23.6 percent. Similar, however less marked, impacts could be seen in wholesale and retail, and insurance, finance and real estate. Performance in

Table 6.4 Variance composition – model with country × industry interaction (in percent)

	Agriculture	Mining	Construction	Manufacturing	Transportation	Wholesale and retail	Insurance, finance and real estate	Services
Firm	26.3	11.9	2.4	40.9	23.6	33.8	28.1	45.6
Country	17.7	7.5	13.5	2.1	0.0	5.5	2.3	0.0
Industry	0.0	8.2	0.0	1.3	5.9	0.0	8.6	1.2
Year	0.6	3.0	0.2	1.1	0.3	0.8	0.2	2.4
Country × industry	4.5	7.5	11.7	0.0	45.0	12.2	19.0	0.0
Error	50.9	61.9	72.1	54.7	25.2	47.7	41.8	50.8
Total	100.0	100.0	100.0	100.0	100.0	100.0	100.0	100.0

Source: Analysis by the authors.

these economic sectors seems to be strongly linked to factors associated to country and industry, leaving less variance explainable by firm idiosyncratic factors than what happens in other economic sectors.

Finally, in the services sector, country effects did not show up in either the simple or the interaction models.

Conclusions

This research investigated the existence and the magnitude of a new class of factor in explaining firms' performance using variance components analysis. Its main finding is that location does have a say in explaining part of the observed variance of performance among firms in different economic and industry sectors, throughout the world. Country does matter when it comes to explaining the dispersion of performance. Although this has been indicated as an important factor in the economic literature (Krugman, 1994), explored in several case studies in the strategy literature (Porter, 1998, pp. 197–287), linked to competition at theoretical level (Kogut, 1991; Porter, 1998, pp. 309–46), this is the first broad statistical assessment of this influence covering 12,592 different firms in 78 different countries.

The statistical nature and the large sample base of this research also allow an assessment of the answer to the second natural question: *how much* does country matter? A broad answer is that country effects are not the main factor in explaining performance variance. Factors associated with the individual firm are still the most important source of explanation of performance dispersion. Country effects compete in the second rank of factors like industry membership. The variance composition varies by different economic sectors. Economic sectors were defined as broad groups of industries (four-digit SIC codes) with some sort of similarity like mining, agriculture, manufacturing, and retail. McGahan and Porter (1997) also highlighted the fact that the variance composition is significantly different among the different economic sectors. Country seems to matter most in economic sectors where production factors are logically more closely associated with geography like agriculture, mining and construction. In agriculture, country effects were able to explain 20.8 percent of total observed variance. In construction, country effects were the most important identifiable factor with 16.9 percent of total variance surpassing firm effects. In mining, country effects accounted for 8.2 percent of total variance while industry and firm effects were at 15.6 percent and 14.0 percent respectively. In manufacturing, by far the largest economic sector considered, encompassing 223 industries, and where most of previous studies were made, country effects accounted for only 2.0 percent of total performance variance. Manufacturing seems to be dominated by firm effects that were able to explain 37.2 percent of total variance while industry accounted for 3.2 percent and year effects for 1.2 percent of total variance. In economic sectors where the activity is more closely related to service and intangibles (like transportation, wholesale and retail, finance and services) country seems to matter less. Only in wholesale and retail, country accounted for 5.0 percent of total variance and in finance for 2.9 percent, in the other economic sectors no effect related to country could be identified.

The country × industry interaction was also explored using an expanded model that included this interaction as a separate effect. The country × industry interaction accounts for variations specific to certain countries and industries. If the particular conditions of a certain country affect (positively or negatively) only certain specific industries, this interaction factor captures this variation. This has certainly a relation to the concept of cluster. If firms belonging to the shoe industry, in Italy, perform better than shoe firms in other regions of the world, this variation in performance would be assigned to this interaction factor. Two aspects must be kept in mind when interpreting the results of this interaction and relating them to the cluster concept. The first relates to the extension of the phenomena. Finding a large percentage of variance assigned to the interaction means that the country combines with industry to give a unique effect extensively, it occurs, in this case, very frequently in the sample of 78 countries and 448 industries. If the interaction phenomenon occurs in just some specific cases, even if it may be very important when it happens, only a small percentage of variance will be explained through the factor. The second aspect relates to the definition of cluster. A cluster is not the interaction of industry and country. Not all firms of the same industry in a certain country need to be members of the cluster. The cluster can also cross borders and include firms of neighboring countries. In addition, the cluster concept includes several related industries. The country × industry interaction captures, thus, only part of the cluster concept. Any percentage of total variance attributable to it should be regarded as highly indicative of a type of "cluster effect."

In manufacturing, where the country effect itself was found to be small, the country × industry interaction could not be detected by the model. In agriculture, mining and construction the interaction was clearly noticeable ranging from 4.5 percent in agriculture to 11.7 percent in construction. If total country influence is considered, summing the percentages of country itself and country–industry interaction, quite significant proportions of total variance were found. In agriculture, it reached 22.2 percent, close to firm effects with 26.3 percent. In mining and construction, it became the most important influence, explaining 15.0 percent and 25.2 percent of total variance respectively. This gives even more support to the statement that country does matter.

In the transportation, retail and finance economic sectors, where the simple model could initially detect a small or non-existent country effect, a surprising result was found. The model with interaction unveiled a significant interaction effect that was able to explain a significant proportion of the total variance left undisclosed by the simpler model. In transportation, the interaction was able to explain 45.0 percent of total variance while firm effects were left with 23.6 percent. The total explained variance, that was 49.2 percent with the simple model, jumped to 74.8 percent when the interaction effect was included. In retail and finance the country × industry interaction also showed up as relevant with 12.2 percent and 19.0 percent respectively.

Besides the identification and preliminary quantification of the country effect and its interaction with industry, this research also offered the opportunity to observe the performance variance composition outside the US in an extensive way since 78 countries were included. In general terms, the findings support the view that the variance of performance on a global basis is not radically different from what was found with

US data. Firm effects dominate the explanation of performance variance. It was not possible to confirm, however, the strong industry influence in economic sectors outside manufacturing as was found by McGahan and Porter (1997). Given the differences in sample and method, this highlights the need of extensive further research in the area to reconcile and generalize the findings.

This chapter also has limitations. The sample cannot be taken as probabilistic sample of all firms in the world and thus external validity is limited. It is, however, such a large sample, that the results are useful even if restricted to it, since it included the most relevant companies in each country. The concept of country also has its limitations. In the database, country was taken as the country where the results are reported. Thus if a global company decided to consolidate its results and report them in the country of origin, this will be the country considered in the study. The large number of companies of 12,592 minimizes this problem, but it must be acknowledged and can be explored in further studies. Industry definition also suffers from a similar fate. Despite any shortcomings of the SIC system in itself, a diversified firm operating in several businesses was assigned to the most typical one. Further analysis comparing the data for the US where both forms of classification are available can also be explored. The dynamic aspect of variance composition is another possibility of extension of the study. This chapter analyzed the period 1998–2001 since the interest was to assess the present situation, but different timeframes can be investigated. The choice of return on assets as an indicator of performance has well-known limitations and other dimensions and measurements can be investigated. Despite the fact that some clear and relevant conclusions were drawn and can be of use in guiding and giving relevance to different streams of strategy research, there is clear opportunity for further study in the area.

Directions for Future Research

This chapter focused on showing that besides industry- and firm-specific elements, country appears as a relevant source of performance variance among firms. This leads to a set of problems that are not usually at stake in the business strategy field. These problems include understanding how and why some countries constitute a more favorable business environment than others do, allowing the firms to perform consistently better. Preliminary answers to these questions can be found in the new institutional economics (North, 1992) and in the development economics (Meier and Stiglitz, 2001). The new institutional economics develops a vision of economic relationships that partly breaks with neoclassical economics assumptions. It agrees with neoclassical theorists in the fundamental issue that economics is essentially built around the rational allocation of scarce resources among alternative ends. However, it takes a divergent approach regarding rationality and the role of institutions. The new institutional economics builds on the bounded rationality concept (Simon, 1945) to postulate that because rationality is limited, and decision makers are imperfect institutions, ideas and ideology matter. New institutional economists argue that institutions impose constraints on human interaction to structure economic behavior. Economic institutions are in that perspective the "rules of the game" of a society, or, in other words, the mechanisms (formal and informal) that structure social life. The ways institutions evolve, in each country, are likely to affect firms' performance in a direct way and the understanding of how these institutions are created and evolve is paramount to understand the differences between countries. On the other hand, some recent developments in development economics can provide other important insights on how to deal with strategy making in different countries. The first generation of economists that targeted development economic processes created models of high mathematical complexity, aiming at structural transformations in the economy, starting from the involvement of the government as planning agent and as catalyst of a change process encompassing economic, social, and institutional aspects. These early models focused the growth of actual per capita income, taking into account that the population was growing and that in many of these countries inflationary phenomena were also persistent. The logical consequence of these models was that the capital accumulation was the first priority (Solow, 2000) and that the state was the key agent in the development process. However, a second generation of development economists focused on a new idea, that economic development depends essentially on individual productive agents that through their abilities, values, and resources actively adapt to the local conditions to increase their personal wealth and the general productivity of the economic system (Sen, 1997). This perspective opens new possibilities of dialogue between economics and the strategic management, from a different perspective, investigating how human capital, resources competencies, entrepreneurship, institutions, development and prosperity are linked in a pluralistic national setting.

In a world where the gap between rich and poor is becoming increasingly wider, such a pluralistic approach must be a priority in the research agenda for strategic management in the coming years.

References

Brush, T. H., Bromiley, P., and Hendrickx, M. 1999. The relative influence of industry and corporation on business segment performance: An alternative estimate. *Strategic Management Journal*, 20: 519–47.

Carroll, G. R. 1993. A sociological view on why firms differ. *Strategic Management Journal*, 14: 237–49.

Chakravarthy, B. S. 1986. Measuring strategic performance. *Strategic Management Journal*, 7: 437–58.

Chang, S., and Singh, H. 2000. Corporate and industry effects on business unit competitive position. *Strategic Management Journal*, 21: 739–52.

Claver, E., Molina, J., and Tari, J. 2002. Firm and industry effects on firm profitability: A Spanish empirical analysis. *European Management Journal*, 20(3): 321.

Donaldson, T., and Preston, L. E. 1995. The stakeholder theory of the corporation: Concepts, evidence, and implications. *Academy of Management Review*, 20(1): 65–91.

Hansen, G. S., and Wernerfelt, B. 1989. Determinants of firm performance: The relative importance of economic and organizational factors. *Strategic Management Journal*, 10: 399–411.

Hawawini, G., Subramanian, V., and Verdin, P. 2003. Is performance driven by industry- or firm-specific factors? A new look at the evidence. *Strategic Management Journal*, 24: 1–16.

Jensen, M. C. 2001. Value maximization, stakeholder theory, and the corporate objective function. *European Financial Management*, 7(3): 297–317.

Kaplan, R. S., and Norton, D. P. 1996. *The Balanced Scorecard: Translating Strategy into Action*. Boston: Harvard Business School Press.

Kogut, B. 1991. Country capabilities and the permeability of borders. *Strategic Management Journal*, 12: 33–47.

Krugman, P. 1994. Location and competition: Notes on economic geography. In R. Rumelt, D. E. Schendel, and D. J. Teece (Eds.), *Fundamental Issues in Strategy: A Research Agenda*. Boston: Harvard Business School Press.

March, J. G., and Sutton, R. I. 1997. Organizational performance as a dependent variable. *Organization Science*, 8(6): 698–706.

Marshall, A. 1920. *Principles of Economics*, 8th edn [1890]. London: Macmillan.

Mauri, A. J., and Michaels, M. P. 1998. Firm and industry effects within strategic management: An empirical examination. *Strategic Management Journal*, 19: 211–19.

McGahan, A. M. 1999. The performance of US corporations: 1981–1994. *The Journal of Industrial Economics*, XLVII(4): 373–98.

McGahan, A. M., and Porter, M. E. 1997. How much does industry matter, really? *Strategic Management Journal*, 18, Summer Special Issue: 15–30.

McGahan, A. M., and Porter, M. E. 1999. The persistence of shocks to profitability. *The Review of Economics and Statistics*, 81(1): 143–53.

McGahan, A. M., and Porter, M. E. 2002. What do we know about variance in accounting profitability? *Management Science*, 48: 834–51.

McNamara, G., Vaaler, P. M., and Devers, C. 2003. Same as it ever was: The search for evidence of increasing hypercompetition. *Strategic Management Journal*, 24: 261–78.

Meier, G., and Stiglitz, J. 2001. *Frontiers of Development Economics: The Future in Perspective*. Oxford: Oxford University Press/World Bank.

Montgomery, C. A., and Porter, M. E. 1991. *Strategy: Seeking and Securing Competitive Advantage*. Boston: Harvard Business School Publishing.

Nelson, R. R. 1991. Why do firms differ, and how does it matter? *Strategic Management Journal*, 12: 61–74.

North, D. C. 1992. Institutions and economic theory. *The American Economist* 36(1): 3–6.

Porter, M. 1990. *The Competitive Advantage of Nations*. New York: The Free Press.

Porter, M. 1994. The role of location on competition. *Journal of the Economics of Business*, 1(1): 35–9.

Porter, M. 1998. *On Competition*. Boston: Harvard Business School Publishing.

Porter, M. 2000. Location, competition, and economic development: Local cluster in a global economy. *Economic Development Quarterly*, 14(1): 15–34.

Powell, T. C. 1996. How much does industry matter? An alternative empirical test. *Strategic Management Journal*, 17: 323–34.

Ricardo, D. 1817. *Principles of Political Economy and Taxation*. Amherst, NY: Prometheus Books, printed in 1996.

Roquebert, J. A., Phillips, R. L., and Westfall, P. A. 1996. Markets vs. management: What drives profitability? *Strategic Management Journal*, 17: 653–64.

Rumelt, R. P. 1991. How much does industry matter? *Strategic Management Journal*, 12: 167–85.

Schmalensee, R. 1985. Do markets differ much? *The American Economic Review*, 75(3): 341–51.

Searle, S. R., Casella, G., and McCulloch, C. E. 1992. *Variance Components*. New York: John Wiley and Sons.

Sen, A. K. 1997. *Resources, Values and Development*. Cambridge MA: Harvard University Press.

Simon, H. 1945. *Administrative Behavior.* New York: Free Press.

Smith, A. 1776. *The Wealth of Nations.* London: Penguin Books, reprinted in 2000.

Solow, R. M. 2000. *Growth Theory: An Exposition.* Oxford: Oxford University Press.

Spanos, A. 1999. *Probability Theory and Statistical Inference: Econometric Modeling with Observational Data.* Cambridge: Cambridge University Press.

Wernerfelt, B., and Montgomery, C. A. 1988. Tobin's q and the importance of focus in firm performance. *The American Economic Review*, 78: 246–50.

CHAPTER SEVEN

The Entrepreneurship and Clusters Foundations of Development: Theoretical Perspectives and Latin American Empirical Studies

Hector O. Rocha

Introduction

The understanding of the relationship between organizations and their contexts has been regarded as critical to foster not only organizational performance but also country competitiveness and development (Thompson, 1967; Lawrence and Lorsch, 1967; Porter, 1990). A special kind of organization – the new and young firm – together with a special kind of context – clusters or geographically proximate groups of firms, governmental and non-governmental organizations in related industries, linked by economic and social interdependencies – have emerged not only as strong lines for research but also as important issues in the policy makers' agenda during the last two decades.

Evidence of this interest in entrepreneurship and clusters can be found in each of the parts of the value chain of creation (i.e. academic and policy research), diffusion (i.e. research and policy publications and popular press), and implementation (i.e. entrepreneurship and cluster initiatives) of new knowledge on entrepreneurship and clusters (see Rocha, 2004a and Van der Linde, 2003 for a review). The evidence is even stronger when the study and diffusion of the phenomena are institutionalized through specialized journals, endowed chairs, international conferences, national policies, and international organisms' policy units (Solvell et al., 2003; Brush et al., 2003). Two representative examples are international organisms and national policies. In effect, relevant international organisms such as the World Bank, the Organization for Economic Cooperation and Development (OECD), the United Nations Industrial Development Organization (UNIDO), and the Inter-American Development Bank (IADB) have created specialized units, launched international conferences, or suggested policy options on entrepreneurship and/or clusters. As to national policies, "hundreds of clusters initiatives have been launched involving virtually all the regions of the world" (Porter, 2003) and a similar conclusion would be reached for entrepreneurship in the next few years (cf. Reynolds et al., 2004; European Commission, 2003).

One of the several reasons explaining this increased interest in entrepreneurship and clusters is that both are two important factors contributing to economic development according to the endogenous development (Garofoli, 1992) and endogenous growth (Romer, 1986) theories. In effect, from the regional standpoint, endogenous development theory stresses entrepreneurship, innovation, and clusters as key factors promoting local development, factors found inside rather than outside the region. From the factors of production standpoint, endogenous growth theory stresses that technological change or productivity increase is a key factor leading to economic growth. Although not explicitly considered by this later theory, entrepreneurship is defined since Schumpeter as an important function for technical change. As to clusters, they are reduced-scale systems of innovation given the positive association between networks within geographical boundaries and knowledge diffusion (cf. Rocha, 2004a for a review).

Given both the empirical and theoretical relevance of entrepreneurship and clusters to economic development, Latin American countries (LACs) are a natural setting for both research and policy making based on these endogenous factors. In effect, LACs face right now the alternative to adopt an entrepreneurial cluster-led strategy to foster firms' performance and regional and national development. After the state-led import substitution strategy between 1950 and 1970 and the macroeconomic liberalization reforms and market-led strategies between 1980 and 2000, local development policies based on private-public partnership with emphasis on entrepreneurship as well as microeconomic rather than macroeconomic reforms appear as the most appealing strategies.

Local development strategies in LACs are appealing for three main reasons. First, they are based on the integration between economic and social goals given that local actors influence the design and implementation of firm strategies and public policies. Second, the high rate of unemployment in LACs calls for more entrepreneurship and clusters given their potential for job creation (Rocha, 2004a). Third and finally, firms and sectors perform very differently even under similar macroeconomic conditions in several LACs (Elstrodt et al., 2002; Porter, 2001) which has led some authors to argue that macroeconomic climate is necessary but not sufficient for competitiveness (Porter, 2001).

This chapter marries the increased interest in entrepreneurship and clusters in general and their potential contribution to development in LACs in particular in order to answer the following research questions: Are clusters conducive to new entrepreneurial activities in LACs? What is the impact of both clusters and new entrepreneurial activities on development in LACs? What are the unique LAC conditions that challenge the arguments underlying the relationship between clusters, entrepreneurship, and development? The focus is limited to the impact of clusters on entrepreneurship and development and on the impact of entrepreneurship on development at three levels of analysis: firm, regional, and national (Figure 7.1).[1]

To answer these questions, this chapter reviews the theoretical arguments and empirical evidence in LACs related to the relationship between entrepreneurship, clusters, and development. Theoretical arguments are taken from the entrepreneurship,

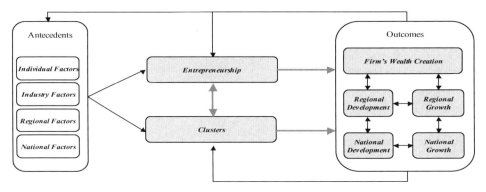

Figure 7.1 Research focus

cluster, and development literature (Rocha, 2004a); the review and assessment of empirical evidence in LACs is done following a matrix approach to literature reviews of empirical studies (Salipante et al., 1982). Empirical evidence is gathered through a snowball approach starting from the search engine Web of Knowledge, meta-studies, and, given the policy nature of the topic, publications and websites of policy-oriented institutions with special focus on Latin America.

Given the regional and socio-economic nature of clusters, this chapter contributes to the analysis of new entrepreneurial activities and development from a regional and socio-economic perspective. The next section conceptually and operationally defines entrepreneurship, clusters, and development. With the concepts defined, the third section summarizes the arguments underlying the relationship between these three phenomena and the fourth section reviews LACs empirical evidence on clusters and entrepreneurship. Finally, the fifth section discusses and summarizes the findings to answer the three research questions of the study and proposes lines for future research and implications for policy making.

Defining the Concepts

Development and growth

Development and growth are often mixed in the literature. However, they convey different realities and therefore different causal mechanisms underlie them. Development is capacity enhancement while growth is increase in outputs (Rocha, 2004a). Another shortcoming in the literature is the focus on the economic side of development and growth, without considering the intrinsic connection between the economic, socio-institutional, natural, and human dimensions (Figure 7.2; Rocha, 2004b).

Economic growth is defined as "a continued increase in the size of an economy, i.e. a sustained increase in output over a period" (Allen and Thomas, 2000) and

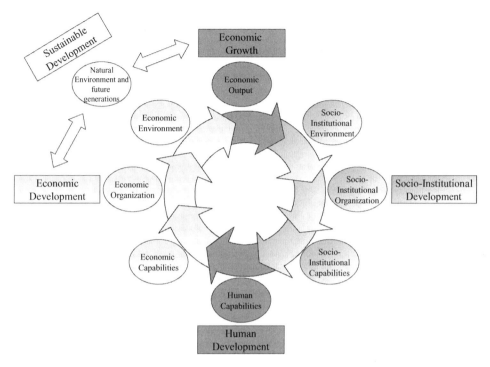

Figure 7.2 Development and growth
Source: Adapted from Rocha (2004b).

generally measured in terms of variation in GDP. Economic development is defined as enhancing the factors of productive capacity of an economy and measured in terms of productivity growth. However, it also includes economic organization such as market structure and industrial organization and economic environment such as macroeconomic variables. Socio-institutional development is the enhancement of the socio-institutional environment (i.e. rules governing social decision making, distribution of capabilities and of income), organization (i.e. structure of networks or relationships), and capabilities (i.e. quality of networks or relationships) (Rocha, 2004b). Finally, human development is defined as "the expansion of human freedom to live the kind of lives that people have reason to value" (Sen, 1997, p. 21). This freedom is achieved by the expansion of people capabilities (Sen, 1997). Development is measured in terms of economic and social indicators such as real income per capita, literacy rate, life expectancy rate, health rate, and people's political participation. A simplified proxy for development is job creation, given the human, social, and economic implications of getting a job. The validity of job creation as a measure of development increases if it is related to outputs – in order to measure economic productivity – and quality jobs – in order to include the human and social dimensions of development (Rocha, 2004b). Quality jobs encompass not only economic (wage level, pension provision, car allowances) and social (holiday entitlements, sick pay, safety and health, working hours, security of employment, child care) benefits but also morale and job satisfaction.

This conceptualization of development and growth can be applied to both national and regional levels. At the firm level of analysis, the concept of firm wealth captures both the output and capability dimensions. In effect, firm wealth is the "capacity of an organization to create benefits for any and all of its stakeholders over the long run" (Post et al., 2002, p. 45). This definition includes as beneficiaries not only the stockholders but also any individual and constituency that contributes to the wealth-creating capacity of the firm. Therefore, both traditional performance indicators and firm linkages to its main stakeholders constitute the indicators of firm development and growth.

Entrepreneurship

Entrepreneurship is the discovery of opportunities and subsequent creation of new economic activity (Low and MacMillan, 1988; Shane and Venkataraman, 2000), often resulting in the creation of new organizations (Schumpeter, 1934, p. 66; Brush et al., 2003).

This definition stresses the idea of venture creation, combining economic, psychological, and sociological perspectives. Entrepreneurship is a multifaceted reality and therefore has been defined from various perspectives, such as entrepreneurship as the entrepreneur (McClelland, 1961) or small and medium-sized enterprises (SMEs) (Brock and Evans, 1989); entrepreneurship as a function, especially as innovation (Schumpeter, 1934) or the discovery, evaluation, and exploitation of future goods and services (Venkataraman, 1997); and entrepreneurship as the creation of new organizations (Gartner, 1989). Each perspective is associated to different disciplines, each one stressing different dimensions of the same phenomenon. In effect, economic perspectives stress the function of entrepreneurship as innovation (Schumpeter, 1934), the discovering and exploitation of opportunities (Venkataraman, 1997), or the alertness to disequilibrium (Kirzner, 1982); psychological perspectives stress the distinguishing traits of entrepreneurs (McClelland, 1961); and sociological perspectives focus on environmental factors affecting the creation of business, such as cultural forces (Aldrich and Waldinger, 1990), environmental selection and evolution of populations (Hannan and Freeman, 1977), networks (Larson, 1992), and regional and national factors (Reynolds et al., 1994; 2002).

Clusters

An extensive historical and intellectual review of the cluster phenomenon shows a lack of agreement on the definition of clusters (Rocha, 2004a). However, this review shows that clusters have three necessary or definitional dimensions (Figure 7.3): geographical proximity, inter-firm network, and inter-organizational or institutional network. Taken together, these dimensions differentiate a cluster from any other socio-economic phenomenon.

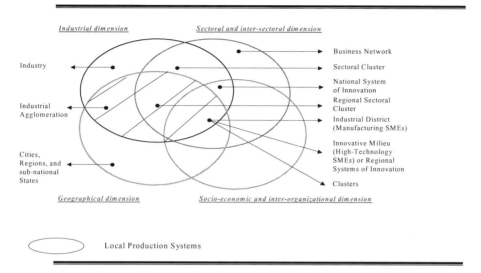

Figure 7.3 Clusters and related phenomena
Source: Adapted from Rocha (2002).

Any conceptual definition of clusters that includes the three constitutive dimensions will have a strong validity. Based on this premise, the present paper defines clusters as a geographically proximate group of firms and associated institutions in related industries, linked by economic and social interdependences (Rocha, 2002, based on Porter, 1998; Rosenfeld, 1997).

This definition captures the essential cluster dimensions and allows distinguishing clusters from other phenomena (Rocha, 2002). In effect, clusters are not only agglomeration of firms, but also networks within geographical boundaries. When only the industrial base is present the phenomenon is an industry; when the industry is relatively concentrated in a region the phenomenon is an industrial agglomeration; when only the geographical dimension is present the phenomenon is a city, a county, or a sub-national state; when only the network dimensions are present the phenomenon is called business and/or social networks; when only the inter-firm network dimension is present in the form of customer-supply relationships, the phenomenon is a sector, value chain, or sectoral cluster (Porter, 1990); when the value chain is integrated in a sub-national geographical space, the phenomenon is a sectoral cluster at the regional level (Feser and Bergman, 2000); finally, when the geographical and network dimensions are present the phenomenon is a cluster. Then, a cluster is a genus including different species. For example, when only manufacturing SMEs are considered, the phenomenon is an industrial district (Becattini, 1979); when only high technology SMEs are considered, the phenomenon is an innovative milieu (Aydalot, 1986).

With entrepreneurship, clusters, and development defined, the next section review the arguments underlying the causal relationships among them.

Reviewing the Arguments

The impact of entrepreneurship on development

The link between entrepreneurship and development has been studied mainly from an economic standpoint, focusing on innovation and economic growth rather than development.

Five theories positively relate entrepreneurship to either economic growth or economic development: Schumpeterian, evolutionary economics, endogenous growth, endogenous development, and competitiveness theories (Rocha, 2004c). First, Schumpeter argues that the entrepreneur is the origin of new combinations – i.e. innovation – and a new firm is the vehicle for disseminating them (Schumpeter, 1934, p. 66). Given that innovation is at the root of economic development, therefore entrepreneurship fosters economic development. Later on, Schumpeter will argue that most innovation is carried out within large corporations through R&D investments (Schumpeter, 1934), which is the starting point of evolutionary economics, which elaborates and formalizes "the Schumpeterian view of capitalism as an engine of progressive change" (Nelson and Winter, 1982, p. 39). Third, also based on Schumpeter's insight, endogenous growth theory (Romer, 1986) includes technological innovation as an endogenous variable in the model explaining economic growth (Rocha, 2004a). Marrying Schumpeter to evolutionary economics and endogenous growth theory, it could be argued that entrepreneurship fosters changes in technology and these, in turn, foster economic growth (Rocha, 2004c). However, in this rationale, entrepreneurship is equated to innovation through R&D rather than to creation of organizations, because the latter is either not considered or treated as an exogenous variable (Rocha, 2004c). Fourth, endogenous development theory (Garofoli, 1992) includes entrepreneurship as an indigenous key factor promoting local development. It focuses on internal factors to the region as the drivers for development, contrary to the emphasis of neoclassical economics on external factors such as foreign direct investment and macroeconomic policies. Fifth and finally, competitiveness theory (Porter, 1990; 2001) places start-ups as a key factor within the context for firm strategy and rivalry, one of the four factors of Porter's competitive diamond. Entrepreneurship increases rivalry and competition, which in turn increases competitiveness and living standards.

From the empirical standpoint, few studies have tested the link between entrepreneurship and economic growth at the national level given data limitations and harmonization of firm birth across countries (Reynolds et al., 2004). Although there is a positive correlation between new firms and national economic growth (Reynolds et al., 2004) regression analysis is needed to isolate the specific impact of entrepreneurship. The situation is different at the regional level, where both cross-sectional (Reynolds, 1994; 1999; Davidsson et al., 1994) and longitudinal (Audretsch and Fritsch, 2002) empirical researches show a positive impact of entrepreneurship on regional development as measured by job creation. In the case of longitudinal studies, the positive impact is registered in the 1990s but not in the 1980s (Audretsch and Fritsch, 2002, p. 121, Van Stel and Storey, 2002, p. 16).

The impact of clusters on development

The impact of clusters on development at the firm, regional, and national levels of analysis have been extensively analysed from the theoretical and empirical standpoint elsewhere (Rocha, 2004a). At the *firm level*, both external economies (Marshall, 1966) and the special competitive (Porter, 1998) and socio-cultural (Becattini, 1979; Saxenian, 1994) environments within clusters foster firm efficiency, innovation, and performance. Also, empirical results show a positive effect of clusters on firm performance and innovation.

At the *regional level*, four theories positively relate clusters to regional development. First, endogenous growth theory argues that clusters promote collective efficiencies, which in turn foster regional development. The sources of collective efficiencies are external economies and a common vision (Schmitz, 1999) based on interaction and cooperation between firms and institutions that operate within the region. Second, endogenous growth theory stresses that technological change or productivity increase, fostered by investments in R&D and knowledge spillovers, is a key factor leading to economic growth. Knowledge spillovers tend to be spatially restricted (Audretsch and Feldman, 1996), especially when they are based on informal ties (Audretsch and Stephan, 1996). Given that "physical proximity and networks, two main components of clusters, foster externalities – and therefore knowledge spillovers as a special kind of externalities – and these externalities foster growth . . . therefore clusters foster growth" (Rocha, 2004a, p. 382). This argument is similar to that of competitiveness theory (Porter, 2001), which argues that clusters affect innovation and therefore competitiveness. Fourth, Krugman's new economic geography argues that increasing returns lead to the clustering of economic activity and the concentration of development in specific areas where the process started due to either chance or historical accident (Krugman, 1991). Then, a process of cumulative causation and inflexibility starts (Arthur, 1989). However, cumulative causation and lock-in effect have negative impacts on regional development in at least four cases: regions with few clusters, clusters specialized in only one industry, and clusters producing congestion effects and social divides – especially in the case of high-technology clusters such as Bangalore, Telecom City, and some other European clusters (OECD, 2002; Keeble and Wilkinson, 2000) – within a region.

At the *national level*, competitiveness theory argues that national competitiveness is based on the quality of the business environment – i.e. Porter's competitive diamond. This environment is enhanced when its factors are geographically concentrated, as it is shown by the concentration of the most international competitive industries in strong clusters (Porter, 1990). Porter demonstrated that his competitive diamond explains much of the variation in overall national productivity, measured in terms of GDP per capita (Porter, 2001). However, given that cluster initiatives imply a policy-led attempt to strengthen regional concentrations, the issue of regional disparities is not taken into account. Thus, regional and national policies should be coordinated to avoid both regional disparities and destructive competition between regions. A more systemic account for the relationship between clusters and economic development is that of the Nordic School, which emphasizes the knowledge and learning dimensions of economic development (Lundvall, 1992) and their embeddedness in specific social and institutional national environments. Both virtuous and vicious circles are a function of the fit or misfit, respectively, between the economic, institutional, and social elements of the innovation system (Lundvall and Maskell, 2000). Therefore, it is the working of systemic interrelation of factors rooted in specific environments that makes development possible. The Nordic School offers an extension of endogenous growth models, which highlight that complementary investments in human capital and R&D are needed for financial and physical capital to produce their expected benefits (Todaro, 2000, p. 101). This has been demonstrated for developing countries, where lower levels of investments in human capital, R&D, and supporting institutions offset the potential high rates of return of investments in financial and physical capital (Ranis et al., 2000).

The impact of clusters on entrepreneurship

The study of contextual factors affecting entrepreneurship is based on the embeddedness perspective of the economic-sociology theory (Polanyi, 1957), the institutional theory (DiMaggio and Powell, 1983), the population ecology theory (Hannan and Freeman, 1977), economics (Geroski, 1995) and competitiveness (Porter, 1990; 1998) theories. This branch of entrepreneurship studies is called demand-side perspective, as opposite to the predominant paradigm until the 1990s, the supply-side perspective, which focuses on the individual traits of entrepreneurs (Thornton, 1999).

Clusters foster entrepreneurship providing established relationships and better information about opportunities; lowering entry and exit barriers; opening up niches of specialization due to the low degree of vertical integration; fostering a competitive climate and strong rivalry among firms that put pressure to innovate due to the presence of close competitors; providing role models and the presence of other local firms that have "made it"; capturing important linkages, complementarities and spillovers from technology, skills, information, marketing and customer needs that cut across firms and industries, which is key to the direction and pace of new business formation and innovation; providing access to physical, financial, and commercial infrastructure; easing the spin-offs of new companies from existing ones; reducing risk and uncertainty for aspiring entrepreneurs; and providing a cultural environment where establishing one's own business is normal and failure is not a social stigma (see, for example, Pyke and Sengenberger, 1992, p. 20; Saxenian, 1994, pp. 30–41, 111–18; Rosenfeld, 1997; OECD, 1998, p. 93; Porter, 1998, pp. 205, 224).

However, these arguments assume that cluster advantages to entrepreneurship are permanent. Taking a dynamic view, some authors argue that the start-up rate increases during the initial stage of a cluster and then it decreases in a more mature stage. The reasons behind this process are different, though. Schumpeter (1934) argues that successful pioneer entrepreneurs remove the obstacles faced by entrepreneurial activity in its early stages. This produces the "clustering of the followers" up to the point of eliminating entrepreneurial profit. Pouder and St. John (1996), referring to high growth clusters in their origination phase of evolution, argue that clusters may be viewed as an incubator of start-ups and spin-offs. At a later stage, congestion effects, mimetic behavior and homogeneity in managers' mental models stabilize entry. Finally, organizational ecology theory argues that at low levels of organizational density legitimation processes dominate and therefore the net founding rate is positive. However, at high levels of density, competition processes dominate and therefore net founding rate decreases (Hannan and Carroll, 1992). Although there was strong initial empirical support to this argument, results differ according to the level of analysis at which the model is specified (Carroll and Wade, 1991; Lomi, 2000).

The dynamic view analyses the net start-up rate and provides different answers to the question about the impact of clusters on entrepreneurship based on the stage of the cluster. However, it faces two limitations. First, from the cluster standpoint, it is based on only one industry and one dimension of clusters – i.e. agglomeration of economic activity. The cluster inter-industrial and inter-organizational dimensions could produce different patterns of start-up evolution. Second, from the entrepreneurship standpoint, it focuses only on the context of entrepreneurship, without considering firm specificities. In particular, population ecology takes as its unit of analysis the population and thus treats foundings as identical additions to homogeneous organizational populations, overlooking the characteristics of new organizations (Baum and Haveman, 1997). This misses two key attributes of entrepreneurship: the role of human volition and organizational learning, and the generation of different outputs at the firm level (Bygrave and Hofer, 1991).

Empirical Evidence in Latin America

The goal of the chapter is to review theoretical arguments and empirical evidence in LACs on the relationship between entrepreneurship, clusters, and development to evaluate how those arguments hold before LACs' specificities. The previous section reviewed the arguments and this section reviews empirical studies on entrepreneurship and clusters in LACs to accomplish that goal. The first part explains the method used for the gathering, organization, and evaluation of empirical studies, and the second part reviews entrepreneurship and cluster empirical studies in LACs and evaluates the applicability of theoretical arguments to LACs' specificities.

Method

The review and assessment of empirical evidence in LACs is done following a matrix approach to literature reviews of empirical studies. A matrix approach aims at gathering information from a number of empirical studies to integrate findings and assess their validity (Salipante et al., 1982, p. 324), with special emphasis on threats to internal and external validity (p. 334).

The methodological bottleneck faced by entrepreneurship and clusters studies in general (cf. Rocha, 2004a for a review) and LACs' empirical studies in particular, prevent fine-grained validity analyses. Therefore, this chapter focuses on a variation of the matrix approach, emphasizing how construct validity at different levels of analysis and LACs' specificities affect both internal and external validity. What follow are the steps of a matrix approach applied to the creation and assessment of LACs on entrepreneurship and clusters.

Defining the review's goals
The goal is to evaluate how the arguments about the relationship between entrepreneurship, clusters, and development apply to the case of LACs given the specificities of entrepreneurship and clusters in LACs.

Four sampling criteria emerge from this goal. First, the studies are empirical – i.e. they include some kind of data or data analysis using either qualitative or quantitative procedures. Therefore, the sample includes both case studies and studies using statistical techniques either in a descriptive or explanatory way using empirical data (Singleton and Strait, 1999; Chandler and Lyon, 2001). Second, the empirical studies match a minimum level of construct validity according to the definition of entrepreneurship and clusters proposed in the present chapter – i.e. new firms rather than SMEs for the case of entrepreneurship and presence of both industry and regional dimensions for the case of clusters. Third, the empirical studies are related to outcomes and these outcomes vary either from a cross-sectional or longitudinal standpoint to reach conclusions on the impact of entrepreneurship and clusters. The source of variability could be time – evolution of the impact over time – or control groups – for example, comparison of outcomes of entrepreneurship to those of established firms, or comparison of outcomes within clusters to those not within clusters or among clusters with different degrees of clustering. Fourth, the studies are original, unless more updated empirical studies are available.

Selecting and obtaining the literature guided by the review's goals. Empirical evidence is gathered through a snowball approach starting from the search engine Web of Knowledge,[2] meta-studies and, given the policy nature of the topic, publications and websites of policy-oriented institutions with especial focus on LACs. The emergent nature of the entrepreneurship and clusters fields means that many sources of information are unpublished. Therefore, an equal emphasis was put on tracking both published and unpublished research.

Empirical studies were obtained using combined keyword searches. The initial sample of studies was 65[3] and the final sample of empirical studies after applying the five selection criteria outlined above is 21, 2 entrepreneurship studies (Table 7.1) and 19 cluster studies (Table 7.2). Two important remarks are in order. First, regarding construct validity, sectoral clusters both at national and global value chain levels without any reference to regional specificities were excluded; on the same vein, all the studies defining entrepreneurship as SMEs were excluded. Second, regarding variability in dependent variable, studies that focus on clusters without measuring their impact either on entrepreneurship or development in terms of either evolution over time or comparison to state or national average for the same industry were excluded.

Identifying substantive findings in each study
The findings were categorized in terms of the impact of both entrepreneurship on development and clusters on entrepreneurship and development.

Grouping of like findings
Given the mixing of levels of analysis in cluster studies, the findings are categorized by levels of analysis – i.e. firm, cluster, regional, and national. The analysis of the findings is done in terms of the relationship between entrepreneurship, clusters, and development.

Assessing the validity of the findings and LACs' specificities
Three types of validity are analyzed: construct validity (i.e. matching between conceptual and operational definition), internal validity (i.e. whether there is a relationship between independent and dependent variable), and external validity (i.e. whether the conclusions can be extended to all type of clusters and beyond LACs). The validity assessment with special focus on LACs' specificities is the object of the following sections.

Empirical studies on entrepreneurship

Table 7.1 shows the only two large-scale studies on entrepreneurship in LACs: the Global Entrepreneurship Monitor (GEM) (Reynolds et al., 2000, 2001, 2002, 2004) and the IADB Report on Entrepreneurship in East Asia and Latin America (Kantis et al., 2002).

GEM is the first international project that focuses on the entrepreneurial process aiming at analysing the determinants, variations, and impact on economic growth of start-ups and new firms (Reynolds et al., 2000). GEM uses representative surveys that identify start-up efforts and new firms in 41 countries, of which five are LACs – Argentina, Brazil, Chile, Mexico, and Venezuela. The sampling frame is people aged 18–64 in each country, and from 1,000 to 16,000 people were interviewed in each country. The main measure of entrepreneurial activity is the Total Entrepreneurial Activity (TEA) prevalence rate, which involves the sum of those individuals involved in the start-up process (nascent entrepreneurs) and individuals active as owner-managers of firms less than 42 months old over people aged 18–64 years-old (Reynolds et al., 2002). The IADB study focuses on the process by which dynamic enterprises in LACs and East Asia are created and developed (Kantis et al., 2002, p. 1). Entrepreneurship is the capacity to create and develop new business ventures and the sampling frame are existing firms between 3 and 10 years old. More than 1,200 founders of new businesses were surveyed in nine LACs (Argentina, Brazil, Costa Rica, Mexico, and Peru) and East Asian countries (Japan, Korea, Singapore, and Taiwan).

Both are outstanding examples of international collaborative research efforts and their goals go well beyond the research focus of this chapter. Therefore, considering the scope of this chapter (Figure 7.1), this section focuses on analysing both projects through the criteria outlined in the previous section.

Construct validity
Entrepreneurship is a young field of study (Cooper et al., 1997) and only recently has entrepreneurship been conceptualized and measured as the creation of organizations. Both studies define entrepreneurship in this way, although GEM takes new

Table 7.1 Latin America: Empirical studies on entrepreneurship

Level of analysis	Entrepren. concept	Study	Entrepreneurship measurement	Time	Space	Industry	Method and sample	Dependent variable	Result
					Scope				
Firm	Capacity to create and develop new business ventures	Kantis, Ishida and Komori, 2002	Firms within 3 and 10 years old.	2001	Argentina Brazil Costa Rica Mexico Peru 4 East Asian countries	Conventional manufacturing Knowledge-based	Quantitative – non-parametric test to find out significant differences Sample of more than 600 founders of new businesses Random sampling method	Employment growth Sales growth Sales per employee % firms that export	Employment: LAC firms employ an average of 15 workers in the first year of operation (vs. 12 in East Asian firms). By the third year, LAC firms employ an average of 26 employees (vs. 30 in East Asian firms). Sales growth: sales volumes in the first year in East Asia is twice that of LACs. By the third year, East Asian firms sell five times more than LACs firms do. Sales per employee: US$ 33,000 by the third year (vs US$ 141,000 in East Asian firms) % firms that export: 6.6% (LACs) vs 20% in first year and 11% (LACs) vs. 27% in third year

Multi-level: country and firm	Creation of new businesses	Reynolds et al. 2000, 2001, 2002, 2004	Total entrepreneurial activity rate: sum of start-ups, new business owners (less than 42 months old) over the number of people 18–64 years old in a region in a given year.[a]	2000–2003	Argentina Brazil Chile Mexico Venezuela 36 additional developed and developing countries	All	Quantitative – parametric and non-parametric tests to find out significant differences Sample: minimum of 1,000 adults in each surveyed country; in addition, a questionnaire sent to a minimum of 36 experts by country	Firm level: expected jobs creation in five years; market impact National level: Entrepreneurial activity (TEA) TEA opportunity TEA necessity Annual new firms jobs as % of existing jobs correlation TEA – GDP growth correlation TEA opportunity – GDP growth correlation TEA necessity – GDP growth	Expected jobs creation: • more than 20 jobs: 19% (LACs) vs 21% (all countries) • no jobs: 4% (LACs) vs 8% (all countries) Expected Market impact • maximum: 1% (LACs) vs. 3% (all countries) • none: 35% (LACs) vs 37 (all countries) Entrepreneurial activity (TEA): 17.85% (LACs) vs. 9% (all countries) TEA opportunity): 11.5% (LACs) vs. 6% (all countries) TEA necessity: 7.08% (LACs) vs.2.5% (all countries) Annual new firms jobs as % of existing jobs: 9% (LACs) vs. 5.5% (all countries) Correlation TEA – GDP growth: 37% Correlation TEA opportunity – GDP growth: 36% Correlation TEA necessity – GDP growth: 44%

[a] There is a *start-up* or nascent entrepreneur when there is a "yes" answer to the following questions (Reynolds et al., 2002): (1) You are, alone or with others, currently trying to start a new business, including any self-employment or selling any goods or services to others; (2) You are, alone or with others, currently trying to start a new business or a new venture for your employer – an effort that is part of your normal work; (3) Over the past 12 months have you done anything to help start this new business, such as looking for equipment or a location, organizing a start-up team, working on a business plan, beginning to save money, or any other activity that would help launch a business? *Additionally*, the person will own all or part of the new business and has not paid salaries during the last 3 months, according to the following questions: (4) Will you personally own all, part, or none of this business; (5) Has the new business paid any full-time salaries or wages, including your own, for more than 3 months? There is a *new business owner or manager* when all the previous conditions are met but salaries have been paid during the last 3–42 months.

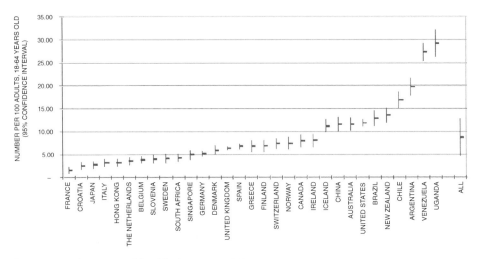

Figure 7.4   Total entrepreneurial activity by country, 2003
Source: Reynolds et al. (2004).

firms less than 42 months old and IADB takes new firms between 3 and 10 years old (Table 7.1).[4]

Internal validity
Table 7.1 shows five outcome measures of entrepreneurship in GEM: three at the national level (human effort devoted to entrepreneurship or percentage of people involved in starting a business, job creation, and economic growth) and two at the firm level (expected job creation and innovative impact on the market). Regarding human effort devoted to entrepreneurship, Figure 7.4 shows the level of entrepreneurial activity for the 31 countries participating in 2003,[5] highlighting that LACs are among the countries with highest levels of entrepreneurship ranging from 15.45 percent (Mexico) to 27.5 percent (Venezuela).[6] The average LACs TEA rate is 17.85 percent compared to 9 percent for all the countries. Given the large sample size, it is possible to infer that more than 50 million people in the five analysed Latin American countries are starting a business or are owner-managers of firms less than 42 months old. However, to understand this higher entrepreneurship rate GEM breaks down the TEA rate by motivation for starting a new business, distinguishing people who become entrepreneurs as a means of either pursuing an opportunity or having a job because there are no better choices. The former is called opportunity entrepreneurship and ranges from 7 percent in Brazil to 16 percent in Venezuela. The latter case is called necessity entrepreneurship and it varies from 5 percent in Mexico to 11.5 percent in Venezuela. This breakdown of the TEA shows that the proportion of necessity entrepreneurship in LACs is 40 percent of the total TEA, while that proportion is 28 percent for all the countries and less than 20 percent for OECD countries.

The other two measures that relate entrepreneurship to national outcomes are job creation and economic growth. As to job creation, the annual rate of new jobs created by new firms as a percentage of existing jobs is 9 percent for LACs compared to 5.5 percent for all countries. As to economic growth, there is a positive statistically significant correlation between TEA and economic growth using different time lags ($r = 0.37$, $r = 0.26$, and $r = 0.34$ for one, two, and three years lag, respectively) confirming that entrepreneurship is associated to economic growth. This association is higher for necessity entrepreneurship ($r = 0.44$, $r = 0.43$, and $r = 0.62$ for one, two, and three years lag, respectively). Although there is not enough data to empirically test the association between entrepreneurship and economic growth in LACs, the fact that the average necessity entrepreneurship in LACs is higher than the world average and that the strongest association to economic growth comes from necessity entrepreneurship suggest that the association between entrepreneurship and economic growth holds for LACs. However, these results should be qualified. In effect, according to GEM, LACs entrepreneurs face worse working conditions as measured in terms of both more working hours and higher proportion of agricultural entrepreneurs.

Finally, regarding the firm level measures, Table 7.1 shows that there are no significant differences between the LACs and world averages in terms of both expected job creation and market innovation. The latter measure shows that most entrepreneurial activity is related to replication of existing activities rather than to the creation of a new market niche or economic sector. The proportion of replication is higher among necessity entrepreneurs than among opportunity ones. Given that in LACs necessity entrepreneurship is higher than opportunity entrepreneurship, replication is higher in LACs. That replication is more common than innovation is consistent with the Schumpeterian idea of clustering of the followers (Schumpeter, 1934) or imitating entrepreneurs (Schmitz, 1989), which is especially true for LACs' entrepreneurs given the relative higher proportion of necessity-driven motivation compared to developed countries.

As to the IADB study, it uses four outcome measures at the firm level of analysis: employment growth, sales growth, sales per employee, and percentage of firms that export. Table 7.1 shows that East Asian firms expand more rapidly in terms of both employees (from 12 to 30 compared to 15 to 26 for LACs) and sales (from a volume twice greater than LACs to a volume of five times more) between the first and third year of operation. As a consequence sales per employee have also expanded more rapidly. Regarding export orientation, the percentage of East Asian firms that export during the first year is 20 percent compared to 6.6 percent in LACs; the gap widens by the third year when the figures reach 27 percent and 11 percent, respectively.

External validity
The similar results among the studied LACs make it possible to infer and generalize to other LACs a positive association between entrepreneurship and economic growth given the higher necessity entrepreneurship rate. However, the arguments related to this association should be qualified according to LACs' specificities when results are to be compared to more developed countries. In effect, LACs are among the highest in terms of entrepreneurial activity and this is a result of both opportunity and

necessity driven entrepreneurship. However, the higher proportion of necessity entrepreneurship is an indicator of new firms created out of higher unemployment rates, which explains why replication of existing activities rather than the creation of new market niches or economic sectors is more pervasive in LACs than in more developed countries. In addition, the quality of the jobs created in LACs seems to be lower than the world average, given the higher proportion of agricultural jobs and long working hours and the lower level of education of the entrepreneurs. These qualifications suggest that LACs should focus more on the association between entrepreneurship and socio-economic development rather than economic growth (Rocha, 2004a). Having more entrepreneurial activity but higher low quality growth leads to a vicious circle that not only hinders innovation but also and most importantly the human and social environment in LACs.

Empirical studies on clusters

Table 7.2 shows the sample of 19 empirical studies on clusters in LACs, which have used political boundaries to define the geographical scope of clusters. These studies cover a total of 146 clusters. What follows is their assessment in terms of construct, internal, and external validity, identifying and grouping the findings in terms of the impact of clusters on development and growth at different levels of analysis.

Construct validity

There is consensus in the literature that to identify clusters it is necessary to conduct both qualitative and quantitative analyses to truly capture the geographical and network dimensions of clusters (Rocha, 2004a). Almost all LAC studies are case based and only three of them consider both dimensions simultaneously. First, Pietrobelli and Rabellotti (2004) measure subjectively 40 clusters in terms of external economies (i.e. the geographical dimension) and joint action (i.e. the network dimension). Second, IDI (2001) maps Argentinean clusters using location quotients and based on the highest values of these quotients infers the presence of industrial districts. A combination of the subjective measures of Pietrobelli and Rabellotti (2004) to quantify the network dimension and the objective measures of IDI (2001) to quantify the geographical agglomeration dimension is the ideal method to measure clusters and get high construct validity. This is attempted in a third study (Rocha et al., 2004), which based on the cluster mapping of IDI (2001) distinguishes between industrial territorial specializations, industrial agglomerations, and clusters. The first two phenomena are identified using location quotients based on firms of all sizes and number of firms within the industrial specialization, while the third phenomenon (i.e. clusters) is identified using the previous agglomeration indicators and three proxies and expert knowledge to measure the network dimensions.

In addition, LAC studies focus on the Italian industrial district paradigm, either to apply this model to LAC cases (Casaburi, 1999; Visser, 1999) or to highlight the differences between the Italian and the LAC model (Rabellotti, 1995; Rabellotti and Schmitz, 1999). This trend has been reverted in the last 5 years and now the focus is more on clusters, which provide a richer framework to analyze local production systems in LACs (cf. Figure 7.3).

Table 7.2 Latin America: Empirical studies on clusters

Level of analysis	Cluster concept	Study	Cluster measurement	Scope			Method and sample	Dependent variable	Result
				Time	Space	Industry			
Firm	Industrial district	Visser, 1999	Expert judgment – boundaries of the cluster defined by the main roads surrounding it	1993	Lima – Gamarra	Garment	Quantitative – non-parametric Qualitative – Case study Random sampling of 130 firms including two-non clustered control groups	Firm performance (several indicators such as employment size and growth, sales and wages)	Clustered firms perform better than non-clustered ones due clustering advantages such as lower costs and information spill-overs
Firm	Local systems	Yoguel and Boscherini, 2001	Political boundaries	Cross-sectional data from different years depending on location	Argentina – Tres de Febrero, Rafaela, Mar del Plata, and Gran Buenos Aires (GBA)	Agricultural foods Auto components Traditional goods Technical progress diffusers	Quantitative – parametric Random sampling of 254 firms (119 in Tres de Febrero; 33 in Rafaela; 41 firms in Mar del Plata; 52 in GBA)	Innovative capacity (composite of six factors: personnel training effort, quality assurance activities, scope of development activities, weight of engineers in development teams, new products, formal and informal	*Local systems or environments where positive externalities prevail lead to higher innovative capacity* Institutional development plays a key role in this kind of local environments. On the contrary, innovative capacity is a function of the size of the firm rather than of

Continued

Table 7.2 *Continued*

Level of analysis	Cluster concept	Study	Cluster measurement	Scope			Method and sample	Dependent variable	Result
				Time	Space	Industry			
								technological cooperation)	the environment in less institutionally developed environments
Firm	Cluster	Zepeda, 2003 (cited in Pietrobelli and Rabellotti, 2004)	Expert judgment and political boundaries	1990–2000	Mexico – Chipilo town	Furniture	Qualitative – Case study	Firm exports Firm employment Number of sub-contractors	After a decade's boom the main firm declared bankruptcy in 2000, affecting the whole cluster Firm exports: from a few hundred thousand dollars to 30 million dollars Firm employment: from 20 employees to 1,500 direct employees and 1,500 indirect employees (sub-contractors' employees) Number of sub-contractors: from 2 to more than 100

Continued

Firm	Industrial district	Rabellotti and Schmitz, 1999	Political boundaries Concentration in terms of sales	1995	Brazil – Sinos Valley Mexico – Guadalajara and Leon	Shoe	Qualitative – case study Quantitative – cluster analysis	Firm performance: Multi-item indicator (Brazil) and product quality (Mexico)	Collective efficiency (local embeddedness) seems to be correlated to performance Performance varies within the same cluster according to size and degree of local embeddedness by firms
Cluster	Cluster	Pietrobelli and Rabellotti, 2004	Expert judgment and political boundaries	1995–2002 (two points in time for production and exports) 2003 (for all other estimations)	Brazil (20 clusters) Chile (2 clusters) Colombia (3 clusters) Costa Rica (1 cluster) Mexico (11 clusters) Nicaragua (1 cluster) Peru (2 clusters)	Traditional manufacturing (15 clusters) Natural resources (11 clusters) Complex systems (9 clusters) Software (5 clusters)	Qualitative – 11 original and 29 reviewed case studies Quantitative – Likert scale to measure main cluster variables Sample of 40 clusters	Production Exports Collective efficiency • external economies • joint action Upgrading (innovation) • product • process • functional • inter-sectoral	Production: increased in 6 cases and decreased in 2 cases between 1995 and 2002 Exports: increased in 6 cases and decreased in 2 cases between 1995 and 2002 Collective efficiency: all the 6 cases with either growing production or exports have an index of either external economies or joint action

Continued

Table 7.2 *Continued*

Level of analysis	Cluster concept	Study	Cluster measurement	Scope			Method and sample	Dependent variable	Result
				Time	Space	Industry			
									above average, while the 2 cases with decreasing exports and production have those indexes below average Collective efficiency: higher in natural resources (8.20) and software (8.70) based on external economies rather than joint action. The latter is generally lacking Upgrading: process and product upgrading in all clusters; functional and inter-sectoral upgrading is lacking Positive association collective efficiency product and

Continued

									process upgrading (2004, p. 45)
Cluster	Local production systems (LPS)	Rocha et al, 2004	Local quotients in terms of plants, expert knowledge, proxies for networks, and political boundaries	1994–2000 (two points in time)	Argentina – All regions and mapping of all local production systems	All manufacturing industries	Census of all firms in manufacturing Total of 717 LPS of which 129 are industrial agglomerations and 98 are clusters	Variation in stock of new firms within and not within each LPS Variation in industrial employment within and not within each LPS	Entrepreneurship is higher within all types of LPS than outside them Regional development is higher within industrial agglomerations and clusters than outside them
Cluster (city level)	Industrial district	Bagella and Pietrobelli, 1997	Expert judgment and political boundaries	1988–1992 (two points in time)	Argentina – Rafaela city	Agro-industry, chemical, industrial and agricultural machinery, auto components	Qualitative – case study	Export propensity (X/total sales)	Rafaela exported 20% of total sales, which is a 300% increase relative to 1988. The national export propensity during the 1980s was only 7% (1997, p. 203)
Cluster (city level)	SME cluster/networks	Ceglie and Dini, 1999	Political boundaries	1993–1996	Honduras	Different industries	Qualitative – Case studies 33 cluster/networks and 300 firms	Total sales growth, employment growth, and investment in fixed asset growth in 6 cluster/networks	Sales increased between 35% and 200% Employment increased between 11% and 50% Fixed assets increased between 10% and 100%

Continued

Table 7.2 *Continued*

Level of analysis	Cluster concept	Study	Cluster measurement	Scope			Method and sample	Dependent variable	Result
				Time	Space	Industry			
Cluster (regional level)	Cluster	Perez-Aleman, 2003	Expert judgment and political boundaries	1981 and 1995 (two points in time)	Chile – South Central Valley Nicaragua – Nueva Guinea city	Tomato processing (Chile) Dairy (Nicaragua)	Qualitative – Case study	Exports (Chile) Product quality (Nicaragua)	Export sales of processed tomato products grew from US$ 2 millions in 1981 to US$ 100 millions in 1995 (2003, p. 794) Raw milk quality highest quality (category A) grew from 0% before 1990 to 95% in 1995 (2003:802)
Cluster	Territorial-sectoral agglomerations	IDI, 2001	Location quotients in terms of employment Political boundaries	1994–2000 (two points in time)	Argentina – All regions and mapping of all industrial agglomerations	All manufacturing industries	Census of small and medium-sized enterprises in manufacturing	Variation in agglomerative propensity Variation in employment within and not within each industrial cluster Churning rate within and not within each	Higher agglomeration propensity within industrial clusters 20% growth in employment within industrial clusters compared to 20% decrease in employment not within industrial clusters Higher churning

Continued

| Region | Industrial district or quasi-district | Paladino and Hasman, 2002 (Quintar et al. 1993) | Expert judgment, and political boundaries | 1980–2001 (different points in time) | Argentina – Rafaela city | Dairy, machinery, car and auto components | Qualitative – case study | % exporting firms
Employment training
Industrial employment growth
Variation in stock of new firms
Unemployment rate
Sanitary satisfaction
Basic needs unmet
Crime rate | % exporting firms: 13.5% vs 6.3% (State)
employment training: 37.5% vs. 16.8%
Industrial employment growth: 20% vs (20%) (State)
Variation in stock of new firms: 13% vs. (11%) (State)
Unemployment rate: 13.8% vs 16.4% (National)
Sanitary satisfaction: 81% vs. 70% (State)
Basic needs unmet: 13.35% vs 18% (State)
Crime rate: 238/10,000 vs 271/10,000 (State) | industrial cluster | rate within some industrial clusters compared to non-clustered firms, but higher employment stability within clusters |

Continued

Table 7.2 *Continued*

Level of analysis	Cluster concept	Study	Cluster measurement	Scope			Method and sample	Dependent variable	Result
				Time	Space	Industry			
Regional (State, county and city level)	Dynamic production systems	Casaburi, 1999	Concentration in terms of production Political boundaries Expert opinion	Different years according to the cluster and indicator	Argentina – Santa Fe state – Rafaela city Chile – Central Valley	Argentina – dairy Chile – fresh fruit	Qualitative – Case study	Exports Productivity Variations in productivity	Central Valley – 15 fold growth in exports (1975–1976) Santa Fe (proxy for Rafaela, p. 45) • highest productivity among the main milk producer regions and the national average • highest productivity growth 1988–1995 (48% vs. 20% national average)

Continued

Multilevel: Firm Cluster	Cluster	Giuliani, 2003	Expert judgment and political boundaries	1995–2000 (cluster) 2002 (firm)	Chile – Colchagua Valley	Wine	Quantitative – Network analysis Census of the whole population (33 firms)	Firm: performance Cluster: plantations and production	Firm performance: variations within the cluster, with higher performances associated to higher absorptive capacities Cluster: plantations doubled and production tripled from 1995 to 2000. However, this together with vertical integration, consumption slowdown and increased competitiveness led to overproduction crisis in 1999.
Multilevel: Firm Region	Industrial district		Political boundaries Concentration in terms of sales and exports	1992–1997 (two points in time)	Brazil – Rio Grande do Sul Sinos Valley cluster	Shoe	Qualitative – Case study	Region level: exports, employment, wages Firm level: SME growth and technical advance	Regional: Export growth, employment growth, wages remained low Firm: evidence of SMEs growing and technically advancing

Continued

Table 7.2 *Continued*

Level of analysis	Cluster concept	Study	Cluster measurement	Scope			Method and sample	Dependent variable	Result
				Time	Space	Industry			
Multilevel: Firm Region	Industrial cluster	Meyer-Stamer, 1998	Political boundaries	1985–1997 (different points in time)	Brazil – Santa Catarina	Textile Metal engineering and electro-mechanical	Qualitative – Case study	Regional level: GDP per capita, exports Firm level: performance and productivity	Before the liberalization reforms (1990s): • Regional level: GDP/capita and export performance has been higher in Santa Catalina than Brazilian average • Firm level: firms within the clusters showed above-average performance and productivity After the liberalization reforms: • Firm level: profitability has decreased

Continued

Multilevel: Firm Cluster	Schmitz, 1999	Political boundaries	1992–1997 (two points in time)	Brazil – Rio Grande do Sul Sinos Valley cluster	Shoe	Quantitative – non-parametric Qualitative – Case study Random sampling of 65 firms	Cluster level: cooperation (bilateral-vertical and multilateral-horizontal); Firm level: performance, product quality and speed	Bilateral vertical cooperation increased and multilateral cooperation collapsed within the cluster after the pressure of globalization in the 1990s Exports decreased Firms' performance decreased Product quality and speed of response increased
Multilevel: Firm Cluster	Rabellotti, 1999	Political boundaries Concentration in terms of sales	1996	Mexico – Guadalajara	Shoe	Quantitative – parametric Qualitative – Case Study Random sampling of 63 firms	Cluster level: Cooperative behavior of firms Firm level: performance (multi-item index obtained with principal component analysis)	Cooperation within the cluster has increased after trade liberalization Cooperation within the cluster positively influences firms' performance

Continued

Table 7.2 *Continued*

Level of analysis	Cluster concept	Study	Cluster measurement	Scope			Method and sample	Dependent variable	Result
				Time	Space	Industry			
Multilevel: Firm Region	Cluster	Meyer-Stamer et al., 2001	Political boundaries Concentration in terms of production and exports Expert opinion	2000	Brazil – Santa Catarina (also Italy – Sassuolo and Spain – Castellon)	Tile	Qualitative – Case study Benchmark of 6 leader firms against firms of the same sector in tile clusters of Italy and Spain	Region level: production growth, exports Firm level: growth, financial situation, technical upgrade, and best practice indicators	Regional: stagnated production growth for the internal market, export growth Firm: export growth, technical upgraded and more productive. Strong financial constraint – technical bankrupt. Compared to European firms, firms within the Santa Catarina Cluster score about 60 (in a scale from 0 to 100) both in best practice and performance.
Multilevel: Firm Cluster	Cluster	Bair and Gereffi, 2001	Political boundaries Concentration in terms of production and exports	1998 and 2000	Mexico – Torreon	Apparel – blue jeans	Qualitative – Case study	Cluster level: production growth, % of exports, employment, cluster divide	Cluster: • production grew from 0.5 (1993) to 6.0 (2000) millions of

Continued

Expert
opinion

Firm level: job
growth, skills,
working
conditions,
wages

garments per
week.
- export share in
  denim grew
  from 1–2%
  (1993) to 15%
  (2000)
- employment
  grew form 12
  (1993) to 75
  (2000)
  thousands
- cluster divide
  between full
  package firms
  and first tier
  supplier (see
  firm level
  variables) and the
  rest

Firm: full
package and first
tier suppliers: job
growth, skill
upgrading,
working
conditions
improvement in
medium and
large firms, and
increase in
wages.

Internal validity

This criterion refers to how valid is the relationship between two variables. Many factors affect the validity of the impact of clusters on entrepreneurship and development at different levels, but two are especially important for LAC cluster studies. First, the sample of cases has to include cluster and non-cluster firms or regions, or regions with different degree of clustering (Rocha, 2004a; Rocha and Sternberg, 2005), if possible controlling by sector. Otherwise, there is no variability in the independent variable. This methodological need is tough to meet but necessary to increase the validity of cluster studies (Schmitz and Nadvi, 1999). Table 7.3 shows that only 11 out of 19 reviewed studies have applied the criterion of variability of independent variable. This confirms that many studies were more interested in analyzing the differences between the Italian industrial district model and LAC agglomerations rather than analyzing the impact of clusters on firm and regional development and growth. Second, the conclusions have to avoid ecological fallacies – i.e. when relationships between properties of geographic areas are used to make inferences about the individual behaviors within those areas (Singleton and Strait, 1999, p. 69).[7] One solution is to analyze the impact of clusters at different levels of analysis, which is the object of the next three sections.

Impact of clusters on entrepreneurship

There is no conclusive evidence on this relationship, although three out of four studies show a positive impact. On the one hand, after an initial boom of new firms in the Chipilo furniture cluster in Mexico, its growth began to slow down when the pioneer firm declared bankruptcy (Zepeda, 2003). On the other hand, three studies show positive impact of clusters on stock of new firms (Paladino and Hasman, 2002), new firm variation (Rocha et al., 2004), and churning rate (births and deaths) (IDI, 2001).

Impact of clusters on firm development and performance

Clusters seem to contribute to firm development – i.e. innovative capacity and upgrading (Yoguel and Boscherini, 2001) – and performance (Visser, 1999; Meyer-Stamer, 1998).

Yet, these results should be qualified. In effect, Table 7.2 shows that several contingencies moderate the relationship between clusters and firm development and performance. First, results could vary according to the stage of the cluster. For example, firms within the Santa Catarina cluster have decreased their profitability after the competitive shock produced by the liberalization process in Brazil (Meyer-Stamer, 1998).

Second, results also vary according to the configuration of the cluster and the degree of embeddedness of the firms. Some clusters present an internal hierarchy such as the blue jeans cluster in Torreon, Mexico (Bair and Gereffi, 2001), which is one of the possible configurations of local clusters inserted in global value chains. This case shows that the gains of the cluster are distributed mainly to the core firms and first tier suppliers, whereas second tier suppliers including SMEs' local subcontractors seem to face at least neutral effects. Similarly, insertion in value chains can

Table 7.3 Internal validity and levels of analysis

		Level of analysis Firm (Unit = firm)	Regional (Unit = region or cluster)	Number of studies
Cluster level of measurement	Dichotomous	Firm outcome = f (in / out cluster) (Visser, 1999; Meyer-Stamer, 1998)	Regional outcome = f (being/not being a cluster) (Bagella and Pietrobelli, 1997; Paladino and Hasman, 2002; Casaburi, 1999; IDI, 2001; Meyer-Stamer, 1998; Bair and Gereffi, 2001; Rocha et al., 2004)	9
	Continuous	Firm outcome = f (degree of clustering of the region / cluster) (Yoguel and Boscherini, 2001)	Regional outcome = f (degree of clustering of the region) (Pietrobelli and Rabellotti, 2004)	2
Number of studies	3	8	11	

prevent functional upgrading – i.e. take on activities with higher value added within the value chain – or create functional downgrading, as in the case of Mexico's furniture industry (Pietrobelli and Rabellotti, 2004, p. 21). In addition, producer-driven global value chains generally source inputs and innovation from foreign companies, not allowing the development of local firms and innovation (D'Avila Garcez, 2001; Humphrey, 2003). Finally, high dependence on a single firm makes firms more vulnerable. For example, SMEs within the furniture cluster in Chipilo were highly dependent on an individual firm; this firm declared bankruptcy, affecting not only the performance but also the existence of its SME suppliers.

More generally, qualitative information shows that firm upgrading depends on the collective efficiency of the cluster, the pattern of governance of the value chain, and the sector in which the firm operates (Pietrobelli and Rabellotti, 2004).[8] For example, collective efficiency – i.e. external economies and joint action – is positively associated to product and to a certain extent process upgrading, but collective efficiency varies according to the type of industry (*ibid.* p. 45). Furthermore, global leaders do not facilitate firm upgrading in complex systems products and natural resources-based clusters, but both product and process upgrading is facilitated by large international buyers in traditional industries such as textile, given that local tacit knowledge and close buyer–producer interaction are critical factors in these industries.

Third and finally, firm development and growth varies even within the same cluster, showing that firm specific capabilities matter. For example, a firm's absorptive capacity was positively associated with its performance (Giuliani, 2003). Other firm specific measures potentially affecting performance are size and degree of embeddedness (Rabellotti and Schmitz, 1999).

Impact of clusters on regional development and growth

At a first glance, Tables 7.2 and 7.3 show a positive impact of clusters on regional development (Pietrobelli and Rabellotti, 2004; Rocha et al., 2004) and growth (for example, Bagella and Pietrobelli, 1997; Paladino and Hasman, 2002).

However, these results have to be qualified. First, clusters upgrade as a function of the degree of collective efficiencies, the governance type of the value chain operating in the cluster, and the sector (Pietrobelli and Rabellotti, 2004), as analyzed in the previous section. Second, clusters could create overproduction when the lack of internal coordination makes clustered firms not to consider demand factors or the potential impact of external factors such as exchange rate and foreign competition, as happened in the Colchagua Valley cluster in the early 1990s (Guiliani, 2003). This usually happens in clusters with good external economies but little joint action (Pietrobelli and Rabellotti, 2004, p. 75) as is evidenced in the lack of statistically significant difference between the impact of industrial agglomerations and clusters on regional development (Rocha et al., 2004). Third and most importantly, clusters could create social divides within the same region, as in the case of the blue jean cluster in Torreon (Bair and Gereffi, 2001). Social divides increase inequality, which is a key indicator of regional development in LACs, the most inequitable in the world (Morley, 2001, p. 8).

Impact of clusters on national development and growth

The sample shows no studies on the impact of clusters on national development and growth. However, it is possible to infer consequences from multinational corporation (MNC) investments and the potential clustering around them. The literature shows more growth with less development, due to the low quality of foreign direct investment (FDI). In effect, MNCs have contributed to Mexico's and Brazil's increased growth in terms of exports.

However, this increased growth is correlated with decreased development due to the low quality of FDI brought by MNC practices (Oxfam, 2002). First, export production is dominated by simple assembly and re-export of imported components, which imply more pressures on the balance of payments, lack of development of local skills and innovation, and lack of opportunities to start new businesses. The Mexican automotive clusters in Chihuahua (Mortimore, 1998) and Puebla (Altenburg and Meyer-Stamer, 1999) are examples of this strategy. Second, increased exports have been linked not only to the lack of innovation but to reduced capacity for research and development and a growing dependence on technology imports. For example, in 1996 MNCs bought up large Brazilian auto-parts producers such as Metal Leve and Cofap and their R&D facilities were then downgraded or closed (Oxfam, 2002). A similar process happened in the Brazilian high-technology sector, where the focus moved from the development of new products to the adaptation of imported products and processes generated by the parent MNC (Cassiolato and Lastres, 1999). As a consequence, import penetration and technological dependence have increased. For example, the Brazilian share of imports in high-tech has doubled to almost three-quarters during the 1990s (Oxfam, 2002). Third, these MNC clusters create social divides not only in terms of salaries but also in terms of lack of integration with the local economy, creating economic enclaves. This is especially true in the case of export-processing zones such as that of the garment industry in the Dominican Republic. Attracted by cheap labor for the assembly of imported goods, MNCs have little incentive to raise the skills of their workforce or to establish linkages with local firms (Oxfam, 2002). Finally, the attraction of some MNCs has been based on economic incentives creating a tax war within sub-national states. For example, Brazilian states attracted automotive MNCs using subsidies and tax breaks generating a bidding war that resulted in the waste of public funds at the national level (Rodriguez-Pose and Arbix, 2001). This strategy not only reduces the amount of public revenues to invest in human capital and infrastructure but also increases the public debt, creating an additional burden for the national economy.

Summing up, LAC clusters of transnational corporations contributed to export success but this contribution was based on low levels of value-added, high levels of import, technological, and market dependence, weak local linkages, and reliance on cheap labor. The exception has been the software and microelectronic industry in Costa Rica, a country that integrated FDI into a national strategy using a selective strategy to attract MNCs based on high quality rather than high quantity investment (Oxfam, 2002).

External validity

This criterion refers to the degree of generalizability of the results. Therefore, the understanding of LAC clusters and cluster studies' specificities is key to evaluate how generalizable are the empirical results among LACs and non-LACs, and across LACs, respectively.

LAC clusters show two specific features: a particular configuration and a low degree of networking. The specific political and macroeconomic LA environment during the last 50 years gave shape to the actual configuration of LAC clusters. The import substitution policy and exogenous development model of the 1950s and 1960s generated little competitive pressure and anti-export bias, concentrating investment in strategic industries in few areas – i.e. growth poles. With little pressure for improvement, diversification rather than specialization was the norm (Altenburg and Meyer-Stamer, 1999). Also, macroeconomic instability fostered vertical integration as a way of coping with uncertainty and transaction costs. These features gave rise to mass-production clusters such as the shoe cluster in Sinos Valley (Schmitz, 1999) and the tile cluster in Santa Catarina (Meyer-Stamer et al., 2001). During the 1980s and 1990s liberalization processes began and a series of competitive shocks affected the industrial landscape of LACs. In effect, "with flexible production systems requiring spatial proximity to enable firms to cooperate intensively, and national policies being liberalized, production sites of large firms increasingly develop the attributes of clusters" (Altenberg and Meyer-Stamer, 1999, p. 1704). Therefore, clusters of transnational corporations emerged as a second type of cluster in LACs, such as the blue jean cluster in Torreon (Bair and Gereffi, 2001) and the auto industry around Puebla (Meyer-Stamer, 1998). Finally, the high rate of unemployment and the particularities of poor regions in LACs gave rise to survival clusters of micro and small-scale enterprises, "which produce low-quality consumer goods for local markets, mainly in activities where barriers to entry are low" (Altenburg and Meyer-Stamer, 1999, p. 1695). The Garment cluster in Lima is an example of this type of cluster (Visser, 1999).

A second specificity of LAC clusters is that they are mostly emergent clusters due to their weak network dimensions. Emergent clusters have the critical mass of firms but lack the necessary interaction among them (Rosenfeld, 1997). The emergent nature of LAC clusters is demonstrated for at least 40 clusters, which show higher external economies (i.e. critical mass) than joint action (i.e. interactions) for all industries (cf. Pietrobelli and Rabelloti, 2004, p. 45). Especially important is the lack of horizontal cooperation, which crystallizes in associations that provide services to the member firms (Brusco, 1992). The low level of horizontal cooperation in LAC clusters indicates that these institutions are weak or inexistent, with few exceptions such as the dairy cluster in Rafaela (Casaburi, 1999) and the salmon farming in Chile (Pietrobelli and Rabellotti, 2004). The low degree of inter-organizational linkages is one of the factors affecting the development of LAC clusters. This problem is heightened in the cases of local clusters inserted in global value chains with hierarchical governance structures, in which large firms are taking the coordinating role in a vertical rather than horizontal direction (Bair and Gereffi, 2001), undermining the role of local institutions in shaping cluster configuration and outcomes.

The specific configuration and the emergent nature of LAC clusters suggest that empirical results on clusters outcomes obtained in other countries cannot be generalizable to LACs. As to the generalization of results across LACs, two methodological issues have to be considered. A first issue is the representativeness of the sample size of firms – in case of firm level studies – and clusters – in case of cluster level studies. Table 7.2 shows that although quantitative analysis dominates at the firm level of analysis, sample sizes are pretty small and therefore non-parametric tests are the norm. As a result, statistical precision is low and results are more exploratory than explanatory. A way to overcome the lack of representativeness is to undertake comprehensive surveys (Pietrobelli and Rabellotti, 2004) and cluster mappings (IDI, 2001; Rocha et al., 2004). A second issue is the application of homogeneous methodologies to compare results across LACs. Standard methods are especially important given that most cluster studies are case based. Attempts to use similar methodologies such as Schmitz (1999) and Pietrobelli and Rabellotti (2004) point at this direction. In the same vein, comparing clusters from developed and developing countries (Rocha et al., 2004) controlling for industrial sectors, as in the case of Meyer-Stamer et al. (2001), Rabellotti (1995), and Rabellotti and Schmitz (1999) is important not only to learn what is achievable for LAC firms and regions but also to identify the specificities of LACs to avoid the direct transferability of models that do not fit the Latin American reality (Humphrey, 1995).

Conclusions and Directions for Future Research

The thrust of the chapter is to review the theoretical arguments and empirical evidence in LACs related to the relationship between entrepreneurship, clusters, and development to answer three specific questions: Are clusters conducive to new entrepreneurial activities in LACs? What is the impact of both clusters and new entrepreneurial activities on development in LACs? What are the unique LAC conditions that challenge the arguments underlying the relationship between clusters, entrepreneurship, and development? The following conclusions aim at answering these questions.

Are clusters conducive to new entrepreneurial activities in LACs?

Only three studies use new firms as outcome measure. First, Paladino and Hasman (2002) show a higher number of new firms within a cluster when compared to the state level. Second, IDI (2001) shows a higher churning rate (births and deaths) within industrial agglomerations compared to non-industrial agglomerations. Third, Rocha et al. (2004) show a positive impact of industrial agglomerations and clusters on the birth of new firms over the period 1994–2000. Although these studies do not analyze cross-sectoral variations, considering the LACs' entrepreneurship and cluster specificities it is possible to hypothesize that start-ups are higher within traditional manufacturing or specialized suppliers' clusters, such as software, given the more flexible governance structures in these types of industries (Pietrobelli and Rabellotti, 2004). On the contrary, clusters inserted in value chains with vertical structures not embedded in the local community, such as some automotive clusters, are likely to hinder the creation of new businesses. In particular, necessity driven entrepreneurship is likely to be higher within survival clusters serving local markets based on the market as coordinating mechanism.

What is the impact of both clusters and new entrepreneurial activities on development in LACs?

The impact of clusters on development was analyzed at three levels, considering both development (i.e. focus on capabilities) and growth (i.e. focus on results). At the firm and regional level of analysis, at a first glance clusters contribute to firm and regional development and growth. However, this conclusion has to be qualified due to opposite results when moderating factors such as stage, configuration, sector, and degree of firm embeddedness within the cluster as well as specific firm features such as absorptive capacity and location within the value chain. Especially important are the governance mechanism and the degree of embeddedness of large firms within the cluster, given that hierarchical coordinating mechanisms coupled with a lack of embeddedness in the region are potential sources of social divides. Social divides increase inequality, which is a key indicator of regional development in LACs, the most inequitable in the world. Clusters could also increase inequality at the national level when they are fostered at the local level based on attraction of low quality FDI and inter-regional competition. These are purely economic and decentralized cluster strategies that increase growth but hinder economic, socio-institutional, and human development because they negatively affect the formation of capabilities and the formation of a stronger socio-economic and institutional organization.

As to the impact of entrepreneurship, while the association between entrepreneurship and growth is positive, the association between entrepreneurship and development is uncertain. In effect, LACs are among the highest in terms of entrepreneurial activity, for both opportunity and necessity driven entrepreneurship. However, the higher proportion of necessity entrepreneurship is an indicator of new firms created out of higher unemployment rates, which explains why replication of existing activities rather than the creation of new market niches is more pervasive in LACs than in developed countries. This is low quality growth, which creates two negative consequences. First, low job quality, which is lower than that of the world average given the higher proportion of agricultural jobs, longer working hours, and the lower level of education of the entrepreneurs. Second, lack of innovative capacities. Innovation is further affected in cases of opportunity driven entrepreneurship when hierarchical governance structures within the value chain or foreign patent practices and laws prevent upgrading of local firms.

What are the unique LAC conditions that challenge the arguments underlying the relationship between clusters, entrepreneurship, and development?

The answer to the previous question shows that there are four LACs' specificities related to clusters and entrepreneurship that qualify the arguments developed at a more general level. In effect, as to clusters, they show two specificities: their emergent nature and special configuration. As to entrepreneurship, LACs also shows two specificities: the higher level of entrepreneurial activity and the relative importance of necessity driven entrepreneurship.

In addition, it is necessary to highlight two issues. First, notwithstanding the importance of micro-economic factors to increase standards of living (Porter, 2001), the general political and macroeconomic environments cannot be overlooked in LACs. This is not only demonstrated by the fact that these environments have strongly shaped the nature of LACs' clusters and entrepreneurship but also by the potential pernicious effects of decentralized development policies that focus predominantly on growth without considering development criteria. Previous experiences based on growth models through either state-led import substitution or market-led liberalization processes were both economic growth-oriented and based on a trickle-down assumption – i.e. the benefits obtained by either the growth poles or the market would trickle down to the less favored regions and people. The fact that LACs are the most inequitable in the world (Morley, 2001; IADB, 1998; 2000) shows that this assumption is wrong.

Second, the specification of what is the end and what the mean and the sequencing implications are extremely important. In effect, developing countries initially favoring economic growth lapse into a vicious cycle, while those with good human development and poor economic growth sometimes move into a virtuous cycle (Ranis et al., 2000). This is especially true for LACs, where development has to occur prior to or simultaneous with improvements in economic growth to reach a virtuous cycle (Ranis and Stewart, 2001). Therefore, the end should be more development rather than growth, given that a focus on capabilities and linkages would prepare the conditions to spread widely the subsequent growth across regions and sectors.

These qualifications suggest that LACs should focus more on the association between entrepreneurship, clusters and socio-economic development rather than economic growth (Rocha, 2004b). Having more entrepreneurial activity and clusters with higher low quality growth and social divides leads to a vicious cycle that not only hinders innovation but also and most importantly the human and social environment in LACs.

Contribution and lines for future research

This chapter provides a regional and socio-economic perspective for the analysis of entrepreneurial activities in LACs, targeting one of the most important challenges and contributions of the entrepreneurship field, i.e. the role of new enterprises in furthering economic progress (Low and MacMillan, 1988; Low, 2001). By including the territorial-sectoral-network dimensions implicit in the cluster phenomenon, this chapter also complements the approaches proposed elsewhere to integrate entrepreneurship and strategic management for wealth creation (Hitt and Ireland, 2000; Hitt et al., 2001). Finally, it proposes tentative answers to questions such as "what are ways to identify clusters, to classify them and to measure differences across them?" and "what are the performance implications of clusters?" that are part of a broader research agenda to analyze entrepreneurship within clusters (Cooper and Folta, 2000; Rocha, 2004a).

The previous analyses suggest that future studies on the relationship between entrepreneurship, clusters, and development in LACs would yield important contributions to research and policy making. Three important considerations related to purpose, content, and methods when designing future research are in order. Regarding purpose (the "what for?"), future studies would have greater contribution if they focus more on the impact of clusters and entrepreneurship on socio-economic capabilities (development) rather than on economic outputs (growth). Regarding content (the "what?"), it is necessary to consider LAC specificities such as the emergent nature and particular configuration of LACs' clusters as well as the causes and consequences of the high level of entrepreneurship, differentiating between opportunity and necessity entrepreneurship. Finally, regarding method (the "how?"), research designs have to consider construct, internal, and external validity issues. Construct validity increases when both the agglomeration and network dimension of clusters are measured. In addition, internal validity improves when research considers comparative research designs and controls for competing variables such as configuration and degree of development of clusters and industry type. Finally, external validity would increase with the use of larger sample sizes and similar methods.

The answer to the previous three questions and the three considerations for future research have at least two important implications for policy making. First, given the potential positive relationship between clusters and entrepreneurship, cluster and entrepreneurship policies should be designed together rather than in an isolated fashion. Second and most importantly, given LACs' specificities, these suggested cluster-entrepreneurship policies should target socio-economic development rather than economic growth (Rocha, 2004b). In effect, fostering entrepreneurship and clusters with higher low quality growth and social divides would lead to a vicious circle that not only would hinder innovation but also the human and social environment in LACs. Policy approaches such as those focusing on vision and capability building with governments playing a subsidiary role are in line with this previous implication (cf. UNIDO, 2001).

It is speculated that entrepreneurship and clusters would have positive impacts in LACs if policy design targets development simultaneously with growth and considers the specificities of LAC clusters and entrepreneurship. *Exclusive* focus on economic growth and potential high-tech clusters and clusters of transnational corporations without considering governance mechanisms, other specific types of LAC clusters, and the nature of necessity based entrepreneurship will both hinder growth in the long run and increase existing disparities in LACs.

Acknowledgments

This chapter has been previously presented at the Strategic Management Society Miniconference on Entrepreneurship and Innovation, Argentina, March 2003, and at the Eleventh United Nations Conference on Trade and Development, June 2004. This research would not have been possible without a grant from IAE – Business and Management School of Austral University (Argentina). The responsibility for everything said in this chapter is the author's alone.

Notes

1 For the *determinants of entrepreneurship* see Reynolds et al. (2004). For the *determinants of cluster upgrading* see Pietrobelli and Rabellotti (2004). For the *impact of development and growth on entrepreneurship* see Rocha (2004a), Reynolds et al. (1994) and Verheul et al. (2001). In this later case, the basic argument is that growth implies a demand effect, which in turn creates new opportunities for the creation of new firms. A more innovation-oriented argument is that customers place new demands on products and services creating opportunities for new technological developments. This increasing demand for new products and services triggers the entrepreneurial process in order to discover and exploit the new opportunities. For the *impact of entrepreneurship on clusters*, see Sengenberger and Pyke (1992), Rosenfeld (1997) and Porter (1998). The basic argument is that entrepreneurship is one of the driving forces of both cluster creation and development. The role of entrepreneurship in the creation of clusters is via spin-offs or the settlement of immigrants, such as the cases of the Toytown cluster in Los Angeles (Rosenfeld, 2002), and the textile and metal engineering and electromechanical clusters in Santa Catarina, Brazil (Meyer-Stamer, 1998). The role of entrepreneurship in the development of clusters is mainly via spin-offs (Sengenberger and Pyke, 1992; Rosenfeld, 1997; 2002) and increasing rivalry, one of the four components of Porter's competitive diamond, due to the entry of new competitors (Porter, 1998).

2 Web of Knowledge is a portal service containing the Web of Science, ISI Proceedings and Journal Citation Reports database. Web of Science coverage dates from 1980, and covers 7,500 journals. Its key feature is that it enables users to identify which author(s) have cited a specific paper since its publication, allowing a snowball effect or to follow "research pathways" in the published literature.

3 From the 65 studies, 40 were paper publications, 5 were conference presentations, 11 were policy documents, and 9 were unpublished documents and websites such as www.isc.hbs.edu, www.unido.org, www.iadb.org, www.eclac.org, and www.worldbank.org.

4 This study asks retrospective questions regarding three stages: inception, start-up, and early development (first three years). A dynamic enterprise was defined as any that reached a size of over 15 employees, but that had no more than 300 at the time of the study. The control group – the less dynamic firms – included new firms with a maximum of 10 employees. The study did not include the segment of informal micro-entrepreneurs, which represent a significant percentage of Latin American firms (Kantis et al., 2002, p. 8). It is estimated that over 80 percent of the business in Latin America and the Caribbean are micro-businesses (IADB, 1998, p. 19). This exclusion prevents the analysis of the impact of entrepreneurship on poorer locations, where micro-enterprises generally operate.

5 Mexico was part of the project until 2002 and its average TEA rate for 2001 and 2002 was 15.45 percent.

6 Comparisons among LACs show that there are clearly three groups of countries for which there are statistical significant differences (p values of means comparison less than 0.05): Venezuela, Argentina and Chile, and Brazil and Mexico (not shown in Figure 7.4). This can be seen comparing the vertical lines for each country in Figure 7.4, which represent the standard errors due to sample size: there is a statistically significant difference whenever there is a gap between two vertical lines, as in the case of Venezuela compared to Argentina. There is no significant difference when there is no gap, as in the case of Argentina and Chile.

7 There are certain conditions under which it is reasonable to make inferences about individuals based on aggregate data; however, it is often difficult to determine whether these conditions are met (cf. Singleton and Strait, 1999, p. 97 for references).

8 This study is at the cluster level of analysis given that collective efficiency, value chain governance, sector, and upgrading are measured and quantitatively analyzed at the cluster level (Pietrobelli and Rabellotti, 2004, p. 45 and Annex 1). To reach conclusions on the impact of clusters on firm upgrading and performance based on quantitative information the variables have to be measured at the firm level of analysis and the sample has to include firms located both inside and outside the cluster or in clusters with different degrees of clustering (collective efficiency) to get variability in the independent variable. This study meets the latter criteria but at the cluster level of analysis, comparing collective efficiency and upgrading across four type of industries (Pietrobelli and Rabellotti, 2004, p. 45). This is why Tables 7.2 and 7.3 classify it at the cluster level. However, given that this study uses both cluster and firm level data (cf. for example 2004, p. 20) and draws on a very rich qualitative information validated by many experts (2004, pp. i, 10), it is possible to qualify the conclusions on the relationship between clusters and firm upgrading and performance using firm level qualitative information.

References

Aldrich, H. E., and Waldinger, R. 1990. Ethnicity and entrepreneurship. *Annual Review of Sociology*, 16: 111–35.

Allen, T., and Thomas, A. 2000. *Poverty and Development into the 21st Century*. Oxford: Oxford University Press.

Altenburg, T., and Meyer-Stamer, J. 1999. How to promote clusters: Policy experiences from Latin America. *World Development*, 27: 1693–713.

Arthur, W. B. 1989. Competing technologies, increasing returns, and lock-in by historical events. *Economic Journal*, 99: 116–31.

Audretsch, D. B., and Feldman, M. P. 1996. R&D spillovers and the geography of innovation and production. *American Economic Review*, 86: 630–40.

Audretsch, D. B., and Fritsch, M. (2002) Growth regimes over time and space. *Regional Studies*, 113–24.

Audretsch, D. B., and Stephan, P. E. 1996. Company-scientist locational links: The case of biotechnology. *American Economic Review*, 86(3): 641–52.

Aydalot, P. (Ed.) 1986. *Milieux Innovateurs en Europe*. Paris: GREMI.

Bagella, M., and Pietrobelli, C. 1997. From SMEs to industrial districts in the process of internationalization: Theory and evidence. In M. P. Van Dijk and R. Rabellotti (Eds.), *Enterprise Clusters and Networks in Developing Countries*. London: Frank Cass, 191–209.

Bair, J., and Gereffi, G. 2001. Local clusters in global chains: The causes and consequences of export dynamism in Torreon's blue jeans industry. *World Development*, 29: 1885–903.

Becattini, G. 1979. Dal "settore industriale" al "distretto industriale." Alcune considerazioni sull' unita d'indagine del'economia industriale. Cited in G. Becattini (Ed.), *Sectors and/or districts: Some Remarks on the Conceptual Foundations of Industrial Economics*. Bologna: Rivista di Economia e Politica Industriale, 123–35.

Brock, W. A., and Evans, D. S. 1989. Small business economics. *Small Business Economics*, 1: 7–20.

Brusco, S. 1992. Small firms and the provision of real services. In F. Pyke and W. Sengenberger (Eds.), *Industrial Districts and Local Economic Regeneration*, Geneva: International Institute for Labour Studies.

Brush, C. G., Duhaime, I. M., Gartner, W. B., Stewart, A., Katz, J. A., Hitt, M. A., Alvarez, S. A., Meyer, G. D., and Venkataraman, S. 2003. Doctoral education in the field of entrepreneurship. *Journal of Management*, 29(3): 309–31.

Bygrave, W. D., and Hofer, C. W. 1991. Theorizing about entrepreneurship. *Entrepreneurship: Theory and Practice*, 16: 13–22.

Carroll, G. R., and Wade, J. 1991. Density dependence in the organizational evolution of the American brewing industry across different levels of analysis. *Social Science Research*, 20: 271–302.

Casaburi, G. G., 1999. *Dynamic Agroindustrial Clusters: The Political Economy of Competitive Sectors in Argentina and Chile*. Basingstoke: Macmillan.

Ceglie, G., and Dini, M. 1999. SMEs cluster and network development in developing countries: The experience of UNIDO. UNIDO – Private Sector Development Branch Working Paper No. 2, 1–25.

Chandler, G. N., and Lyon, D. W. 2001. Issues of research design and construct measurement in entrepreneurship research: The past decade. *Entrepreneurship: Theory and Practice*, 25(4): 101–13.

Cooper, A., and Folta, T. 2000. Entrepreneurship and high-tech clusters. In D. L. Sexton and H. Landstrom (Eds.), *The Blackwell Handbook of Entrepreneurship*. Oxford: Blackwell, 348–67.

Cooper, A. C., Hornaday, J. A., and Vesper, K. H. 1997. The field of entrepreneurship over time. In P. D. Reynolds (Ed.), *Frontiers of Entrepreneurship Research*. Wellesley, MA: Babson College, Center for Entrepreneurial Studies, 1–12.

D'Avila Garcez, C. M. 2001. Multinational enterprises and local systems of innovation: The case of the automotive industry in Brazil. The DRUID Winter Conference, Copenhagen, Denmark, January.

Davidsson, P., Lindmark, L., and Olofsson, C. 1994. Small firms, business dynamics and differential development of economic well-being. *Small Business Economics*, 7: 301–15.

DiMaggio, P. J., and Powell, W. W. 1983. The iron cage revisited: Institutional isomorphism and collective rationality in organizational fields. *American Sociological Review*, 48: 147–60.

Elstrodt, H., Ordorica Lenero, P., and Urdapilleta, E. 2002. Micro lessons for Argentina. *The McKinsey Quarterly* 2: 1–6.

European Commission 2003. *Green Paper: Entrepreneurship in Europe*. European Commission – Enterprise Publications.

Feser, E. J., and Bergman, E. M. 2000. National industry cluster templates: A framework for applied regional cluster analysis. *Regional Studies*, 34: 1–19.

Garofoli, G. 1992. *Endogenous Development in Southern Europe*. Averbury: Aldershot.

Gartner, W. B. 1989. "Who is an Entrepreneur?" is the wrong question. *Entrepreneurship Theory and Practice*, 13: 47–68.

Geroski, P. A. 1995. What do we know about entry? *International Journal of Industrial Organization*, 421–40.

Giuliani, E. 2003. Knowledge in the air and its uneven distribution: A story of a Chilean wine cluster. DRUID Winter Conference 2003 (www.druid.dk), 1–34.

Hannan, M. T., and Carroll, G. R. 1992. *Dynamics of Organizational Populations: Density, Legitimation, and Competition*. New York: Oxford University Press.

Hannan, M. T., and Freeman, J. 1977. The population ecology of organizations. *American Journal of Sociology*, 82: 929–64.

Hitt, M. A., and Ireland, R. D. 2000. The intersection of entrepreneurship and strategic management research. In D. L. Sexton and H. Landstrom (Eds.), *The Blackwell Handbook of Entrepreneurship*. Oxford: Blackwell, 45–63.

Hitt, M. A., Ireland, D. R., Camp, M. S., and Sexton, D. L. 2001. Guest editor's introduction to The Special Issue Strategic Entrepreneurship: Entrepreneurial Strategies for Wealth Creation. *Strategic Management Journal*, 22: 479–91.

Humphrey, J. 1995. Industrial reorganization in developing-countries: From models to trajectories. *World Development*, 23: 149–62.

Humphrey, J. 2003. Globalization and supply chain networks: The auto industry in Brazil and India. *Global Networks*, 3: 121–41.

IDI (Instituto para el Desarrollo Industrial) 2001. La Evolucion Territorial-Sectorial de las PYMIS Argentinas (1994–2000). IDI – Observatorio Permanente de las PyMIs Argentinas.

IADB (Inter-American Development Bank) 1998. *Facing up to Inequality*. Washington, DC: IADB.

IADB (Inter-American Development Bank) 2000. *Development beyond Economics*. Washington, DC: IADB.

Kantis, H., Ishida, M., and Komori, M. 2002. Entrepreneurship in emerging economies: The creation and development of new firms in Latin America and East Asia. Inter-American Development Bank Policy Report, 1–123.

Keeble, D., and Wilkinson, F. 2000. *High-technology Clusters, Networking and Collective Learning in Europe*. Aldershot: Ashgate.

Kirzner, I. M. 1982. The theory of entrepreneurship in economic growth. In C. A. Kent, D. L. Sexton, and K. H. Vesper (Eds.), *Encyclopedia of Entrepreneurship*. Englewood Cliffs, NJ: Prentice Hall, 272–7.

Krugman, P. 1991. *Trade and Geography*. Cambridge, MA: MIT Press.

Larson, A. 1992. Network dyads in entrepreneurial settings: A study of the governance of exchange relationships. *Administrative Science Quarterly*, 37(1): 76–104.

Lawrence, P. L., and Lorsch, J. W. 1967. *Organization and Environment*. Boston, MA: Harvard Business School Classics.

Lomi, A. 2000. Density dependence and spatial duality in organizational founding rates: Danish commercial banks, 1846–1989. *Organization Studies*, 21: 433–61.

Low, M. B. 2001. The adolescence of entrepreneurship research: Specification of purpose. *Entrepreneurship Theory and Practice*, 25: 17–26.

Low, M. B., and MacMillan, I. C. 1988. Entrepreneurship: Past research and future challenges. *Journal of Management*, 14: 139–61.

Lundvall, B.-A. 1992. *National Systems of Innovation: Towards a Theory of Innovation and Interactive Learning*. London: Pinter.

Marshall, A. 1966. *Principles of Economics*, 8th edn. London: Macmillan.

McClelland, D. C. 1961. *The Achieving Society*. Princeton, NJ: Van Nostrand.

Meyer-Stamer, J. 1998. Path dependence in regional development: Persistence and change in three industrial clusters in Santa Catarina, Brazil. *World Development*, 26: 1495–511.

Meyer-Stamer, J., Maggi, C., and Seibel, S. 2001. Improving upon nature: Creating competitive advantage in ceramic tile clusters in Italy, Spain and Brazil. INEF Report, Universitat Duisburg 54.

Morley, S. A. 2001. Distribution and growth in Latin America in an era of structural reform: The impact of globalisation. OECD Development Centre Technical Papers, 1–36.

Mortimore, A. 1998. Getting a Lift: Modernising industry by way of Latin American integration. *Transnational Corporations*, 7: 97–136.

Nelson, R., and Winter, S. 1982. *An Evolutionary Theory of Economic Change*, Cambridge, MA: Harvard University Press.

OECD 2002. *International Conference on Territorial Development: Local Clusters, Restructuring Territories, and Environment-Enterprises-Districts*. Paris, France: OECD – DATAR.

Oxfam 2002. *Rigged Rules and Double Standards. Trade, Globalisation, and the Fight against Poverty.* Oxfam Report, www.maketradefair.com.

Paladino, M., and Hasman, A. 2002. *Rafaela: Un Exito mas Alla de lo Economico.* IAE, Business and Management School, Austral University, 1–35.

Perez-Aleman, P. 2003. Decentralised production organisation and institutional transformation: Large and small firm networks in Chile and Nicaragua. *Cambridge Journal of Economics,* 27: 789–805.

Pietrobelli, C., and Rabellotti, R. 2004. Upgrading in clusters and value chains in Latin America: The role of policies. Inter-American Development Bank Policy Report, 1–126.

Polanyi, K. 1957. *The Great Transformation: The Political and Economic Origins of our Time.* Boston: Beacon Press.

Porter, M. E. 1990. *The Competitive Advantage of Nations.* London: Macmillan.

Porter, M. E. 1998. *On Competition.* Boston, MA: Harvard Business School Press, 197–288.

Porter, M. E. 2001. Enhancing the microeconomic foundations of prosperity: The current competitiveness index. In K. Schwab, M. Porter, and J. Sachs (Eds.), *The Global Competitiveness Report 2001–2002.* New York: Oxford University Press, 52–73.

Porter, M. E. 2003. Foreword. In O. Solvell, G. Lindqvist, and C. Ketels (Eds.), *The Cluster Initiative Green Book.* Stockholm: Ivory Tower AB, 1–92 (www.clusterresearch.org).

Post, J. E., Preston, L. E., and Sachs, S. 2002. *Redefining the Corporation: Stakeholder Management and Organizational Wealth,* 1st edn. Stanford, CA: Stanford University Press.

Pouder, R., and St. John, C. H. 1996. Hot spots and blind spots: Geographical clusters of firms and innovation. *Academy of Management Review,* 21, 1192–225.

Pyke, F., and Sengenberger, W. 1992. *Industrial Districts and Local Economic Regeneration.* Geneva: International Institute for Labour Studies.

Quintar, Aída, et al. 1993. Rafaela: un cuasi-distrito italiano "a la Argentina." Buenos Aires, CEPAL, Documento de Trabajo CFI-CEPAL, no 35.

Rabellotti, R. 1995. Is there an industrial district model: Footwear districts in Italy and Mexico compared. *World Development,* 23: 29–41.

Rabellotti, R. 1999. "Recovery of a Mexican Cluster: Devaluation Bonanza or Collective Efficiency," *World Development,* 27(9), 1571–85.

Rabellotti, R., and Schmitz, H. 1999. The internal heterogeneity of industrial districts in Italy, Brazil and Mexico. *Regional Studies,* 33: 97–108.

Ranis, G., and Stewart, F. 2001. Growth and human development: Comparative Latin American experience. *Developing Economies,* 39: 333–65.

Ranis, G., Stewart, F., and Ramirez, A. 2000. Economic growth and human development. *World Development,* 28: 197–219.

Reynolds, P. 1994. Autonomous firm dynamics and economic growth in the United States, 1986–1990. *Regional Studies,* 28: 429–42.

Reynolds, P. D. 1999. Creative destruction: Source or symptom of economic growth? In Z. Acs, B. Carlsson, and C. Karlsson (Eds.), *Entrepreneurship, Small and Medium-Sized Enterprises and the Macroeconomy.* Cambridge: Cambridge University Press, 97–136.

Reynolds, P. D., Bygrave, W. D., and Hay, M. 2002. *Global Entrepreneurship Monitor – 2002 Executive Report.* Kauffman Center for Entrepreneurial Leadership.

Reynolds, P. D., Bygrave, W. D., Autio, E. et al. 2004. *GEM Global 2003 Executive Report.* Kauffman Center for Entrepreneurial Leadership.

Reynolds, P. D., Camps, S. M., Bygrave, W. D., Autio, E., and Hay, M. 2001. *Global Entrepreneurship Monitor – 2001 Executive Report.* Kauffman Center for Entrepreneurial Leadership.

Reynolds, P. D., Hay, M., Bygrave, W. D., Camps, S. M., and Autio, E. 2000. *Global Entrepreneurship Monitor – 2000 Executive Report*. Kauffman Center for Entrepreneurial Leadership.

Reynolds, P., Storey, D. J., and Westhead, P. 1994. Cross-national comparisons of the variation in new firm formation rates: An editorial overview. *Regional Studies*, 28: 343–46.

Rocha, H. O. 2002. Entrepreneurship and development through clusters. A theoretical model. Presented at the British Academy of Management, London.

Rocha, H. O. 2004a. Entrepreneurship and development: The role of clusters – A literature review. *Small Business Economics*, 23(5): 363–400.

Rocha, H. O. 2004b. The relationship among clusters, entrepreneurship, and development: Evidence from Latin American Countries and Germany. Presented at the Plenary Session on Building Competitive Export Capacity of Developing Countries Firms and at the Round Table on Best Practices in the Promotion of Clusters and Global Value Chains, XI United Nation Conference for Trade and Development, Sao Paulo, 14–18 June.

Rocha, H. O. 2004c. Entrepreneurship and regional development: The role of clusters. Unpublished dissertation. London Business School, 1–346.

Rocha, H. O., Reynolds, P. D., Donato, V., and Haedo, C. 2004. Local production systems, entrepreneurship and regional development: Theoretical arguments and empirical evidence from Argentina. Presented at the Babson – Kauffman Entrepreneurship Research Conference, Glasgow, 3–6 June.

Rocha, H. O., and Sternberg, R. 2005. Entrepreneurship: The role of clusters – Theoretical perspectives and empirical evidence from Germany. *Small Business Economics*, 24(3): 267–92.

Rodriguez-Pose, A., and Arbix, G. 2001. Strategies of waste: Bidding wars in the Brazilian automobile sector. *International Journal of Urban and Regional Research*, 25, p. 134.

Romer, P. 1986. Increasing returns and long-run growth. *Journal of Political Economy*, 94: 1002–37.

Rosenfeld, S. 1997. Bringing business clusters into the mainstream of economic development. *European Planning Studies*, 5: 3–23.

Rosenfeld, S. 2002. Creating smart systems: A guide to cluster strategies in less favoured regions. *European Union – Regional Innovation Strategies*. 1–35.

Salipante, P., Notz, W., and Bigelow, J. 1982. A matrix approach to literature reviews. *Research in Organizational Behaviour*, 4: 321–48.

Saxenian, A. 1994. *Regional Advantage. Culture and Competition in Silicon Valley and Route 128*. Cambridge, MA: Harvard University Press.

Schmitz, H. 1999. Global competition and local cooperation: Success and failure in the Sinos Valley, Brazil. *World Development*, 27: 1627–50.

Schmitz, H., and Nadvi, K. 1999. Clustering and industrialization: Introduction. *World Development*, 27: 1503–14.

Schmitz, J. A. 1989. Imitation, entrepreneurship, and long-run growth. *Journal of Political Economy*, 97: 721–39.

Schumpeter, J. A. 1934. *The Theory of Economic Development*. Cambridge, MA: Harvard University Press.

Sen, A. 1997. *Development Thinking at the Beginning of the 21st Century*. Development Economics Research Programme, STICERD, LSE.

Sengenberger, W., and Pyke, F. 1992. Industrial districts and local economic regeneration: Research and policy issues. In F. Pyke and W. Sengenberger (Eds.), *Industrial Districts and Local Economic Regeneration*. Geneva: International Institute for Labour Studies, 3–29.

Singleton, R. A., and Strait, B. C. 1999. *Approaches to Social Research*, 3rd edn. Oxford: Oxford University Press.

Solvell, O., Lindqvist, G., and Ketels, C. 2003. *The Cluster Initiative Green Book*. Stockholm: Ivory Tower AB (www.cluster-research.org), 1–92.

Thompson, J. D. 1967. *Organizations in Action*. New York: McGraw-Hill.

Thornton, P. H. 1999. The sociology of entrepreneurship. *Annual Review of Sociology*, 25: 19–46.

Todaro, M. 2000. *Economic Development*, 7th edn. Essex, England: Addison-Wesley.

UNDP (United Nations Program for Development) 1992. *Human Development Report 1992*. Oxford: Oxford University Press.

UNIDO (United Nations Industrial Development Organization) 2001. *Development of Clusters and Networks of SMEs – The UNIDO Programme*. Vienna: UNIDO.

Van der Linde, C. 2003. The demography of clusters: Findings from the cluster meta-study. In J. Brocker, D. Dohse, and R. E. Soltwedel (Eds.), *Innovation Clusters and Interregional Competition*. Berlin: Springer-Verlag, 130–49.

Stel, A. van, and Storey, D. 2000. The relationship between firm birth and job creation. Tinbergen Institute Discussion Paper TI02-52/03. Rotterdam: Erasmus University.

Venkataraman, S. 1997. The distinctive domain of entrepreneurship research: An editor's perspective. In J. Katz and J. Brockhaus (Eds.), *Advances in Entrepreneurship, Firm Emergence, and Growth*, Greenwich, CT: JAI Press.

Verheul, I., Wennekers, S., Audretsch, D., and Thurik, R. 2001. *An Eclectic Theory of Entrepreneurship: Policies, Institutions, and Culture*. Zoetermeer: EIM Business and Policy Research.

Visser, E. 1999. A comparison of clustered and dispersed firms in the small-scale clothing industry of Lima. *World Development*, 27: 1553–70.

Yoguel, G., and Boscherini, F. 2001. The environment in the development of firms' innovative capacities: Argentine industrial SMEs from different local systems. Mimeo.

Zepeda, M. E. 2003. Segusino: Auge y Caida de la Exportacion de Muebles. In C. Pietrobelli and R. Rabellotti (Eds.), *Upgrading in Clusters and Value Chains in Latin America: The Role of Policies*. Washington, DC: Inter-American Development Bank, 93–5.

CHAPTER EIGHT

The Political Foundations of Inter-firm Networks and Social Capital: A Post-Communist Lesson

Gerald A. McDermott

For more than a decade scholars of economic sociology, organizational theory, business strategy, complexity theory, and political economy have found great purchase in the related concepts of social capital and socio-economic networks. Much of the debates have centered on the ways in which the social structure and norms in which firms and individuals are embedded, constrain and enable action (Powell and Smith-Doerr, 1994; Podolny and Page, 1998; Portes, 2000; Burt, 2000; Kogut, 2000). This line of research is not without its limitations, namely that accounts of social capital and networks can often be over-socialized, static, and binary. (See for instance the critiques of Granovetter, 1985; Sabel, 1993; and Salancik, 1995.) In particular, Salancik (1995, p. 348) argued that "[a] network theory should . . . propose how adding or subtracting a particular interaction in an organizational network will change coordination among actors in a network." Recently, several authors have taken up this challenge by analyzing the evolution of network structures with changes in inter-firm ties as strategic responses to largely economic and technological changes (Burt, 2000; Powell et al., 2002; Uzzi et al., 2002; Baum et al., 2003).

This chapter attempts to account for both continuity and change in network structures and relationships by analyzing how a country's political approach to institution building alters network reproduction. The extant approaches may lead to static and over-socialized views of networks since they largely take socio-economic relationships as prior to and independent of the political-institutional setting. In turn, networks are largely self-governing, since the attendant norms, power structures, and resource distribution comes mainly from repeated interactions and a deep history among the member firms themselves. In contrast, the *embedded politics* approach offered here understands inter-firm networks as *socially and politically* constructed. That is, while firm level actors may develop tenacious socio-economic relationships, the authority structure of a network, which governs dispute resolutions and the distribution of resources, emerges from the ways certain constituent firms align themselves with public institutions.

By arguing that firms are embedded in concrete socio-*political* networks, my approach attempts to reconcile the tension in economic sociology and political economy about the co-evolution of the social foundations and the political-institutional architecture for economic activity. For instance, scholarship on inter-firm networks is in many ways grounded in the work of Karl Polanyi (1944), who emphasized the social embeddedness of economic activity (Granovetter, 1985; Uzzi, 1997). But Polanyi also argued that modern economic organization was the product of high politics and state action. These dual currents have been at the center of recent research on economic development (Evans, 1995; Biggart and Guillen, 1999), industrial districts (Piore and Sabel, 1984; Locke, 1995; Herrigel, 1996), and firm strategy and organization (Fligstein, 2001; Guillen, 2001; Henisz and Delios, 2001; Lounsbury, 2001). Moreover, in addressing the social and political factors shaping network evolution, one, in turn, revisits the origins of power and the authority structure in an economic network, be they derived from the technological characteristics of an industry, economic resources, the density and strength of social ties, or the politics of the state and regulatory agencies. (See, for instance, Hamilton and Biggart, 1988; Oliver, 1990; Pfeffer, 1992; Ostrom, 1995; Rosenkopf and Tushman, 1998; Burt, 2000; Kogut, 2000; Rowley et al., 2000; Fligstein, 2001.)

Examining an emerging market democracy gives a unique setting, in which governments are experimenting with new institutional forms and roles while firms are attempting to reproduce or change their existing networks. In countering an anemic, economistic view of development and post-communist transformations, several scholars have emphasized how inter-firm networks with longstanding social ties can shape the distribution of new resources (Rona-Tas, 1997; Ostrom, 1995) and be sources of decentralized knowledge and problem solving (Stark, 1996; Putnam et al., 1993; Spenner et al., 1998). Yet such research can over-emphasize the stable reproduction of network structures over time.

The Czech Republic, for instance, was often used as evidence that norms of reciprocity and structural positions attendant to communist era socio-economic networks could be stably reproduced and determine the strategies and governance rules of firms in the post-communist era (Chavance and Magnin, 1997; Stark and Bruszt, 1998; Allio et al., 1997). After a decade of transformation, however, the economic and organizational outcomes undercut the expectations of these approaches. By the late 1990s, the Czech capital markets had collapsed under the weight of investment fund mismanagement and self-dealing, and economic growth and output lagged significantly behind countries like Poland and Hungary. Moreover, a close examination of Czech manufacturing reveals that while firms attempted to reproduce past industrial networks, the process was highly unstable and led to significant structural changes in networks. Stable governance came to networks only through the intervention of the government.

In order to account for both continuity and change in the Czech networks, my embedded politics approach links the micro-level attempts at network reproduction with the macro-level politics of institution building during periods of transformation by focusing on the authority structure of the network. First, the power a firm or plant may have over assets and the creation of rules and norms is derived from one's position in the value-chain, such as a critical supplier or purchaser, as well as the strength of one's ties to local public actors, such as bank and party-council officials during communism. (A network may be more hierarchical or more egalitarian, depending on the mix of these two factors.) Yet during transformation as firms and plants clash over restructuring strategies and asset control, the dissolution of certain political institutions can undermine the relative authority of network members and thus much of the prior social norms for conflict resolution.

Second, network stability and tipping points for change come from the way the state balances two aims: maintaining insulated, centralized control over institutional policies and experimenting with new roles of conflict mediation and risk sharing to address crises and institutional short falls (Fligstein, 2001, pp. 40–3). As a country begins with the former aim, network reproduction grows unstable as old authority structures wither and no new institutional mechanisms for risk sharing and conflict mediation are in place. When and how the government reverses course and begins institutional experiments via backing negotiated restructurings will determine the structural and substantive changes of networks. In many ways, this approach follows the work of Keith Provan and his collaborators (Provan and Milward, 1995, 2001). In highly uncertain and newly emerging environments, network coordination and stability depends on the level of centralized and legitimized control over decision making and resources. Legitimized authority within a network is often a product of changes in the political-institutional context. For a transforming country like the Czech Republic, attempts by the government to insulate political power by dissolving old institutions and replacing them simply with rules grounded in self-enforcing incentives can easily lead to intra-network conflict and fragmentation. Subsequent attempts by the government to avert an economic collapse and build mechanisms of risk sharing and conflict mediation will favor certain network firms over others, thus changing the structure and substantive rules of network governance. In other words, while firms may try to reproduce their old network ties, political approaches by the government toward insulating policy-making power and building new institutions to regulate the economy will have a direct impact on the authority structure of a given network.

The next section describes the data and methodology. The following section analyzes the emergence of Czech industrial networks during communism. The fourth section examines the immediate attempts by the respective firms to reproduce their network ties and embrace privatization. Subsequent sections then focus on the points of instability and change. Both networks faced powerful internal conflicts over asset control and restructuring strategies that could not be mediated by either reference to old ties or contractual and ownership means. Intra-network conflict resolution required political intervention – assistance by public institutional actors to facilitate workouts and the reorganization of the network itself. The last section concludes the chapter.

Data and Methodology

The chapter examines in detail the evolution of two leading Czech industrial networks during and after communism. These two networks were flagships of Czech industry during the twentieth century and were viewed even by *The Wall Street Journal* (1996) as the future corporate leaders of post-communist East Europe. The analysis follows the comparative case method that controls alternative explanatory variables and highlights the degree to which differences and similarities in network evolution depend on the social and political ties of firms (Ragin, 1987; Eisenhardt, 1989). As all the firms involved were in mechanical engineering and subject to the same laws and unions, I am able to control for technological, unit labor cost, and legal factors. Moreover, as they respectively represent ideal-types of different dominant network forms in the former Czechoslovakia, a matched pair analysis allows one to control for the impact of traditional network factors. That is, a matched pair analysis shows not only how pre-existing social ties may lead to divergent privatization and restructuring strategies but also how political and institutional factors produce similar problems of network instability and determine change.

I formed the structured case studies by examining sectoral and national financial, production, and privatization data and conducting approximately 150 structured and unstructured interviews mostly in the Czech language with relevant ministerial, bank, and firm managers from 1993 to late 1996. Archival and contemporary records on firm finances, legal structure, production, and privatization methods were used to define the economic structure of sectors, contracting relationships, and restructuring strategies and outcomes. I conducted at least two interviews during 1993 to 1996 with relevant actors. The interviews focused on defining (1) the qualitative and structural dimensions of past network relations among firm and political actors and (2) the extent to which economic factors, existing professional and contracting ties, and current state policy shaped the choice of strategies of the relevant firm, plant, and bank managers.

Networks and Social Capital under Communism

In the 1980s, economic sociologists examined how the failures of central planning and the shortage environment led managers and workers to develop greater flexibility via informal horizontal ties and norms of reciprocity (Burawoy, 1985; Stark, 1986; Voskamp and Wittke, 1991). In communist Czechoslovakia, similar patterns of network formation could also be found, namely within industrial associations (VHJs) – meso-level planning structures that managed particular industrial branches (McDermott, 2002). VHJs integrated firms with related production to increase technological synergies and decrease the number of unfilled inter-firm orders. As VHJ directorates gained greater responsibility to guide production, member firms and plants gained greater independence from the central organs of the state. Constituent customers and suppliers, managers and work teams forged direct informal ties and rules to adapt production to the exigencies of plan failure and shortage. Firms and plants developed broad production profiles of final and intermediate products and forged tight inter-unit technical and economic links as sub-contractors and collaborators in R&D.

Further research on communist economies revealed, however, that political-institutional factors were directly shaping production methods and bargaining power (Szelenyi, 1988; Prokop, 1996; Dornisch, 1997; Stark and Bruszt, 1998, Ch. 4; Woodruff, 1999; Jacoby, 2000). McDermott (2002, Ch. 2) showed how alliances

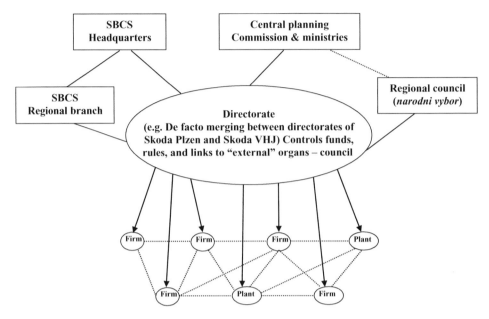

Figure 8.1 Hierarchical network (e.g. Skoda VHJ)
Note: Solid lines are stronger links than broken lines.

between certain firms, central bank branches and especially regional Party councils shaped the authority structures of VHJ networks (McDermott, 2002, Ch. 2). Communist regimes had created three parallel planning structures – one for the economy via VHJs, a second for the management finances through which state bank regional branches provided working capital and investment credits, and a third for territorial administration through which sub-national Party councils managed political and social welfare matters. These structures overlapped in different ways but with VHJs as the nexus points. For instance, council officials could block the appointment of top managers. Councils and VHJ firms together administered housing, health, cultural, and training assets that were on the books of the firms but under the jurisdiction of the councils. Over time, certain VHJ managers forged alliances with their relevant regional or district councils and bank branches to gain resources and to develop informal rules of economic governance for the respective region.

The importance of the alliances becomes immediately apparent when we try to distinguish different types of networks and how they evolved during communism. First, Figures 8.1 and 8.2 show two typologies of industrial networks, hierarchical and polycentric, represented respectively by the VHJs Skoda and TST. Each VHJ averaged in the 1980s about 30,000 employees and 20–25 member firms. Within their respective VHJs, the networks differed in their production traditions, nodes of power, and distribution of decision-making rights, even though both VHJs had the same legal organizational form (a *koncern*) and were both in mechanical engineering.

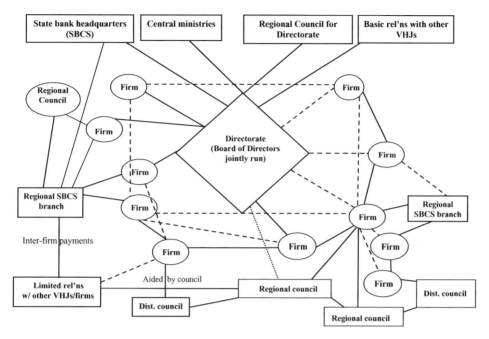

Figure 8.2 Polycentric network (e.g. TST VHJ)
Note: Solid lines are stronger links than broken lines.
Source: McDermott (2002, Ch. 2).

Within Skoda, there were several heavy engineering production programs, such as locomotives, power plant equipment, heavy machinery, forged steel parts, and gearboxes. Firms and plants were incorporated as both final producers and mutual sub-contractors. Decision making for production and finances was centralized at the level of the directorate, which set the framework for lower level bargaining among members and overtly favored certain members' production needs over those of other members. Within TST, member machine tool producers had fewer sub-contracting links between themselves, collaborating only on certain parts and the R&D conducted by two member firms. Decision making was decentralized, with member firms keeping their own financial accounts and running the directorate largely through consensus.

A key reason for these structural differences was the variation in the ways that certain member firms forged alliances directly with the administrative councils and indirectly with corresponding bank branches. For instance, the firm, Skoda Plzen, dominated the directorate of Skoda VHJ. This grew out of the alliance that Skoda Plzen forged with the powerful regional council of Western Bohemia. The alliance allowed Skoda Plzen top management to control all channels outside of their VHJ to other VHJs, government actors, and the banking system. Such control afforded

Skoda Plzen management the authority to dominate even other large firms within the VHJ, like having the firm for nuclear power equipment take orders from a turbine plant of Skoda Plzen. In TST, most member firms developed direct links to regional bank branches and regional/district administrative-communist party councils. These linkages aided firms in managing inter-firm debts, mediating delivery disputes with non-TST firms in the region, and acting as sources of countervailing bargaining power *vis-à-vis* one another, the TST directorate, and the central state ministries.

These different patterns of firm-council alliances had a clear impact on the repro-duction of network reproduction when the communist state dissolved the VHJ system in the late 1980s. Similar to strategies of VHJs in steel, trucks, and aircraft manufacturing, Skoda became a consolidated, single firm. To fight off independence battles of member firms, Skoda Plzen used its ties to the regional and city councils who aided Skoda Plzen to convert the remaining member firms of the old VHJ into its own plants, which it alone vertically commanded. Plants would have no legal powers and no individual accounts, while the head office kept control of, among other things, foreign trade relations, R&D, and credit links to the state commercial banks. The contrasting form of network reproduction that TST pursued was also found in electronics, pump manufacturing, and chemical sectors. With the aid of their already decentralized financial accounts and their relevant regional and district coun-cils, TST firms pushed to become separate, independent state-owned firms, with all attendant rights and privileges. Yet because each firm lacked financial strength and direct foreign trade experience, the firms again called on the aid of their political allies and collectively bargained with the central state to have the former directorate of TST (with its personnel and facilities) become head office of their "own" voluntary branch association, which they all would control.

The critical point here is that if one were to view the inter-firm and inter-plant net-works as autonomous from their political-institutional contexts, then one might be tempted to conclude that existing patterns of intra-network resource control and norms of reciprocity would directly determine network reproduction and the new patterns of economic governance during a future period of transformation. From an embedded politics view, however, the continuity of the distribution of power and group cohesion is more fragile, since both are functions of a network authority struc-ture that grew out of the relationships certain managers had largely with sub-national political actors. Alterations in the authority structure of a network emerge not simply from new economic incentives but more so from changes in the political-institutional environment, like the reorganization of the central and sub-national governments, privatization rules, and financial regulations. The politics surrounding the way the state attempts to develop new institutional designs would force changes in industrial networks and economic governance.

Revolution and Reproduction

By the early 1990s, the Czech lands had two noticeable characteristics: a political approach to transformation based on a depoliticization strategy (Frydman and Rapaczynski, 1993; Boycko et al., 1995) and a concerted effort by firms to repro-

duce their old network ties. Depoliticization is the ability of the state to eschew negotiations with economic and social actors about the initial institutional designs and
their subsequent revisions by insulating a powerful "change team" from society to
impose rapidly a new set of rules that should directly guide actors toward efficient
resolution of restructuring conflicts (McDermott, 2002). Vaclav Klaus, first as
Finance Minister and then as Prime Minister, built a coalition to follow this strategy.
New transformation laws created a strong, insulated policy apparatus by minimizing
the interventions of parliament and special interest groups, limiting the powers of
workers councils, dissolving regional councils, and reducing the powers and resources
of district and fragmented municipal governments. The new self-enforcing rules for
economic restructuring came in the form of mass privatization via vouchers (privatizing over 1,800 firms and banks in less than 4 years), one-time recapitalization to
strengthen banks, and a strict bankruptcy law based on liquidation of defaulting
debtors. As a result, over 400 investment funds emerged almost overnight as the
principal vehicles for corporate governance, and the Czechs led the region in private
ownership of industrial and banking assets (European Bank for Reconstruction and
Development (EBRD), 1994, 1996; World Bank, 1996).

The Czech depoliticization approach also created strong incentives for existing
industrial networks to reproduce and protect themselves from outside interference.
First, the combination of new financial constraints, a collapse of stable markets, and
government avoidance of directly restructuring firms allowed for the continuation of
a rigid and segmented industrial structure (McDermott, 2002, Ch. 3). Surveys
showed that the lack of new sources of sales, inputs, and financing led firms and
plants to work with their few existing suppliers and customers to gain resources and
reorganize production.[1] Second, the priority of rapid privatization with limited government intervention also provided an opportunity for managers to try to maintain
control over the firm. Research shows that privatization projects from incumbent
management won out by far over those of outsiders (Buchtikova and Capek, 1993;
Svejnar and Singer, 1994; Kotrba, 1994). Moreover, managers thought the use of
vouchers would allow them to retain decision-making powers while their pursuit
of joint ventures (JVs) would bring needed foreign capital.[2]

These general tendencies, however, were mediated by the change in the political
and institutional environment. While network firms fought over conflicting strategies
to increase consolidation to weather the economic turbulence or to break up into
multiple independent firms, the past forms of conflict resolution dissolved with alterations in the network authority structures. Formerly powerful members no longer
monopolized external channels. Regional councils were dissolved with no replacement, the planning system was disassembled, ministries were diluted of resources,
and the transforming state banks faced new regulations. Plants and units also had the
right to submit their own privatization projects to the government. Subsequently,
two patterns of reproduction emerged.

Members within former hierarchical networks, such as Skoda, appeared to strike
an initial compromise: to privatize the group as a whole in the form of a holding
company, combining the use of voucher and foreign partners (see Table 8.1). The
holding structure allowed a diffusion of authority and a sharing of common resources.
Units became subsidiaries or divisions, with decision-making power over production

Table 8.1 Sample of Czech holdings and their privatization strategies

Firm/Sector	Employment, organization, 1991[a]	Original privatization project and strategy[b]	Main foreign partnerships	Government action taken as of 1995
Škoda/ Engineering	34,231 employees (2.3%) 25 plants to be subsidiaries.	48.5% – 1st wave vouchers 42.1% – in FNM for FI 5% – City of Plzeň Create JVs with FIs for different production groups or divisions.	Plan double JV with Siemens. Fails in 1992.	1992 equity tenders with Czech firm and banks lead to negotiated restructuring model. MPO sits on board. Process lasts over $2\frac{1}{2}$ years before equity transferred to Czech firm and banks.
ČKD/ Engineering	21,776 employees (1.5%) Holding of 18 subsidiaries (a.s.)[c].	49.2% – 1st wave vouchers 41.6% – in FNM for FI Create divisions from subsidiaries. Pursue JVs with FIs.	Plan JV with AEG for transport division. Fails in 1993. Plan JV for Kompresory with DBB. Fails in 1993–4.	1994 equity tender with Czech firm leads to negotiated restructuring model. Czech banks to finance, with state loan guarantees. MPO sits on board. $1\frac{1}{2}$ years before equity transferred.
Aero/ Aircraft	19,820 employees (1.4%) Holding of 11 subsidiaries (a.s.)[c].	49% – 1st wave, vouchers 48% – in FNM for FI and 2nd wave vouchers Create recreational and military divisions and pursue JVs or partial buyouts of subsidiaries or divisions.	Plan JVs with Fairchild, Pratt &Whitney, and Hamilton Std. All fail by 1993.	By December 1993 three failed attempts at financial restructuring and debt-equity swaps. 1994 plan: Government and Czech banks share ownership of holding and certain subsidiaries, while seeking FIs. MPO and banks manage holding and subsidiaries.

Continued

Firm / Sector	Employment & ownership	Privatization	Plan	Outcome
Poldi Kladno/ High grade steel	16,471 employees (1.2%) Holding of 19 subsidiaries (a.s.)^c Creates two main steel subsidiaries: Poldi I & II.	97% – in FNM for FIs. Plan a JV for Poldi I&II, and partial equity sales or JVs of other subsidiaries with different FIs.	Plan JV for Poldi I&II with consortium led by Maison Lazard. Fails by May 1993.	1993 equity tender of Poldi I&II to Czech firm, while FNM and Czech bank retain control of Poldi Holding. 1995–6 FNM and bank sue Czech firm for embezzlement. Poldi Holding reclaims Poldi I & II.
Tatra Kopřivnice/ Heavy trucks	14,685 (1.0%) Holding of 7 subsidiaries.	97% – 1st wave vouchers. Create JVs in assembly and parts.	Plan JVs with IVECO for assembly and Detroit Diesel for engines. Both fail by 1993.	1993–4 failed attempt to create new foreign manager-owner. MPO creates new department to help run Tatra. Orchestrates sale of Tatra to Škoda Plzeň in 1995–6. Czech banks finance.
Liaz/Medium trucks	8,606 employees (0.6%) 9 plants to become subsidiaries (a.s.)^c of new holding.	42.9% – 1st wave vouchers 51.1% – in FNM for FI; Create JVs for subsidiaries. Focus on engine upgrades and modular vehicle design.	Plan simultaneous JVs for assembly and parts with Mercedes consortium. Fails by December 1993.	MPO runs restructuring of Liaz along with Tatra. Orchestrates sale of Tatra to Škoda Plzeň in 1995–6. Czech banks finance.

Notes:

[a] Percentages in parentheses are firm employment as a share of total Czech industrial employment in 1991.

[b] Shares left in FNM to attract a direct foreign investor (FI) via a future sale or JV. Percentage of shares not noted are those left by law in a fund for restitution compensation.

[c] a.s. = Czech equivalent of joint-stock company; s.r.o. = Czech equivalent of limited liability company.

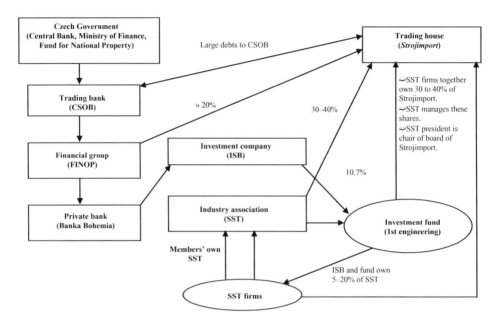

Figure 8.3   Network ties in the Czech machine tool industry, 1992–3
Note: Direction of arrow denotes direction of ownership. Percentages denote ownership share.
Source: McDermott (2002, Ch. 5).

changes and new independent financial accounts. The holding became an "internal, regulated market," providing critical resources each lacked on its own: financing and mutual subsidization through internal credit, strategic management for common production programs, foreign trade and partnership contacts, and shared labor and production facilities. In the meantime, members, collectively or individually, would formulate restructuring strategies and find foreign partners to gain needed investment, market niches, and know-how.

Members of a polycentric network, like the ex-TST VHJ, chose distinctly different privatization strategies that built on their earlier efforts to further decentralization but support group cohesion. First, the 40 firms entered the first wave of privatization as individual entities mainly via vouchers. Second, they grafted indirect equity and financial alliances onto their past social ties. They converted the directorate of their former VHJ into the headquarters of new machine tool association, SST, in which each firm was a part owner. As can be seen in Figure 8.3, SST used its past professional ties to create overlapping equity stakes with FINOP and CSOB, the Czech leaders of international trade finance, and their new private bank, Banka Bohemia, in key investment funds and foreign trade companies. SST and the new equity links would provide members with strategic sectoral information and a common coordinating structure in areas where individually they were weak, such as in foreign trade, shared trademarks, critical inputs, vocational training, and development loans.

At first glance, we can see that the old network patterns were durable. Despite having similar technologies, aggregate employment, and end markets as well as being subject to the same laws, policies, and trade union (Kovo), the members of the ex-Skoda and the ex-TST VHJ networks chose different privatization strategies and initial organizational forms. Moreover, both groups were conscious about the importance of maintaining cohesion, by using holding structures and associations that would be supported by new private external partners, such as through FDI JVs and local financial organizations. To the extent that networks are more or less self-governing entities, then one would expect that any future conflicts over restructuring would be resolved by the continuity of pre-existing power distribution and norms of reciprocity. Moreover, the Czech ability to rapidly privatize and establish the requisite legal regime offered network actors the additional dispute resolution tools of contracts and ownership.

But if one fast-forwards the story a few years, one finds that although pre-existing inter-firm and inter-unit relationships would distinctively structure the ensuing patterns of restructuring conflicts, the use of old social ties, contracts, and equity were insufficient. For holding companies like Skoda, members were unable to resolve collective decisions about how new asset boundaries would be drawn, new rights distributed, liabilities divided, and investment directed. By 1992–3, virtually all the prospective JVs between foreign partners and holdings collapsed. By 1995, the SST network had fragmented and most firms bordered on insolvency. For members of both groups the attempt to preserve their past social relationships, reinforce them with new governance mechanisms of equity and contracts, and also replace past public external partners with new private ones did little to promote cooperation and restructuring. In the end, the central government would have to step in to mediate internal disputes and provide financial support for restructuring. Indeed, by the mid to late 1990s the pre-existing network structures would be reversed for each. The previously hierarchical structure of Skoda would end up with a significantly weaker central office and fiercely independent member firms. The previously polycentric structure of TST/SST would end up with a single strong member firm that owned several others and controlled the rest via its hold over the association headquarters, subcontracting, and available credit.

The Limits of Continuity: The Conflict over Network Restructuring

To answer the aforementioned challenge by Salancik (1995), this section and the next must demonstrate for both sets of firms how Klaus's political approach to transformation altered institutional variables that (1) undermined network stability despite concerted attempts to combine new contractual methods with past social ties, and (2) led to new network structures. I first show how for both Skoda and then the TST/SST coordination would falter since the depoliticization approach of the Czech government not only eliminated traditional political allies of certain firms but also provided no institutional substitute to mediate disputes and share risk.

Reinforced linkages and disharmony in the Skoda network

By 1989, the production profile of Skoda Plzen accounted for 91 different product groups across more than 20 plants.[3] Intra-network conflicts over asset control and restructuring strategies emerged in Skoda from the contradiction between the reinforcement of inter-unit production and financial links and the multiple restructuring experiments pursued by members. If the inherited scope and flexibilities were sources for unit autonomy, the overlapping supply links with relatively narrow technical specifications constrained individual discretion. Intra-holding sub-contracting links remained vital for the flow of production across different common programs as well as those of individual units.[4] They also provided cross-subsidization in a liquidity constrained economy. The importance of these internal links, however, varied according to one's place in the network. In turn, managers held different views over production interdependencies, which provoked clashes over such critical restructuring issues as asset control, spin-offs, new sub-groups, and plant closings.

First, although many units faced strong incentives to increase their independence from the group, such actions threatened their own and joint production programs. Yet attempts at greater independence only led to increased hold-up problems within the holding. As these plants focused more resources on their own priorities, the common production programs mentioned above and inter-unit supplies suffered. Moreover, the rapid insolvency and loss of key components by several self-liberated previously profitable members of Skoda and other holdings further restrained the ambitions of holding units to spin-off.[5]

Second, the scope of plant level production and density of multiple production links impeded the clear definition of new divisions for the main programs. Since several units often produced key inputs for multiple programs using the same facilities and personnel, members fought over the control of these suppliers. Third, given the production interdependencies and the lack of clear outside sourcing, holding members could not reach agreement over the closing of large loss-making intra-holding suppliers.

The growing intra-holding stalemate was to a certain degree the result of high uncertainty – the uncertain returns on individual production and organizational experiments undermined the credible guarantees that members could give to one another or a bank to gain needed cooperation for components or financing. Yet why, despite the conscious construction of the holding company and the existence of historical social ties, could network members not overcome these gaps in credibility and coordination? The answer, from an embedded politics view, was that the Klausians' depoliticization approach toward institutional change had radically altered the authority structure of the old network and not provided institutional mechanisms to resolve such disputes.

First, Czech policy efforts to centralize power effectively had eliminated a critical source of socio-political power and order. As experiments began to foster potentially conflicting strategies and change the position of units within the group, the authority structure of the network was thrown into question: how should new boundaries around assets be drawn and who had the rights to decide them? Under the former hierarchical network, a key firm supported by the regional council possessed the

political and social resources to aid a resolution to conflicts – be it by force or compromise. After 1989, no such actor was around. The dissolution of regional councils
and the weakening of district and municipal councils eliminated a source of power
for some members and a source of external resources and mediation for the group
as a whole. Indeed, the aggregate and holdings data on privatization show that firms
solicited the aid of local municipalities by offering them free transfers of significant
equity stakes.[6] Yet the changes in the systems of territorial administration and taxes
effectively left municipalities with little control over political and financial resources
(McDermott, 2002).

Second, depoliticization provided networks with two private sources of capital and
authority – the main Czech banks and foreign direct investors – as new substitutes
for external partners. But such new ties had to be forged via contracts and not
through any form of government mediation and risk sharing.

With the highest domestic bank debt to GDP ratio in the region, Czech banks
and industrial firms were highly interdependent. Yet the main banks refrained from
leading restructuring. Given the lack of bank restructuring experience and weak
capital structures, providing large amounts of capital under high uncertainty was
highly risky. At the same time, given their limited client base, liquidation was equally
risky. Depoliticization viewed government supported workout institutions, such as in
Chapter 11 or special agencies developed in Poland, as an anathema and simply an
invitation for never-ending handouts (see McDermott, 2004).

Foreign direct investment (FDI) via JVs was a primary objective of holding strategies. Proposed JVs proliferated since voucher privatization had taken sales of whole
sets of assets out of state control and since foreign investors wanted to learn more
about Czech management and were interested in a sub-group of holding units (Gulati
and Gargiulo, 1999). But by 1993 virtually all prominent JVs collapsed and foreign
investors withdrew (see Table 8.1). The primary reason was that the Klausians refused
to help build credible commitments about asset control and investment between the
Czech managers and foreign investors.

The bell weather JV was between Skoda and Siemens and was viewed at the time
to be the bell weather for future FDI. With Czech privatization rules already restrict-
ing government intervention into deals that did not contain outright sales by and
revenues to the state, such participation was tantamount to revising Czech privatization policy and the clear roles of government organs. The Klausians saw this as
antithetical to their designs and control over policy. As they gained increasing political power and control over policy from late 1991 through their victory in the June
1992 parliamentary elections, the Klausians blocked efforts by the Minister of Industry to allow the government to become a financial and negotiating partner. After the
elections, the Minister of Industry was ousted and the talks with Siemens collapsed.
In September 1992, Skoda's management board resigned and the holding shut down
three major units and defaulted on its loans.

Fragmentation in SST

As discussed above, SST firms were poised in 1990–1 to join the growing trend in
machine tool firms becoming paradigmatic examples of SME creation and flexible

specialization (Piore and Sabel, 1984; Acs and Audretsch, 1990; Acs et al., 1991; Herrigel, 1996). While their decades of experience, polycentric structure, embrace of privatization all pointed to ideal conditions for becoming an entrepreneurial and adaptive network (Larson, 1992), SST's new supporting investment alliances would provide crucial finance and information (refer again to Figure 8.3). By 1995, however, the machine-tool network had fragmented and most firms bordered on insolvency. The attempt by SST members to reinforce their past social relationships with equity ties and contracts and also replace past public external partners with new private financial ones did little to promote cooperation and restructuring.

First, the uncertainties of new production experiments created restructuring conflicts between interdependent firms. Given the lack of knowledgeable suppliers and the high costs of total in-house production, SST firms turned to one another for the development or sub-contracting of certain components and the cost sharing of exporting and importing (especially for CNC electronics). Since the strategies of new product development entailed significant risks and often conflicted with one another, no firm could give the contractual guarantees to the others to forego their own plans and invest in those of the solicitor. For instance, even when the solicitor demonstrated that the trial runs were for a credible international client, the small production volumes and poorly defined future revenue streams undermined the credibility of the project. In turn, the potential SST suppliers refused to alter their own component production for the benefit of the solicitor.[7]

Second, the supporting equity alliances failed to provide needed financing to overcome the hold-up problems among members. Even with the government's partial recapitalization and debt-relief for the banks, CSOB, like the other "big five" Czech banks, still had weak capital bases and tight financial links with industrial and trade firms. But the big Czech banks found it too risky to lead bankruptcies or finance restructuring via the available governance mechanisms of contracts, liquidations, and ownership (debt-equity swaps) (Hoshi et al., 1998). In turn, the big banks refused to provide credit lines directly to firms or via new banks like Banka Bohemia, and SST firms languished. Indeed, in 1994, regulators closed four of the five largest de novo banks, including Banka Bohemia.

By tying network reorganization to the politics of institution building, an embedded politics approach can make sense of the failure of past social relations and new equity ties to mediate the disputes among SST firms. First, the depoliticization agenda radically altered the network authority structure that underpinned the inherited social capital between firms. A key reason for the development of polycentric network during communism was that relevant central bank branches and regional/district administrative party councils had provided many firms of the old VHJ network with political and material resources for bargaining power *vis-à-vis* other machine tool firms and the central state ministries. Bent on centralizing power during transformation, the Czech government literally and figuratively eliminated the traditional external partners for the firms, removing the power structure that supported the past informal decision-making rules and norms of reciprocity.

Second, to sustain its insularity, the Czech government impeded the development of new institutions for restructuring. Once mass privatization was implemented and banks were partially recapitalized, private contracts and a bankruptcy regime emphasizing liquidation were to induce restructuring. Any alternative policies, such as leasing firms, selling assets with typical conditions of restructuring, or promoting workouts as part of bankruptcy, would have linked ownership change and restructuring and required government oversight. Moreover, to do so would have demanded empowering different public actors, be they ministries or sub-national governments, with the necessary discretion and resources to share some of the risks and create rules for the relevant parties to negotiate over time the restructuring of both operations and financing. Czech transformation policy, however, strongly curtailed any such delegation of power and public-private deliberations.

Politics and the Reconstitution of Order in Networks

If depoliticization undermines network stability, then the next key issue is the identification of the political and institutional conditions that can reconstitute a new authority structure of a network. The notion that state policy and institutional rules can define and legitimize the distribution of resources and the paths of development has been a central theme of students of technological change (Piore and Sabel, 1984; Rosenkopf and Tushman, 1998), business groups (Guillen, 2001), the modern corporation (Fligstein, 2001), and modes of capitalist growth (Hall and Soskice, 2001). But because transforming economies are developing both institutional forms and policy domains (Fligstein, 2001), the distribution of political power is a prevailing factor in how state policy is formed and thus authority structures constituted. That is, any exploration of a new role for public actors demands a reconfiguration of political control. In turn, three conditions of the mode, timing, and consistency of state action toward network reorganization can be defined.

First, to the extent that the government can delegate public agencies to forge negotiated solutions to restructuring with network actors, it would have to share some financial risks and mediate intra-network disputes. As Provan and Milward (1995, 2001) have shown in their analysis of mental health service networks, while such actions would clearly favor certain network actors and alter the balance of power among them, state provision of resources and legitimacy can improve stability. Who those actors would be would depend on the state of disrepair in the network (timing) and the policy resources available to the public agencies at the moment of government action. Second, consistent with the work on institutional development (e.g., Dorf and Sabel, 1998; Fligstein, 2001), timing is often a function of moments of crisis. Third, the consistency needed for different public actors to learn and build on their institutional experiments depends on coalition politics. That is, since coherent policy change and institutional experiments demands a change in the distribution of policy-making power from the status quo (depoliticization in this case), the key political leaders need to cede power to other political actors. To the extent they are unwilling to do this, institutional development is retarded, threatening the newly found stability of the network authority structures.

In what follows, crises would impel the Klausians to shift policy and engage members of Skoda and SST, leading to a dramatic change in the network authority structures. But coalition politics would eventually undermine steps toward regulating the market and network development.

Stabilizing Skoda

The shut down and default of Skoda in September 1992 triggered an immediate response from the reluctant Klausians. Given the size of holding companies and the close interdependencies between industrial firms and the few main Czech banks, Skoda's collapse threatened to bring down the banking system and damage whole sectors and regions. The Klausians had two resources at its disposal: the shares of Skoda Holding that remained in the privatization agency for the proposed JV (about 40 percent) and the existing bank debts of Skoda related to communist-era programs. Skoda in turn became the first case for Klausians to support negotiated restructurings and a model for its future engagement with other holdings.

This trial and error experiment started with a failed attempt to use a public tender and incentive contracts but ended with a multi-level governance structure that both limited self-dealing and altered the authority structure of the existing network. The initial tender chose two delegates: a firm of ex-Skoda managers, Nero, and a consortium of Skoda's two largest creditor banks, KB and IB. The incentives were that the parties could receive the remaining equity at reduced prices and that the government would absorb some of the old large debts. But the parties failed to cooperate as the banks were unwilling to invest in Skoda projects without greater transparency and improved coordination among the Skoda members. In turn, the government remained a partner for almost 3 years by combining the tools of delegation and deliberation to alter the balance of power in the network and to improve multi-party monitoring.

The government delegated to Skoda's new central management team of Nero the authority to rebuild the internal organization of the firm, namely increasing the power of the newly formed subsidiaries and transparency. The banks had to finance this reorganization, but gained direct access to the subsidiaries and valuable collateral. Deliberations emerged by the government using debts and the vague pricing of shares to provoke the parties to reveal information about their actions and monitor one another's progress in meeting their restructuring obligations. The ensuing pattern of negotiations set the foundations for two levels of interlinked structured deliberations that governed restructuring (see Figure 8.4). In the "external" triangle the government, the banks, and the central management team exchanged information and control rights in deliberating each other's contribution to debt restructuring, decentralization, and financial transparency. In the "internal" triangle Skoda's Center, the banks and the subsidiaries similarly exchanged information and control rights in negotiating debts, transfer prices, and project finance.

In many ways, the government's use of the dual monitoring triangles resembled public-private workout institutions in advanced developed nations and was an effective means of restructuring the holding companies (Hayri and McDermott, 1998). This may not be surprising. Provan and Milward (1995, 2001) argue that network effectiveness can improve in newly emerging institutional environments when state control is direct and network integration is centralized. Moreover, state intervention

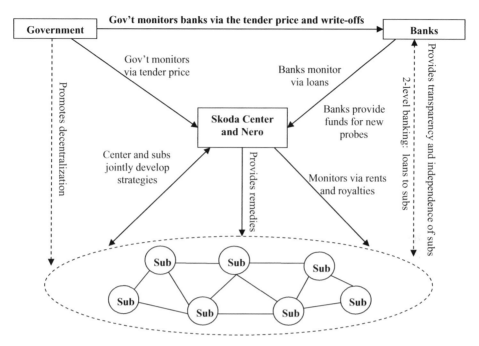

Figure 8.4 Monitoring triangles for Skoda restructuring
Source: McDermott (2002, Ch. 4).

and the combination of deliberation and delegation can improve the legitimacy of the new organizational form in the eyes of the participants. By 1995, Skoda's debt had fallen to 50 percent of its 1992 level, revenues had increased over 50 percent, and employment was increasing significantly. Skoda's rebound was even recognized by independent observers such as the stock market, the international business media (e.g., *The Economist* and *The Wall Street Journal*),[8] and international banks that would go on to finance new Skoda ventures.

But the combination of delegation and deliberation also forced a radical change in the authority structure of Skoda. The holding that grew out of a hierarchically com-manded network was now very decentralized. Key decisions were reached through collaboration not fiat. No longer did a single member monopolize outside economic and political channels. Rather, government oversight and the monitoring triangles empowered subsidiaries by granting them greater legal rights and giving them the space to develop greater operational autonomy and stronger direct links with outside banks, clients, and suppliers.

Stabilization of SST through state-backed domination

With the SST network fragmenting and bordering on insolvency, one member firm, ZPS, would use its "brokerage" position (Burt, 1992) to launch a strategy to dom-inate the others and control key financial institutions. Between 1992 and 1995, ZPS more than doubled its total sales and exports by redesigning several of its final and semi-finished products and often selling them at or below cost to gain market share. ZPS had cultivated a new network of its former employees as well as those of the past regional council and big banks. This new network, referred to locally as the "Zlin Mafia," had at its core ZPS, the independent and rapidly growing investment fund PPF, and a newly found but also rapidly growing bank, Pragobanka. Managers from all three sat on each other's boards. As SST relationships fragmented, ZPS found it too risky to engage its initial strategy of gradually spinning off certain plants and utilizing other SST firms for sub-contracting. Instead, ZPS sought to impose its own order over the network and acquire other SST firms by mid-1995. The question, of course, was how they would obtain control of the other firms, given that the big five Czech banks and the dominant investment funds had proven useless as sources of direct financing.

The answer is that a well-placed network can be used for self-dealing and domination as easily as it can be used for collaborative production. The turning point toward domination and increased instability becomes apparent when one exposes the "brokerage" concept to the dynamics of a political-institutional setting. ZPS generated its advantageous "brokerage" position by leveraging its participation in SST with its conscious efforts to rebuild and convert its own local socio-political network into a source of sales and financing. Yet, brokerage is a two-way profession and depends still on the integration of supporting public institutions. On the one hand, the broker needs a reasonably stable core network (SST) to put existing assets and information to new uses without taking full responsibility for them. On the other hand, as the core network collapses and total control becomes paramount to the broker's entrepreneurial aspirations, the broker (ZPS) demands ever more resources to consolidate its position (and avoid default). Without institutionalized mechanisms to forge negotiated management of common assets and liabilities or to constrain individual ambitions, the broker's private allies (PPF et al.) had to mimic the broker's domination strategy to capture any available financial resources, albeit through manipulation.

ZPS and its local allies, in turn, used their elaborate network of new banks and investment funds to gain strategic control of ZPS shares, to manipulate share prices of ZPS and other companies, as well as to channel financing to ZPS from bank depositors, notably the partially privatized Czech Insurance Company. At the same time, it sought to control the SST board and its engineering investment fund mentioned above (see Figure 8.3). With its new finances, the aid of PPF, and influence over SST's fund, ZPS orchestrated a series of takeovers of four of the largest SST member firms. At the same time, PPF began to buy up stakes in the Czech Insurance Company and went public with charges that main banks had unjustly privileged positions in the privatization plans for remaining shares of the company.

Ultimately, such a scheme can lead to systemic failure, when the state can no longer ignore the damage. Just as ZPS was attempting to complete its conquest with the acquisition of two more SST firms and PPF was battling the main Czech banks in 1996, regulators seized one of their allied banks, declared an emergency at the Czech Insurance Company, and placed Pragobanka on a watch list. The domination strategy for the broker had reached back into the heart of the public domain.

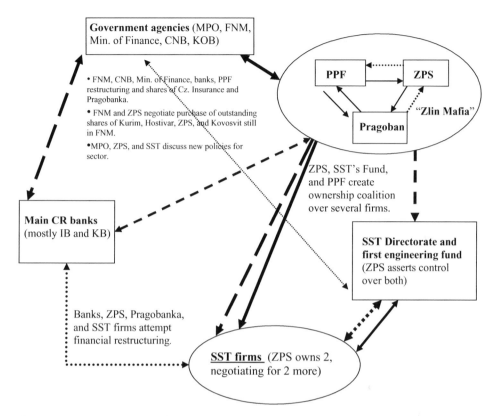

Figure 8.5 New control structure of SST, 1996
Note: Arrows denote direction of control. Thick solid lines denote a stronger link and control than thin, dashed lines.
Source: McDermott (2002, Ch. 5)

The Klausians were, however, much more reluctant to intervene. The government had little immediate bargaining leverage as it had no equity in ZPS and virtually all SST firms. Leverage could only come from new policy initiatives and further empowerment of relevant agencies (like those previously involved in Skoda). But such changes were no longer politically viable. By early 1996 with the holdings and main banks stabilized, political infighting within the ruling coalition and the pending general elections in June led Klaus to declare an end to transformation policies and to reconsolidate his party's control over the relevant economic agencies and ministries. In turn, the Klausians sought an expeditious solution to the new crisis via appeasement. PPF and the main banks were given joint control of the Czech Insurance Company and, with ZPS, of Pragobanka. The Ministry of Industry also invited ZPS and its subservient SST directorate to participate in discussions over the future of the sector.

In turn, the Czech government's delayed and weak response to the crisis effectively reinforced the Zlin Mafia's control over SST (see Figure 8.5). The once polycentric structure of ex-TST firms now looked very hierarchical. The past consensus decision making was replaced with the power and fiat of a much more powerful ZPS.

Epilogue

Klaus's return to depoliticization in 1996 underscored how the contentious politics of unpacking public power could impact network stability. To reconsolidate his hold on power, he curtailed the discretionary power of the central ministries and agencies that were under the control of other coalition parties. These were the principal public actors engaged in new initiatives that began with the Skoda intervention and who were responsible for correcting the abuses of firms like ZPS and PPF. Subsequently, as the government withdrew from Skoda and other holdings, it simply left them to be governed by the same capital markets and bankruptcy rules that had hindered restructuring in the first place. No new institutional policies were pursued to promote workouts, effective investor protection, FDI, and exports. In turn, firms like Nero, which was the manager-owner group running the center of Skoda, and ZPS were left in a poor governance and regulatory regime and resorted to undertaking dubious investments. Klaus's government collapsed in mid-1997. In the wake of the 1997–8 Asian and Russian crises, both Skoda and ZPS became insolvent. Creditors of both firms tried and failed for a year to form voluntary standstill agreements to reorganize the assets. In 1999, Skoda, ZPS, several holdings, and the main banks entered into a new public-private restructuring and reprivatization agency that was created by the newly formed social-democratic government. Once again, the Czechs would embark on rebuilding their economic institutions while restructuring their industrial networks.

Concluding Remarks

This chapter has argued for a more political constructionist approach to analyzing the reproduction and change in inter-firm networks and their attendant social capital, particularly during periods of institutional transformation. If one assumes that structural and relational variables as being prior to and virtually autonomous of the political-institutional environment, networks and social capital can appear largely self-governing and static. The industrial networks examined in the chapter indeed were imbued with long histories, strong socio-economic ties, and specific distributions of resource control. They were also subject to the same laws and unions and similar technologies and economic shocks. Yet, as we saw, these networks were not self-governing – historical socio-economic ties, repeated interactions, and the use of contracts and ownership were insufficient to help network firms and plants resolve restructuring conflicts and gain investment.

In pointing out these deficiencies, the aim of the chapter was not to discard simply socio-economic variables, but rather to show how their interaction with political-institutional variables help identify factors of continuity and change. On the one hand, the social and economic ties of the respective networks clearly shaped the organizational and privatization strategies during the initial period of transformation. Firms and plants within hierarchical networks, like Skoda Plzen, tended to reinforce their subcontracting and financial ties, and elected to privatize themselves together as a holding company through the use of the vouchers and joint ventures with foreign strategic investors. Firms and plants within polycentric networks, like TST/SST, elected to privatize themselves individually as well as build an association and set of equity alliances with new banks and investment funds.

On the other hand, the politics of institution building had profound impacts of the authority structures of industrial networks, in turn the adaptability and reconfiguration of the networks when faced with new economic uncertainties. By advancing their depoliticization approach to institution building, the Klausians centralized political power, severely weakened subnational governments, and offered virtually no mechanisms to promote collective workouts. For firms this meant that the existing authority structures of respective networks were radically altered and members had few resources at their disposal for forging new, stable structures for internal governance. Only when the government intervened by sharing some of the risks and mediating disputes did restructuring proceed. For Skoda, this intervention brought stability by supporting a new, multi-polar authority structure that changed the configuration of the former hierarchical network. Yet for SST, coalition politics and limited resources led to a weak government response that provided temporary stability via solidifying the Zlin Mafia's control over the once multi-polar structure of SST.

In many ways, the argument presented here reflects a recent current in economic-sociology and political economy to show how government policy shapes the organizational forms and social capital in underdeveloped economic settings. For instance, Guillen (2001), Fligstein (2001), and Hamilton and Biggart (1988) have shown how the variation in development policy impacts the creation of new corporate forms. In their analysis of Russian and Czech capital markets, Kogut and Spicer (2002) have demonstrated how government approaches to regulatory institutions can embolden or weaken the extended chains of trust that are vital for investment and governance. In his analysis of the economic revival of subnational regions in northern Brazil and southern Italy, Locke (2001) has argued that government enforcement of standards and licenses is vital to enable inter-linked firms to develop durable mechanisms of collaboration. Both Fligstein (2001) and Hamilton and Biggart (1988) have shown how state policy and interest group politics shape the control structures and governance norms of corporations. And most similar is the work of Provan and Milward (1995, 2001), who show the frailty of decentralized networks and the importance of direct state intervention in nascent institutional settings.

My embedded politics approach pushes this line of work further by making a more explicit link between the struggles over the distribution of public power and economic networks. First, the authority structure of an inter-firm network, in turn the constituent pattern of associationalism and resource distribution, is derived from the ways certain network firms gain resources and privileges from public institutions. Second, the political approaches governments take to build new institutions will alter the authority structures of networks but vary the stability and reconfiguration of networks. To the extent that political leaders are able to empower and monitor a variety of public actors to experiment with new institutional roles, network firms would appear more likely to extend their time horizons and pursue negotiated modes of reorganization (McDermott, 2004). To the extent that political leaders seek to insulate and centralize public power, fragmentation and winner-take-all strategies are likely to prevail in the network.

In sum, this chapter points to new areas of research on the origins and evolution of social capital and networks. To begin with, researchers should try to identify how the authority structures and informal rules of networks emanate from specific institutional supports and public policy. From there, one can examine network change in two ways. One is to examine how existing institutional and political variables inhibit and enhance network adaptation to external technological and economic shocks. The other is to analyze how different political approaches to institutional reform impact the stability and adaptation of the economic networks themselves.

Acknowledgments

The author would like to thank the Reginald H. Jones Center of the Wharton School and the URF of the University of Pennsylvania for their generous financial support and thank the participants in the seminars at EGOS 2003 and the Jones Center. The usual exculpations apply.

Notes

1 For instance, in a 1991–2 survey of managers in over 60 major manufacturing firms, 85 percent of the firms continued to produce only for their past few customers, and 25 percent devoted all of their production to a single customer. In addition, 80 percent of the firms had almost fully internalized R&D, input and parts production, and distribution and marketing activities, but could no longer support such integration. Seventy percent said that the only alternative was to cooperate with their past customer to develop new processes and products. The survey included firms mainly from the engineering, metal working and steel sectors. Their size ranged from 500 to 20,000 employees. Together the firms accounted for over 5 percent of industrial employment, 5 percent of turnover and 8 percent of capital assets in the CSFR. Forty percent of firms were located in Bohemia, 30 percent in Moravia, and 30 percent in Slovakia. See Mihola et al. (1991), Mihola and Havlin (1992).

2 For instance, the above mentioned survey indicated that only 6.5 percent and 8 percent of managers believed that vouchers would, respectively, improve production and financial health of the firm and help generate investment capital. Over 50 percent of the managers surveyed asserted their primary interest was to maintain or increase their independence and decision-making rights over wages and disposal of assets *vis-à-vis* the center. Only 10 percent believed that privatization and vouchers would allow "the influence and interests of new outside owners to be felt." At the same time, over 70 percent said they could gain needed financing and know how, which vouchers lacked, by creating partnerships with foreign firms.

3 These groups roughly correspond to the 3-digit level of the SIC system. See McDermott (2002, Chs. 2 and 4).

4 For instance, between 1986 and 1993, average production for customers outside the group accounted consistently for over 70 percent of total output. Between 1986 and 1990 inputs from outside the group, however, accounted consistently for only 21 percent of production value. From 1991 through 1993 this share dropped to about 12 percent. See McDermott (2002, Ch. 4) for details.

5 In 1989–90, such units as Skoda Export and Skoda Praha of Skoda Plzen, Jihostroj, Jihlavan, Mikrotechnica, and Technometra of Aero, Slany, Naftovy Motor, Slavia, and Kutna Hora of CKD Praha, and Motorpal in trucks all had strong production and sales programs outside of their respective groups and decided to become independent firms. Almost all were insolvent by 1993. Statistical analysis of privatization shows there were a very small number of industrial spin-offs, which also performed significantly worse than their former parents (see Kotrba, 1994; and Lizal et al., 1995).

6 Data on the first wave of privatization projects for joint-stock companies show that 11 percent of equity (on average) was proposed as free transfers to local municipalities (making it the third largest category, behind vouchers and FNP holdings). See Kotrba (1994) and Lastovicka et al. (1994). Holdings, such as Skoda Plzen and Poldi Kladno, had originally proposed 5 percent of equity to be transferred to their respective municipalities.

7 Similar fates met efforts to clarify firm specializations, collaborate in exports and imports, and use the vocational training system. An added fear was that firms were beginning to encroach on one another's traditional product lines. See McDermott (2002, Ch. 5).

8 See *The Economist* (February 18, 1995); *The Wall Street Journal* (May 8, 1996).

References

Acs, Z., Audretsch, D., and Carlsson, B. 1991. Flexible technology and firm size. *Small Business Economics*, 3(4): 307–21.

Acs, Z., and Audretsch, D. 1990. *Innovation and Small Firms*. Cambridge, MA: MIT Press.

Allio, L., Mariusz, M. D., Mikhailov, N., and Weimer, D. L. 1997. Post-communist privatization as a test of theories of institutional change, in D. L. Weimer (Ed.), *The Political Economy of Property Rights: Institutional Change and Credibility in the Reform of Centrally Planned Economies*. Cambridge: Cambridge University Press.

Baum, J., Shipilov, A., and Rowley, T. 2003. Where do small worlds come from? *Industrial and Corporate Change*, 12: 597–725.

Biggart, N. W., and Guillen. M. 1999. Developing difference: Social organization and the rise of the auto industries of South Korea, Taiwan, Spain, and Argentina. *American Sociological Review*, 64(5): 722–47.

Boycko, M., Shleifer, A., and Vishny, R. 1995. *Privatizing Russia*. Cambridge, MA: MIT Press.

Burawoy, M. 1985. *The Politics of Production: Factory Regimes under Capitalism and Socialism*. London: Verso.

Burt, R. 1992. *Structural Holes: The Social Structure of Competition*. Cambridge, MA: Harvard University Press.

Burt, R. 2000. The network structure of social capital. *Research in Organizational Behavior*, 22: 345–423.

Butchtikova, A., and Capek, A. 1993. Privatization in the Czech Republic: privatization strategies and priorities. Paper presented at the conference on sources of privatization in Eastern Europe, in Budapest, 21–22 May.

Chavance, B., and Magnin, E. 1997. Emergence of path-dependent mixed economies in Central Europe. In A. Amin and J. Hausner (Eds.), *Beyond Market and Hierarchy: Interactive Governance and Social Complexity*. Cheltenham: Edward Elgar.

Dorf, M. C., and Sabel, C. F. 1998. A constitution of democratic experimentalism. *Columbia Law Review*, 98(2): 267–473.

Dornisch, D. 1997. An ecology of projects: regional restructuring and network recombination in transforming Poland. PhD Dissertation. Cornell University.

Economist, The 1995. Something clunky out East. February 18.

European Bank for Reconstruction and Development (EBRD). 1994, 1996. *Transition Report*. London: EBRD.

Evans, P. 1995. *Embedded Autonomy: States and Industrial Transformation*. Princeton, NJ: Princeton University Press.

Fligstein, N. 2001. *The Architecture of Markets: An Economic Sociology of Capitalist Societies*. Princeton, NJ: Princeton University Press.

Frydman, R., and Rapaczynski, A. 1993. Privatization in Eastern Europe: Is the state withering away? *Finance and Development*, 30(2): 10–13.

Granovetter, M. 1985. Economic action and social structure: The problem of embeddedness. *American Journal of Sociology*, 91: 481–510.

Guillen, M. 2001. *The Limits of Convergence: Globalization and Organizational Change in Argentina, South Korea, and Spain*. Princeton, NJ: Princeton University Press.

Gulati, R., and Gargiulo, M. 1999. Where do interorganizational networks come from? *American Journal of Sociology*, 104(5): 1439–93.

Hall, P., and Soskice, D. (Eds.) 2001. *Varieties of Capitalism: The Institutional Foundations of Comparative Advantage*. Oxford: Oxford University Press.

Hamilton, G., and Biggart, N. 1988. Market, culture, and authority: A comparative analysis of management and organization in the Far East. *American Journal of Sociology*, 94(supplement): S52–S94.

Hayri, A., and McDermott, G. 1998. The network properties of corporate governance and industrial restructuring: A post-socialist lesson. *Industrial and Corporate Change*, 7(1): 153–93.

Henisz, W., and Delios, A. 2001. Uncertainty, imitation and plant location: Japanese multinational corporations, 1990–96. *Administrative Science Quarterly*, 46(3): 443–75.

Herrigel, G. 1996. *Industrial Constructions: The Sources of German Industrial Power*. New York: Cambridge University Press.

Hoshi, I., Mladek, J., and Sinclair, A. 1998. Bankruptcy and owner-led liquidation in the Czech Republic. In E. Balcerowicz, C. Gray, and I. Hoshi (Eds.), *Enterprise Exit Processes in Transition Economies*. Budapest: CEU Press.

Jacoby, W. 2000. *Imitation and Politics: Redesigning Germany*. Ithaca: Cornell University Press.

Kogut, B. 2000. The network as knowledge: Generative rules and the emergence of structure. *Strategic Management Journal*, 21: 405–25.

Kogut, B., and Spicer, A. 2002. Capital market development and mass privatization are logical contradictions: Lessons from Russia and the Czech Republic. *Industrial and Corporate Change*, 11(1): 1–37.

Kotrba, J. 1994. Czech privatization: Players and winners. CERGE-EI Working Paper No. 58.

Larson, A. 1992. Network dyads in entrepreneurial settings: A study of the governance of exchange relationships. *Administrative Science Quarterly*, 37: 76–104.

Lastovicka, R., Marcincin, A., and Mejstrik, M. 1994. Privatization and opening the capital markets in the Czech and Slovak Republics. CERGE-EI Working Paper No. 54.

Lizal, L., Singer, M., and Svejnar, J. 1995. Manager interests, breakups, and performance of state enterprises in transition. In J. Svejnar (Ed.), *The Czech Republic and Economic Transition in Eastern Europe*. San Diego: Academic Press.

Locke, R. M. 1995. Building trust. Paper presented at the Annual Meetings of the American Political Science Association, Hilton Towers, San Francisco, CA, September 1.

Locke, R. 2001. "Building Trust." Paper presented at the Annual Meetings of the American Political Science, Hilton Towers, San Francisco, California, September 1.

Lounsbury, M. 2001. Institutional sources of practice variation: Staffing college and university recycling programs. *Administrative Science Quarterly*, 46: 29–56.

McDermott, G. 2002. *Embedded Politics: Industrial Networks and Institutional Change in Post Communism*. Ann Arbor: University of Michigan Press.

McDermott, G. 2004. Institutional change and firm creation in East-Central Europe: An embedded politics approach. *Comparative Political Studies*, 37(2): 188–217.

Mihola, J., and Havlin, V. 1992. Volne ruce pro rozhonovani. *Hospodarske noviny*, January 31.

Mihola, J., Havlin, V., and Skala, M. 1991. Adaptace podniku v prvnich mesicich transformace cs. Ekonomiky. Ustredni ustav narodohospodarskeho vyzkumu, Prague. Mimeo.

Oliver, C. 1990. Determinants of inter-organizational relationships: Integration and future direction. *Academy of Management Review*, 15: 241–65.

Ostrom, E. 1995. Self-organization and social capital. *Industrial and Corporate Change*, 4(1): 131–59.

Pfeffer, J. 1992. *Managing with Power: Politics and Influence in Organizations*. Boston, MA: Harvard Business School Press.

Piore, M., and Sabel, C. 1984. *The Second Industrial Divide: Possibilities for Prosperity*. New York: Basic Books.

Podolny, J., and Page, K. 1998. Network forms of organization. *Annual Review of Sociology*, 24: 57–76.

Polanyi, K. 1944. *The Great Transformation: The Political and Economic Origins of our Time*. Boston: Beacon.

Portes, A. 2000. The two meanings of social capital. *Sociological Forum*, 15(1): 1–12.

Powell, W., and Smith-Doerr, L. 1994. Networks and economic life. In N. Smesler and R. Swedberg (Eds.), *The Handbook of Economic Sociology*. Princeton, NJ: Princeton University Press.

Powell, W., White, D., Koput, K., and Owen-Smith, J. 2002. Practicing polygamy with good taste: The evolution of interorganizational collaboration in the life sciences. Working Paper, Stanford University, November 25.

Prokop, J. 1996. Marketization in Russia's Regions, 1990–1994. Doctoral Dissertation, Department of Government, Harvard University.

Provan, K. G., and Milward, H. B. 1995. A preliminary theory of interorganizational network effectiveness: A comparative study of four community mental health systems. *Administrative Science Quarterly*, 40(1): 1–33.

Provan, K. G., and Milward, H. B. 2001. Do networks really work? A framework for evaluating public-sector organizational networks. *Public Administration Review*, 61(4): 414–23.

Putnam, R., Leonardi, R., and Nanetti, R. 1993. *Making Democracy Work: Civic Traditions in Modern Italy*. Princeton: Princeton University Press.

Rona-Tas, A. 1997. *The Great Surprise of the Small Transformation: The Demise of Communism and the Rise of the Private Sector in Hungary*. Ann Arbor: University of Michigan Press.

Rosenkopf, L., and Tushman, M. L. 1998. The coevolution of community networks and technology: Lessons from the *Flight Simulation Industry*. *Industrial and Corporate Change*, 7(2): 311–46.

Rowley, T., Behrens, D., and Krackhardt, D. 2000. Redundant governance structures: An analysis of structural and relational embeddedness in the steel and semiconductor industries. *Strategic Management Journal*, 21: 369–86.

Sabel, C. 1993. Constitutional ordering in historical perspective. In F. Scharpf (Ed.), *Games in Hierarchies and Markets*. Boulder, CO: Westview Press.

Salancik, G. R. 1995. Wanted: A good network theory of organization. *Administrative Science Quarterly*, 40: 345–49.

Spenner, K. I., Suhomlinova, O. O., Thore, S. A., Land, K. C., and Jones, D. C. 1998. Strong legacies and weak markets: Bulgarian state-owned enterprises during early transition. *American Sociological Review*, 63(4): 599–618.

Stark, D. 1986. Rethinking internal labor markets: New insights from a comparative perspective. *American Sociological Review*, 51: 492–504.

Stark, D. 1996. Recombining property in East European capitalism. *American Journal of Sociology*, 101: 993–1027.

Stark, D., and Bruszt, L. 1998. *Post-Socialist Pathways: Transforming Politics and Property in Eastern Europe*. New York: Cambridge University Press.

Svejnar, J., and Singer, M. 1994. Using vouchers to privatize an economy: the Czech and Slovak Case. *Economics of Transition*, 2(1):43–64.

Szelenyi, I. 1988. *Socialist Entrepreneurs*. Cambridge: Polity Press.

Uzzi, B. 1996. The sources and consequences of embeddedness for the economic performance of organizations: The network effect. *American Sociological Review*, 61: 674–98.

Uzzi, B. 1997. Social structure and competition in interfirm networks: The paradox of embeddedness. *Administrative Science Quarterly*, 42: 35–67.

Uzzi, B., Spiro, J., and Delis, D. 2002. Emergence: The origin and evolution of career networks in the Broadway musical industry, 1877 to 1995. Working Paper, Northwestern University, December.

Voskamp, U., and Wittke, V. 1991. Industrial restructuring in the former GDR. *Politics and Society*, 19(3): 241–79.

Wall Street Journal, The. 1996. Czechs offer peek at new corporate East. May 8, sec. A10.

Woodruff, D. 1999. *Money Unmade: Barter and the Fate of Russian Capitalism*. Ithaca: Cornell University Press.

World Bank. 1996. *From Plan to Market*. New York: Oxford University Press.

CHAPTER NINE

External Networks of Entrepreneurial Teams and High Technology Venture Performance in Emerging Markets

Balagopal Vissa and Aya S. Chacar

With the demonstrated importance of new ventures to the economic health of a country and the extremely high failure rate of new ventures, social network researchers have tried to examine the positive impact of social networks on new venture performance. The impact of social networks on venture outcomes is likely to be particularly prominent in emerging economies because social ties often work as substitutes for nonexistent markets and other institutional voids that are endemic in such contexts (Khanna and Palepu, 1997; Peng and Luo, 2000). Network research highlights the importance of the focal actor's position in social structure as a key driver of performance (e.g. see Adler and Kwon, 2002; Burt, 2000; Portes, 1998 for a review). This stream of research argues that network positions that allow access to actors that are otherwise disconnected provide information and control benefits (Burt, 1992). These arguments, applied to a new venture's entrepreneurial team suggest that teams with appropriately structured external contact networks would confer performance advantages to their venture (e.g. Aldrich and Zimmer, 1986; Birley, 1985; Nohria, 1992).

Extant research on social networks and new venture performance focuses on the structure of entrepreneurs' social networks but places less emphasis on the quality of network ties. As Coleman (1990) and Nahapiet and Ghoshal (1998) remind us, both network structure and network quality are important dimensions of social capital. In fact, we will argue in this chapter that structure and quality do not act independently of each other. The structural dimension of social capital determines the volume and diversity of resources that are potentially accessible via the social network while the quality of network ties allows for better utilization of network-based resources. We argue that heterogeneity in the access and use of informational and other resources available through external network ties have a significant impact on venture performance outcomes.

Research on new ventures traditionally focused on failure as the outcome of interest. However, more recent research (e.g. Baum et al., 2000) seeking to understand the drivers of performance differences among surviving start-ups provides evidence of considerable variation in the early growth of start-ups, with some ventures flourishing while others languish. In this study, we first examine the relationship between entrepreneurial teams' external network structure and the growth of their ventures. We then examine how the quality of the entrepreneurial teams' network ties moderates the relationship between network structure and venture growth. Growth is an important performance outcome because it confers ventures with economies of scale, increased power, profits, and the ability to withstand environmental changes.

We contribute to the entrepreneurship literature by providing a better understanding of how entrepreneurial teams' social networks are a source of venture heterogeneity. Past studies on the impact of entrepreneurial teams have been relatively under-socialized (Granovetter, 1985) since they focus on the team composition and internal processes and ignore the social structure in which the team is embedded. In contrast, this study assumes that economic action is embedded in social relations and focuses on how the social structure in which the team is embedded both enables and constrains economic action. In addition, we make a methodological contribution by correcting for two significant measurement problems that have beset past research in this area; biases introduced by measurement of categories of network as opposed to individual networks and the lack of data on the relationship between network contacts.

We also contribute to the social networks literature in two ways. First, we stress the importance of the quality of network ties which is in consonance with the growing literature on the micro-sociology of value creation (e.g. Lawler and Yoon, 1998). Second, we extend social network analysis to the team level, an understudied area of research.

Theory and Hypotheses

Organizational researchers have attributed numerous benefits to social networks in general, including informational and other resource acquisition benefits (e.g. Burt, 1992; Coleman, 1990; Granovetter, 1973), and more specifically to the social networks of new venture founders (e.g. Aldrich and Zimmer; 1986; Birley, 1985). We review extant research below, focusing on the theoretical and empirical limitations.

On the theoretical side, current research is potentially mis-specified as it typically focuses on the structure of the founders' social network but ignores the important moderating impact of the quality of network ties. On the empirical side, the execution of empirical tests on the impact of founders' networks on new venture performance has two limitations. First, research has measured the founders' social network structure based on the categories of contacts they have (e.g. family and business advisers), rather than their individual contacts, leading to measurement biases (Burt, 2000). Second, the structure and quality of relations between contacts is not measured, making it impossible to construct adequately the measures that characterize the entrepreneurs' ego-centric network. The precise structure and quality of ties is important for a number of reasons: Granovetter's (1985) notion of embeddedness implies that economic action is influenced by the specific structure and quality of ties, while Burt (1992) and Coleman (1990) also emphasize the importance of the specific structure of ties in influencing action.

Network structure as a driver of venture performance

Burt (1992) suggests that there are two main benefits to networks that affect performance outcomes for the focal actor: information and control. Network ties act as conduits of information providing the focal actor with valuable information in a timely manner either directly from the network contact or by receiving referrals from trusted others. More specifically, Aldrich and Zimmer (1986) suggested that the new venture founders' relations with members of their role set such as customers, suppliers, advisers, venture capitalist, family etc., affects their ability to access resources in pursuit of opportunity.

Thus, entrepreneurial teams embedded in information-rich networks would gain informational advantages such as knowledge spill-over benefits on best practices, market intelligence on customer needs, competitor moves, failed technological approaches, new supply sources etc. In addition, the external network contacts may increase the strategic alternatives available for selection because external contacts may provide insights that extend beyond the entrepreneurial team's own limited skills base. Considering the uncertainty in managing a new venture, these informational advantages would result in superior strategic decision making by the team and thereby superior venture performance.

More specifically, all else being equal, the larger the entrepreneurial team's external network, the greater the information benefits. In general, more network contacts should deliver greater information and advice leading to better decision making and thereby superior performance.

H1: The size of the entrepreneurial team's external network is positively associated with new venture performance.

In addition to size, social network research has emphasized another structural aspect – sparseness. Network sparseness is the extent to which network contacts are themselves not connected to each other and allow access to a greater variety of information. The information flowing through a sparse network is less likely to be redundant and more likely to be novel if contacts are themselves not connected to each other (Burt, 1992). This is also the essence of Granovetter's (1973) argument that weak ties bridging otherwise disconnected social groups are more valuable as sources of new information than strong ties, which are typically densely interconnected and hence offer redundant information. Benefits accrue to the entrepreneurial team largely because sparse networks bring access to a wider circle of information and advice on potential new markets, innovations, technology trends, sources of funding, skilled human resources etc., which are valuable in entrepreneurial activity. Burt

(1992) also stresses the importance of control benefits of being centrally positioned to bring otherwise disconnected and disorganized contacts together. While this is an important benefit within large, established firms, it is unlikely that entrepreneurial teams in new ventures could be powerful enough to gain control benefits in having sparse external networks. We therefore emphasize only the information benefits of sparse external networks. More formally:

> H2:   The sparseness of the entrepreneurial team's external network is positively associated with new venture performance.

Structure versus quality of network ties

While the mainstream research on the founders' social network has emphasized the importance of the structural aspects of such network, more recent research has pointed to the importance of the social network's quality. In fact, Nahapiet and Ghoshal (1998) have described the broader "social capital" concept as multi-dimensional. In their conceptualization, the first dimension of social capital is the structure of one's social network, which is in line with past research (e.g. Burt, 1992; Granovetter, 1973). Structural features include the number of ties one has to key contacts and the extent to which these contacts are themselves connected, which serve as proxies for the extent to which resources are available to the focal actor. The second dimension of social capital which they label as "Relational" encompasses the quality of one's network ties. The quality of ties refers to how one perceives his or her contacts as opposed to simply who knows whom. While Nahapiet and Ghoshal (1998) suggest that network quality has a direct and independent impact on performance, we argue that in addition to the direct performance effect, the quality of ties also moderates the impact of network structure on performance. We characterize the relational dimension of social capital using the two attributes of *contact trustworthiness* and *relational closeness*. We examine each of these relational attributes in turn.

Contact trustworthiness

Of the two dimensions of relational quality, we believe trust is especially important in network ties that span firm boundaries. Trust is needed because exchanges of information and knowledge are subject to a high level of hazard (Arrow, 1974; Teece, 1986) and trust is associated with lower levels of opportunism in an exchange transaction (Williamson, 1996). Within established firms, division of labor, hierarchy of authority, and behavioral rules strongly constrain member's actions, attenuating the threat of opportunism (Aldrich, 1999). In contrast, actions outside of established firms are not so constrained and the higher threat of opportunism implies that the interpersonal trust is likely to have a strong impact on the resources accessed through the external network.

Trust has been variously defined and is complex in character (Rousseau et al., 1998). In a recent review, Rousseau et al. (1998) summarize their overview of a multi-disciplinary and multi-level review of the uses of trust by offering the following definition: "Trust is a psychological state comprising the intention to accept vulnerability based upon positive expectations of the intentions or behaviour of another." While the literature on trust recognizes deterrence-based trust as well as reputation effects, we focus on inter-personal trust (Rousseau et al., 1998; McAllister, 1995), since this form of trust is perhaps more relevant for a discussion of social capital at the level of individuals and groups. This is because trust in specific others in an individual's contact network is mainly constructed through personal interactions and direct experience with the other party. The antecedents of interpersonal trust include perceived integrity of others, their competence in ongoing exchanges and the predictability of others through the alignment of goals and values (Butler, 1991).

From the perspective of the entrepreneurial team members, high levels of trust in the network contact enable the team to act on the basis of the contact's advice and information, enabling superior strategic decision making and thereby performance. More formally:

> **H3:**   Contact trustworthiness of the entrepreneurial team's external network is positively associated with new venture performance.

In this chapter, we would like to emphasize that structure and quality do not act independently of each other. The structural dimension of social capital establishes the boundary conditions for the volume and diversity of available resources, identifying the potential to access valuable resources. The quality of network ties on the other hand, determines how effectively the resources that are potentially available for value creation will actually be utilized.

We have argued that the advice and information provided by network contacts enables the entrepreneurial team to take superior strategic decisions and thereby improve performance. However, it is often difficult to establish the authenticity of information flowing in from external networks in a new venture setting. This is because of the high degree of uncertainty that characterizes the venturing process. The entrepreneurial team needs to convince different stakeholders of the viability of the new venture based on their own vision for the market and commitment to the venture. They need to achieve this in spite of the lack of resources, legitimacy and non-existent track record of the venture. Simply put, the entrepreneurial team needs to come to grips with significant uncertainty as it "discovers" the market demand function and the production function for the new venture.

This endemic uncertainty surrounding the new venture is likely to be especially problematic for entrepreneurial teams with large and sparse networks because of their greater volume of non-redundant information. In contrast, in dense, small networks, information is likely to be mostly redundant, making it easier to check its veracity. Contact trustworthiness greatly reduces the need to establish the authenticity of information since the greater integrity and competence of highly trustworthy contacts makes it unnecessary to do so. Hence, all else being equal, contact trustworthiness is likely to be far more important for large, sparse networks than for small, dense networks. More formally:

> H4a: Contact trustworthiness of the entrepreneurial team's external network moderates the effect of network size on venture performance. Network size is more likely to be positively associated with superior venture performance for teams with greater contact trustworthiness than for teams with lower contact trustworthiness.
>
> H4b: Contact trustworthiness of the entrepreneurial team's external network moderates the effect of network sparseness on venture performance. Network sparseness is more likely to be positively associated with superior venture performance for teams with greater contact trustworthiness than for teams with lower contact trustworthiness.

Relational closeness

Similar arguments have also been presented about the impact of relational closeness between the focal actor and her social network (Marsden and Campbell, 1984). Relational closeness refers to the extent of personal intimacy and familiarity in a relationship. Contacts with greater relational closeness have a greater motivation to be of assistance (Granovetter, 1982) and hence the resources that they control are typically more easily accessible to the focal actor. Contacts with greater relational closeness are thus more likely to offer valuable resources such as private information or expert advice or referrals to the entrepreneurial team and this in turn should lead to improved performance. More formally:

> H5: Relational closeness of the entrepreneurial team's external network is positively associated with new venture performance.

We have argued that the volume of information flowing through the network is influenced by relational closeness. Contacts with greater relational closeness are more likely to share private information or expert knowledge or provide referrals because they are motivated to help the entrepreneurial team.

While large and sparse networks have a greater potential for the flow of non-redundant information, the volume of such a flow is likely driven by relational closeness. In contrast, in small, dense networks, relational closeness would also increase the volume of information flow but this information is more likely to be overlapping and redundant. All else equal, greater relational closeness will therefore have a greater performance impact when entrepreneurial teams have larger more sparse networks. More formally:

> H6a: Relational closeness of the entrepreneurial team's external network moderates the effect of network size on venture performance. Network size is more likely to be positively associated with superior venture performance for teams with greater relational closeness than for teams with lower relational closeness.

H6b: Relational closeness of the entrepreneurial team's external network moderates the effect of network sparseness on venture performance. Network sparseness is more likely to be positively associated with superior venture performance for teams with greater relational closeness than for teams with lower relational closeness.

Methods

Empirical setting

To test the hypotheses, we conducted an investigation of how the social network of entrepreneurial teams of Indian software ventures influenced the growth performance of the venture. The software industry is highly technology intensive, with firms facing intense competitive pressures due to rapid technological innovations from new entrants as well as incumbents. This feature of the industry suggests that external ties could convey important market-related information and knowledge that has performance consequences. Focusing on ventures from a single industry helps control for a variety of industry specific effects that could potentially confound the impact of entrepreneurial teams on venture performance outcomes. Further, research on emerging economies suggests that social networks often substitute for non-existing economic institutions that are endemic in such settings (Khanna and Palepu, 1997; Peng and Luo, 2000). In essence, these arguments suggest that the informational and other benefits of external ties are likely to be far greater in an emerging economy setting, thus maximizing the chances of observing their performance consequences.

We identified new software ventures by their entry into industry and entrepreneurial association lists in India. Specifically, we identified 470 ventures that were less than 6 years old[1] and were members of either a trade association – National Association of Software and Service Companies (NASSCOM) – or a prominent networking organization for high technology entrepreneurship – the IndUS Entrepreneurs (TiE). The 6-year upper limit is consistent with past research on identifying new firms (e.g. Zahra et al., 2000). NASSCOM is the only industry association of software firms in India and has a membership of about 900 firms accounting for about 98 percent of industry revenues. TiE is headquartered in Silicon Valley and has local chapters in many Indian cities.

In order to gain contextual understanding of the phenomenon, we conducted in-depth fieldwork with the venture of two start-ups followed by interviews with the chief executive officers (CEOs) of five other ventures. The participants at this stage of the research were a convenience sample drawn from individuals attending networking events conducted by TiE that volunteered to take part in the research. The in-depth fieldwork involved five interviews lasting about two hours each with members of the top management teams of the two ventures. The interviews with the CEOs of five other ventures were for a total of 2 hours per CEO spread over two or three sessions. In addition, participants also filled out various survey instruments.

Interview questions were initially open-ended and grew in detail over time, seeking to understand how participants scanned the environment for information and their decision making procedures. The interviews reaffirmed the relevance of examining the link between external networks, internal team process and performance outcomes in this setting and the richness of contextual detail enabled a grounded specification of the model, constructs, and survey items. A pilot survey was used to refine the wording of items, layout of the instrument, and the length of the survey.

The final mail survey packet was addressed to the CEOs of the 470 ventures in the sampling frame in January 2002. The survey packet contained three mail surveys, one marked "CEO Questionnaire" and the other two marked as "Team Member Questionnaire." The venture team was operationalized by asking the CEO to identify a maximum of two most important managers of the venture that were crucial for strategic decision making. This sampling approach is similar to that of Simons et al. (1999) and trades off the difficulty in obtaining complete team data against the risk of omitting team members. This approach is also similar to that of Smith et al. (1994) in asking the CEO to identify the members of the top management team. Including the CEO and two other managers whom the CEO identifies as the most important participants in strategic decision making helped ensure that the sampling plan captured the most relevant data effectively. Further, it seems reasonable to restrict the venture team to three individuals since the median venture in our sample was fairly small with 29 full-time employees.

The mail survey protocol followed Dillman's (2000) guidelines to maximize response rates. Of the 470 survey packets sent out, 462 were eligible for completion (eight ventures had either closed down or changed addresses) and 110 (24 percent) ventures responded with at least one survey while 97 (21 percent) ventures had returned all the surveys (i.e. CEO Questionnaire and Team Member Questionnaire(s)). The final sample consisted of data from 84 (18 percent) ventures that was complete in all respects. The final response rate (18 percent) was considered sufficient and in line with typical response rates for mail survey methods (Rossi et al., 1983). Endorsement of the research project by NASSCOM and two local chapters of TiE was of significant help in achieving a satisfactory response rate. We tested for response bias on age and location since size data were not available for the entire sampling frame. We found no evidence of sampling bias based on age. We also found that the distribution of responses across geographic locations was slightly skewed, with disproportionate responses from two cities. However, the average ventures in these two cities did not significantly differ from the sample average on size or performance, suggesting that the skewness in geographic location may not pose a problem.

Methods and measures

Using Rousseau's (1985) classification, this chapter develops a cross-level model of the phenomenon since it specifies the causal effect of variables at one level of analysis on variables at a different level of analysis. While the dependent variable is venture growth performance – a variable at the firm level of analysis, the independent variables are at the team level of analysis.

We use validated scales from the literature wherever available for the independent and control variables. All the data used in the analysis were collected through the survey instrument administered to the CEO and the other entrepreneurial team members.

We regressed venture growth performance on the control variables, main effect variables and interaction terms in sequential steps. Robust standard errors were used throughout to control for heteroskedasticity.

Venture performance

Since accounting profit is unlikely to be disclosed and no stock market based measures exist, new venture performance as measured by venture growth has arguably been the single most important indicator of new venture performance used in past research (e.g. Baum et al., 2000; Chandler and Hanks, 1993; Zahra, 1993). We operationalized venture growth performance as the percentage change in the venture's sales revenues from 2000 to 2001 as reported by the CEO to an independent networking association's representative.

Network variables

To draw up individual entrepreneurial team members egocentric external network, we asked respondents the following name generator: "Please write the names of a maximum of five most important people, not employed by your company, that you rely on for valuable advice, guidance or information relevant to the company." Respondents could list up to five contacts and the maximum possible number of contacts in an entrepreneurial team's external network is thus limited to 15. This limitation is in line with past studies in the networks literature (e.g. Aldrich et al., 1987; Burt, 1992).

The networks of the individual team members are added up to obtain the team's network. The approach followed in building up the entrepreneurial team's network from the networks of individual team members is illustrated through an example. Figure 9.1 shows the contact network of Chris and Carol – the entrepreneurial team members of the focal venture. Carol reports three network contacts, of which there is one indirect tie (between Tom and Craig, shown as a dotted line). Chris also reports three network contacts, with one indirect tie (between Tom and Jack, shown as a dotted line). The procedure we used in constructing the team's network from the individual entrepreneurial team members' networks is as follows.

We first added the network ties of all team members. Duplicate ties to the same external contact were counted as one tie. This generated the entrepreneurial team's external network. In the example, though Tom is tied to both Chris and Carol, the tie is counted as one tie in the team's network. The non-duplicate ties are added up and the final network of the entrepreneurial team has five network contacts: Craig, Jay, Jack, Pete, and Tom.

Team network size

The entrepreneurial team's external network is assembled from the egocentric networks of the individual team members as given in the example above. *Network size*

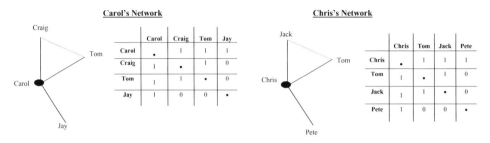

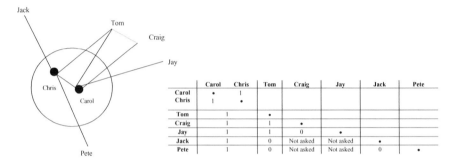

Figure 9.1 Deriving the team's networks from members' networks

is defined as the total number of ties in the entrepreneurial team's external network and ranges from 0 to 15. *Team network size* should be positive and significant if hypothesis H1 is supported.

Team network sparseness

Following Burt (1992), each team member was asked whether he or she thought there was a tie between each pair of contacts (i.e. indirect ties) in their egocentric network. This methodology assumes that there are no systematic biases in the way team members perceive relations between their network contacts. The second assumption is with regard to unknown data on some indirect ties. In the example given above, we do not know if Jay and Jack have a tie or if Pete and Jay have a tie, because neither Chris nor Smith can be asked to assess whether such a relationship exists (they can only be asked to assess indirect ties between contacts they had named in their *own* individual networks). There is, however, no reason to believe that the extent of indirect ties for unreported contacts should differ *systematically* from the extent of ties for reported contacts.

Following the methodology in Hansen et al. (2000), we make the assumption that the proportion of indirect ties among the possible number of indirect ties that are unknown equals the proportion of estimated indirect ties among the possible number of indirect ties that respondents were asked to assess. We calculate the *adjusted* maximum number of indirect ties as:

Adjusted maximum number of indirect ties = $N * (N - 1)/2 - X$

where N is the number of network contacts in the team's network (five in the example) and X is the number of ties between contacts that could not be assessed (the four 'not asked' cells in Figure 9.1). Network sparseness is then calculated as follows:

Network sparseness = $1 -$ (No. of reported indirect ties $/$
Adjusted max. No. of indirect ties)

Network sparseness should be positive and significant if hypothesis H2 is supported.

Contact trustworthiness
We measured contact trustworthiness as follows. We first measured inter-personal (i.e. dyadic) trust in an individual team member's network. We did this by selecting and adapting items used in Johnson-George and Swap's (1982) scale for measuring trust in a specific other as well as McAllister's (1995) scale for affect and cognition based trust. Dimensions of inter-personal trust include perceptions of honesty, competence, and goal alignment. We asked individual team members to choose from five Likert-type items regarding their network contact, focusing on integrity, competence and reliability of the network contact. Factor analysis revealed that the five items loaded on to a single factor. We then calculated contact trustworthiness of the entrepreneurial team's external network as the average of individual team members' trust in their network contact using the formula given below:

Contact trustworthiness = $\Sigma\Sigma \, DT_{ij} / \Sigma \, c_i$

where DT_{ij} is the dyadic trust between team member i and external network contact j in the team member's network; and c_i is the total number of external contacts in the network of team member i. *Contact trustworthiness* will be positive and significant if hypothesis H3 is supported. Respectively, *contact trustworthiness × network size* and *contact trustworthiness × network sparseness* should be positive and significant if hypotheses H4a and H4b are supported.

Relational closeness
The second dimension of tie quality is relational closeness (Marsden and Campbell, 1984), measured for the entrepreneurial team's external network based on the individual team member's network using the formula given below:

Relational closeness = $\Sigma\Sigma \, TS_{ij} / \Sigma \, c_i$

where TS_{ij} is the relational closeness (measured on a 1–4 Likert scale) of team member i with external network contact j in the team member's external network; and c_i is the total number of external contacts in the external network of team member i. *Relational closeness* will be positive and significant if hypothesis H5 is supported. Respectively, *relational closeness × network size* and *relational closeness × network sparseness* should be positive and significant if hypotheses H6a and H6b are supported.

Control variables

We controlled for competitive intensity in the new venture's market, venture size, venture age, team size, prior start-up experience and functional diversity in the entrepreneurial team, since these variables have frequently been identified as factors that can influence venture growth performance (e.g. Birley and Stockley, 2000; Eisenhardt and Schoonhoven, 1990; Roure and Keeley, 1990). *Competitive intensity* was measured by a two-item Likert-type scale in the specific software market in which the new ventures operates. *Venture size* was the number of full-time equivalent employees in December 2000. *Venture age* was measured as the number of months from the date of legal incorporation of the venture. Of the 84 ventures in the final sample, ten ventures had two-member entrepreneurial teams while the rest had three-member teams. We controlled for team size using a dummy for two-member teams. *Prior start-up experience* was measured as the average number of times team members had started a new venture prior to the current one. *Functional diversity* was measured using the entropy index (Teachman, 1980).

Model and analysis

We use ordinary least squares (OLS) regressions methods to test the hypotheses developed. In order to correct for the multi-collinearity that arises when testing moderated relationships among continuous variables, the relevant independent variables were centered before the interaction terms were generated (Aiken and West, 1991). Centering involved subtracting the sample mean from each independent variable, leaving the sample distribution unchanged, but with a mean of zero. The interaction terms were generated by multiplication of the mean centered variables. The centering procedure is preferable because it yields readily interpretable coefficients and significantly reduces multi-collinearity between the main terms and the interaction terms.

Results

Descriptive statistics and correlations of all the variables are presented in Table 9.1. The average venture is 3.9 years old, with 70 employees and an entrepreneurial team of 2.9 members. Eighty-three percent of CEOs also identify themselves as founders,[2] while 49 percent of the other team members are also founders. The average team member is male, 37 years of age and has software industry work experience of 6.4 years. The average team network size is 9.2 contacts and the maximum is 14 contacts. Venture age and size are negatively correlated with venture performance while network size and network sparseness are positively correlated with venture performance.

Table 9.2 presents the OLS regression estimates of the impact of the entrepreneurial team's external networks on venture growth. While model 1 of Table 9.2

Table 9.1 Descriptive statistics and correlation matrix[a]

Variable	Mean	S.D.	(1)	(2)	(3)	(4)	(5)	(6)	(7)	(8)	(9)	(10)
1. Venture growth (log)	0.20	0.20	1									
2. Competitive intensity	3.9	0.87	−0.09	1								
3. Venture size	70	108	−0.24*	0.05	1							
4. Venture age	3.9	2.4	−0.21*	−0.11	0.02	1						
5. Two person team dummy	0.12	0.32	−0.03	−0.07	−0.17	0.21†	1					
6. Prior start-up experience	1.6	1.4	−0.08	0.09	−0.15	0.02	−0.10	1				
7. Functional diversity	0.47	0.21	0.32**	−0.17	−0.17	0.0	−0.12	−0.19†	1			
8. Network size[b]	0.0	3.2	0.24**	−0.06	−0.16	−0.19	−0.29*	−0.09	0.17†	1		
9. Network sparseness[b]	0.0	0.22	0.34**	0.02	−0.17	−0.13	−0.0	−0.29**	0.15	0.28**	1	
10. Contact trustworthiness[b]	0.05	0.68	0.07	0.13	0.20	−0.0	−0.04	0.08	−0.08	−0.23*	−0.05	1
11. Relational closeness[b]	−0.02	0.46	0.04	0.04	−0.10	0.11	−0.06	0.11	0.09	0.07	0.05	0.22*

[a] Reported correlations are Pearson coefficients with $N = 84$ observations.

[b] Mean centered variables.

† $p < 0.10$; * $p < 0.05$; ** $p < 0.01$.

Table 9.2 Regression analysis of effects of entrepreneurial teams' external networks on venture performance[a]

	Model 1 Controls	Model 2 N/w structure	Model 3 N/w quality	Model 4 Full model
Competitive intensity	−0.01	−0.01	−0.01	−0.004
	(0.03)	(0.03)	(0.03)	(0.025)
Venture size	−0.0003*	−0.0002	−0.0003*	−0.0001
	(0.0002)	(0.000)	(0.0002)	(0.0001)
Venture age	−0.018*	−0.015*	−0.018*	−0.01[†]
	(0.008)	(0.08)	(0.008)	(0.008)
Two-member team dummy	0.005	0.03	0.005	0.02
	(0.09)	(0.08)	(0.09)	(0.08)
Prior start-up experience	−0.006	0.005	−0.008	0.006
	(0.01)	(0.011)	(0.01)	(0.01)
Functional diversity	0.268**	0.24*	0.268**	0.16[†]
	(0.11)	(0.12)	(0.11)	(0.11)
Network size		0.01[†]		0.007
		(0.006)		(0.006)
Network sparseness		0.22*		0.167[†]
		(0.11)		(0.116)
Contact trustworthiness			0.02	0.038
			(0.03)	(0.033)
Relational closeness			0.006	−0.011
			(0.05)	(0.054)
Sparseness × Relational closeness				−0.007
				(0.19)
Sparseness × Contact trustworthiness				0.488**
				(0.191)
Network size × Relational closeness				−0.009
				(0.011)
Network size × Contact trustworthiness				0.005
				(0.008)
Model F	5.9**	6.6***	4.4**	4.3**
R^2	0.20	0.27	0.20	0.36
N	84	84	84	84

[a] Unstandardized regression coefficients with standard errors in parentheses. All models estimated using OLS regression with robust standard error. Dependent variable is the logarithm of revenue growth. Interacting variables have been mean centered.
[†] $p < 0.10$; *$p < 0.05$; **$p < 0.01$; ***$p < 0.001$ (one tailed tests).

presents the base model, models 2–4 present results for the network structure, network quality and their interaction effects introduced in a stepwise fashion to the base model.

The base model that includes only the control variables is significant and has considerable explanatory power. As can be seem, the control variables explain about 20 percent of the variance and the regression as a whole is significant. *Venture size* and *venture age* are negatively related to growth while *functional diversity* is positively related to growth. *Competitive intensity, prior start-up experience* and team size, proxied by the *two member team dummy* are not statistically significant.

Model 2 examines the impact of our two network structural variables *network size* and *network sparseness*. Model 2 shows that *network size* has a positive and significant effect on venture growth, suggesting strong support for H1. We also find that *network sparseness* is positive and significant, strongly supporting H2 that teams with sparse external networks have a positive influence on performance.

Turning to the two network quality variables – *contact trustworthiness* and *relational closeness* – we find that both of them are positive but not significant at conventional levels, suggesting that network quality may not have a direct effect on performance outcomes, indicating no support for H3 and H5. Model 4 presents the results of the full model that includes the interaction effect between network structure and network quality. *Network sparseness × contact trustworthiness* is positive, suggesting that high trust network contacts enable team members to leverage the informational advantages of sparse networks, supporting H4b. The other interaction terms between structure and quality variables are not significant, showing lack of support for H4a, H6a, and H6b. The main effects of network size and network sparseness still remain the full model, albeit with reduced significance. Overall, our results suggest that the structure of entrepreneurial teams' external advice network has a significant direct effect on venture growth, while contact trustworthiness is an important moderator. Teams with sparse networks can better leverage the benefits of network sparseness when their contacts are also highly trustworthy.

Discussion and Conclusion

The main goal of this study was to determine whether the combined effect of network quality and network structure is a driver of new venture performance. We find that this is partially the case, with network sparseness combined with contact trustworthiness being positively correlated with new venture growth. The joint effect of network size and contact trustworthiness, however, is not significant. We speculate that contact trustworthiness is likely to be more important in sparse networks where there is greater non-redundancy of information. When information sources are less non-redundant, as is likely to be the case in larger networks, trustworthiness may not be as important as the same information could be obtained and verified from multiple sources.

Surprisingly, however, we do not find the relational closeness aspect of tie quality to be important. Past research has hypothesized that closeness is an indicator of the willingness of network contacts to provide the information or resources needed by the focal actors. Our results could be driven by the particular setting of our data. Most of the network contacts in our study were labeled by respondents as customers, suppliers, investors, or formal advisers rather than "friends or family." We speculate that this strong task orientation of the advice network could be one reason for non-significance of relational closeness. Finally, our empirical strategy of examining separately the impact of the structure and quality of network ties builds on recent research by Galunic and Moran (1999) and could be a useful approach for future research on entrepreneur's personal networks.

More generally, this study supports the notion that the social networks of new ventures' top management are an important source of new venture performance heterogeneity. Empirical research in the entrepreneurship literature has examined the impact of the personal networks of the founder(s) on venture performance, with mixed results. For example, Hansen (1995) and Ostgaard and Birley (1996) find that personal networks are significant drivers of venture growth. Reese and Aldrich (1995), however, report that general features of the personal network, such as time invested and the scope of the network, do not seem to affect venture performance. Bruderl and Preisendorfer (1998), using tighter statistical controls, find that strong ties in the personal network of founders are more important than weak ties. One explanation given for these mixed results, alluded to earlier in the chapter, is the methodological limitations of past research. This chapter corrects for these methodological biases and finds strong positive effects of entrepreneurial teams' networks on performance, strengthening the view that entrepreneurs' networks matter for performance. Our results are also consistent with the broader organizational research showing that sparse networks provide performance benefits. For example, research has shown that sparse and non-redundant networks are beneficial for job promotion (e.g. Burt, 1992) and in career development (e.g. Higgins and Kram, 2001).

There are a number of potential limitations that could affect our conclusions. First, since this a cross-sectional study, there is a possibility of reverse causality, i.e. instead of network sparseness driving venture growth it could be that teams from successful ventures could have more sparse networks. While there is no independent way to confirm the age of ties, we are reassured here as to the validity of our conclusions by the fact that the average duration of ties was greater than 6 years and no network tie was less than one year old, suggesting that the network ties were temporally antecedent to the performance variable examined in this study.

As in other network studies, a second limitation is potential endogeneity. It could be that both sparseness and performance were outcomes of unobserved variables such as, say, IQ (i.e. intelligent individuals could have sparse networks and cause successful ventures). Unfortunately, we are unable to correct for such a possibility at present.

A third limitation of this study relates to the generalizability of our results to other countries than India. While the advantage of this study is that it examined the relationship between network characteristics and new venture performance in an emerging market, we do not know at the present the degree of generalizability across institutional environments. Future comparative research, or simple replication in different institutional environments, is needed here.

Finally, in spite of all the above-mentioned limitations, an important contribution of this chapter is the empirical evidence that top management teams differ systematically in the structure of their external advice ties, in ways that matter for venture performance outcomes. More interesting is the finding that teams with greater contact trustworthiness are systematically better at exploiting their network resources. A great deal of research in strategy has focused on how management teams are an important source of firm heterogeneity (Castanias and Helfat, 1991). At a fundamental level, this research identifies some of the mechanisms by which management teams in an emerging economy setting use their social capital as drivers of firm heterogeneity.

Notes

1 Data on venture age provided by NASSCOM and TiE did not match self-reported age for seven ventures, which were more than 6 years old. We retained these ventures (with their self-reported age) in our sample to improve degrees of freedom, but our reported results are robust to dropping them.
2 Founders were defined as individuals who were significantly involved in start-up activities and who own a large equity stake in the venture.

References

Adler, P., and Kwon, S. 2002. Social capital: Prospects for a new concept. *Academy of Management Review*, 27(1): 17–40.

Aiken, L., and West, S. 1991. *Multiple Regression: Testing and Interpreting Interactions*. Newbury Park, CA: Sage.

Aldrich, H. 1999. *Organisations Evolving*. Thousand Oaks, CA: Sage.

Aldrich, H., and Zimmer, C. 1986. Entrepreneurship through social networks. In D. L. Sexton and R. W. Smilor (Eds.), *The Art and Science of Entrepreneurship*. Cambridge, MA: Ballinger.

Aldrich, H., Rosen, B., and Woodward, W. 1987. The impact of social networks on business founding and profit: A longitudinal study. In N. C. Churchill et al. (Eds.), *Frontiers of Entrepreneurship Research*. Wellesley MA: Babson College, Center for Entrepreneurial Studies, 154–8.

Arrow, K. 1974. *The Limits of Organization*. New York: Norton.

Baum, J., Calabrese, T., and Silverman, B. 2000. Don't go it alone: Alliance network composition and start-ups performance in Canadian biotechnology. *Strategic Management Journal*, 21: 267–94.

Birley, S. 1985. The role of networks in the entrepreneurial process. *Journal of Business Venturing*, 1: 107–17.

Birley, S., and Stockley, S. 2000. Entrepreneurial teams and venture growth. In D. L. Sexton and H. Landström (Eds.), *The Blackwell Handbook of Entrepreneurship*. Oxford: Blackwell.

Bruderl, J., and Preisendorfer, P. 1998. Network support and the success of newly founded businesses. *Small Business Economics*, 10: 213–25.

Burt, R. 1992. *Structural Holes*. Cambridge, MA: Harvard University Press.

Burt, R. 2000. The network structure of social capital. In R. Sutton and B. Staw (Eds.), *Research in Organisational Behaviour*. Greenwich, CT: JAI Press.

Butler, J. K. Jr. 1991. Towards understanding and measuring conditions of trust: Evolution of a conditions of trust inventory. *Journal of Management*, 17: 643–63.

Castanias, R. P., and Helfat, C. E. 1991. Managerial resources and rents. *Journal of Management*, 17(1): 155–71.

Coleman, J. 1990. *Foundations of Social Theory*. Cambridge, MA: Harvard University Press.

Chandler, G., and Hanks, S. 1993. Measuring the performance of emerging businesses: A validation study. *Journal of Business Venturing*, 8(5): 391–408.

Dillman, D. 2000. *Mail and Internet Surveys: The Tailored Design Method*. New York: Wiley.

Eisenhardt, K., and Schoonhoven, C. 1990. Organisational growth: Linking founding team, strategy, environment and growth among US semi-conductor ventures, 1978–1988. *Administrative Science Quarterly*, 35: 504–29.

Galunic, C., and Moran, P. 1999. Social capital and productive exchange, LBS Working Paper.

Granovetter, M. 1973. The strength of weak ties. *American Journal of Sociology*, 78: 1360–80.

Granovetter, M. 1982. The strength of weak ties: A network theory revisited. In N. Lin and P. Marsden (Eds.), *Social Network Analysis*. New York: Sage.

Granovetter, M. 1985. Economic action, social structure and embeddedness. *American Journal of Sociology*, 91: 481–510.

Hansen, E. 1995. Entrepreneurial networks and new organisation growth. *Entrepreneurship Theory and Practice*, 19(4): 7–19.

Hansen, M., Podolny, J., and Pfeffer, J. 2000. So many ties, so little time: A task contingency perspective on the value of social capital in organisations. Paper presented at the annual meetings of the Academy of Management, Toronto.

Higgins, M., and Kram, K. 2001. Reconceptualizing mentoring at work: A developmental network perspective. *Academy of Management Review*, 26(2): 264–88.

Johnson-George, C., and Swap, W. 1982. Measurement of specific interpersonal trust: Construction and validation of a scale to assess trust in a specific other. *Journal of Personality and Social Psychology*, 43: 1306–17.

Khanna, T., and Palepu, K. G. 1997. Why focused strategies may be wrong in emerging markets. *Harvard Business Review*, 75(4): 41–51.

Lawler, E., and Yoon, J. 1998. Network structure and emotion in exchange relations. *American Sociological Review*, 63: 871–94.

Marsden, P., and Campbell, K. 1984. Measuring tie strength. *Social Forces*, 63: 482–501.

McAllister, D. 1995. Affect and cognition based trust as foundations for interpersonal co-operation in organizations. *Academy of Management Journal*, 38: 24–59.

Nahapiet, J., and Ghoshal, S. 1998. Social capital, intellectual capital and the organisation advantage. *Academy of Management Review*, 23: 242–66.

Nohria, N. 1992. Information and search in the creation of new business ventures: The case of the 128 Venture Group. In N. Nohria and R. Eccles (Eds.), *Networks and Organisations*. Boston, MA: Harvard Business School Press, 240–61.

Ostgaard, T., and Birley, S. 1996. New venture growth and personal networks. *Journal of Business Research*, 36: 37–50.

Peng, M., and Luo, Y. 2000. Managerial ties and firm performance in a transition economy: The nature of a micro-macro link. *Academy of Management Journal*, 43(3): 486–501.

Portes, A. 1998. Social capital: Its origins and applications in modern sociology. *Annual Review of Sociology*, 24: 1–24.

Reese, P., and Aldrich, H. 1995. Entrepreneurial networks and business performance: A panel study of small and medium sized firms in the research triangle. In S. Birley and I. MacMillan (Eds.), *International Entrepreneurship*. London: Routledge.

Rossi, P., Wright, J., and Anderson, A. 1983. *Handbook of Survey Research*. New York: Academic Press.

Roure, J., and Keeley, R. 1990. Predictors of success in new technology based ventures. *Journal of Business Venturing*, 5(4): 201–21.

Rousseau, D. 1985. Issues in cross level research. In B. M. Staw and L. L. Cummings (Eds.), *Research in Organisational Behavior*. Greenwich, CT: JAI Press.

Rousseau, D. M., Sitkin, S. B., Burt, R. S., and Camerer, C. 1998. Not so different after all: A cross discipline view of trust. *Academy of Management Review*, 23(3): 393–404.

Simons, T., Pelled, L., and Smith, K. 1999. Making use of difference: Diversity, debate, and decision comprehensiveness in top management teams. *Academy of Management Journal*, 42(6): 662–73.

Smith, K., Smith, K., Olian, J., Smis, H., O'Bannon, D., and Scully, J. 1994. Top management team demography and process – the role of social integration and communication. *Administrative Science Quarterly*, 39(3): 412–38.

Teachman, J. 1980. Analysis of population diversity. *Sociological Methods and Research*, 8: 341–62.

Teece, D. 1986. Profiting from technological innovation: Implications for integration, collaboration, licensing and public policy. *Research Policy*, 15: 285–305.

Williamson, O. 1996. *Mechanisms of Governance*. New York: Oxford University Press.

Zahra, S. 1993. Environment, corporate entrepreneurship, and financial performance: A taxonomic approach. *Journal of Business Venturing*, 8(4): 319–40.

Zahra, S., Ireland, D., and Hitt, M. 2000. International expansion by new venture firms: International diversity, mode of market entry, technological learning, and performance. *Academy of Management Journal*, 43(5): 925–51.

CHAPTER TEN

Entrepreneurial Innovation in Standards-based Industries: Insights from Indian IT Product Firms

T. R. Madanmohan

New business creation and entrepreneurial "churning" (Reynolds and White, 1996) are increasingly recognized as being among the most important sources of development and growth of a country's economy. In particular, the future welfare of a country seems to depend on its capacity to exploit the numerous opportunities connected to information technology, telecommunication, biotechnology and life sciences. All these industrial sectors exhibit what economists term as network markets. The basic block of network markets is the consumer's willingness to adopt a product as a part of a community of users. On the demand side, the more customers join a network, such as a telecommunications service, the higher the incentive for other customers to join. On the supply side, the larger a network becomes in terms of users and also in size of assets deployed, the easier it is for a company to lower costs and prices. Because of the strong positive-feedback elements, these markets are prone to the "winner-takes-all" phenomenon. With significant modularization and network externalities in these industries, standards – especially compatibility standards – are emerging as the most important dimension of competition.

Historical analyses of recent standards in the information and communication technologies (ICT) sector suggest the crucial role the standards-based firms play (Burg, 2001). Standards-based firms, part of the larger technological community, participate in standard definition, development, and deployment. They also undertake implementation, develop extensions, train and re-skill developers, and participate in institutionalization of the standard. These firms create a community of supply structures that support the technology development by standardizing new variants that affect the success of a standard. Standards-based firms not only have the potential of creating new industries, but they also provide innovation inputs to established industries and contribute to their revitalization. There are several growth-related management challenges that are specific to standards-based firms. The technical knowledge possessed by employees and the extent to which its management can participate in the evolution and the adoption and institutionalization of the standard plays a prominent role for the identification of business opportunities for standards-based firms. Owing to the inherent uncertainty of technical knowledge and the uncertainty of the value that technical knowledge has for meeting compatibility requirements of customers, standards-based firms face more uncertainty than many other types of technology-based firms. Due to the high rate of technological developments and institutional dynamics surrounding standardization it becomes necessary for these firms to continually identify new opportunities for growth and at the same time deal with the increased complexity of a larger consortia/standard-setting organization.

While many aspects of growth in technology-based start-ups have been investigated (Garnsey, 1998), the interaction between technology (standards) and growth has not received much attention. Cooper (1993) notes that entrepreneurship research has not advanced very far in its quest for predicting new venture performance and growth. Growth is a process, and better understanding of the process itself is likely to lead to better understanding of its outcome. A missing step towards better understanding of firm growth within the field of technology entrepreneurship is the development of a conceptualization of the growth process. This is especially true for the study of standards-based firms where no studies of the growth process exist. For appropriate conceptualization of the growth process for standards-based firms it has to take into account the relationship between standards evolution and the dynamics of the technological community, internal technical knowledge and growth. Analysis of their initiation, entrepreneurial trajectory followed and development of resources and capabilities assumes research significance, as no entrepreneurial literature exists in firms that are concomitantly subject to standards in network industries. Although one of the purposes of entrepreneurship research is to understand how opportunities to manifest future goods and services are discovered, created, and exploited (Venkataraman, 1997), little research has been done on the entrepreneurial process of "complementary" firms in network industries. An analysis of these firms has more value to many firms in countries such as Ireland, India, and China that are engaged in traditional software services business, but want to move up the value chain by developing standalone products and services. This chapter focuses on the entrepreneurial evolution process, but has its starting point in technological adaptation, resource exploitation and capability development as aggregate outcomes of entrepreneurship. The chapter is therefore concerned with those activities and contexts of entrepreneurship that relate to the identification and exploitation of opportunities for technological innovation in standards-based markets. This chapter aims at contributing to the development of scientific knowledge about the entrepreneurial process in firms in high-tech and knowledge-based sectors that are evolving in tandem with a standard.

Network Industries, Standard-based Firms and Entrepreneurial Innovation: Selected Literature Review

A standard is understood as a set of technical specifications adhered to by a set of producers, either tacitly or as a result of a formal agreement (David and Greenstein, 1990). A standard attempts to strike a balance between the user requirements, technological possibilities, producers, and societal costs. In emerging industries standards play an important role of ensuring supplier specialization and part repair or replacement strategies (Economides, 1989). It also reduces uncertainty along the technical dimension, and thus eliminates the role of marketing characteristics such as brand name/manufacturer's reputation in the marketplace (David and Greenstein, 1990). Standards may be classified into product versus non-product or based on their content into private or open standards. From the point of view of the ICT sector, standards can be classified as product or service standards or horizontal and vertical standards. TCP/IP protocols, operating systems such as Windows, XML, etc. are examples of technology product horizontal standards, in that they are applicable in many industries. Standards that are applicable to a specific industry are vertical standards; they not only have narrower applicability but also focus more on data and business processes. Service standards refer to specific service processes such as recognition, validation, and QoS (Quality of Service) related to a specific process or an industry.

Standards emerge through two broad processes: *de jure* and *de facto* standardization. *De jure* standardization concerns standards promulgated by legislative bodies or voluntary standards published by independent organizations (David and Greenstein, 1990). *De facto* standards emerge when a standard arises from a standardization struggle between different technologies, each of them sponsored by a firm or a coalition of firms (David and Greenstein, 1990). While *de jure* standards are important to trade, recent history in ICT industries has shown that it is the *de facto* standards that matter from the point of view of competition. Moreover, *de facto* standardization is far more challenging for companies, since they can play an active role in the process of standardization (David and Greenstein, 1990). Standard-setting organizations based on degree of strategic purposes can be classified as research consortia, specification consortia, and strategic consortia (Updegrove, 1993). A research consortium connotes a cooperative research effort among companies, universities, industries, and/or government, typically aimed at helping the participants maintain their leadership position. Specification groups such as XML/EDI (Electronic Data Interchange) or OMG (Object Management Group) are essentially concerned with development of a usable, robust standard for the benefit of the industry. Essentially apolitical, many of these groups are formed and funded by vendors, some are formed through the efforts of end-users to lower acquisition costs. Due to the absence of proprietary pressures, the output of these consortia tends to be responsive to broad practical and economic considerations, often representing the broad consensus of the industry. Finally, strategic consortia are formed and funded by a small number of companies for their individual benefit in order to promote the adoption of certain technology as open technology. In recognition of this, governments, standard-setting bodies, and incumbent firms support the creation of new standards. Well-known recent examples include US-led CDMA and Europe-driven TDMA in telecommunications, a consortia led by Bluetooth and IEEE supported 802 technology for short-range wireless and Microsoft led NET platform versus SUN led open standard Java.

Network innovations are explained by adopting a technology community framework (Van de Ven and Garud 1989; 1994). Accordingly, technologies and institutional frameworks "co-produce" each other. Governments, standard-setting bodies, firms, and individuals define, standardize, and regulate the variety and selection of technologies. Tushman and Rosenkopf (1992), define "technological community" as the set of organizations that are stakeholders for a particular technology or product class. This includes suppliers, manufacturers, user groups, government agencies, standards bodies and professional associations. According to Tushman and Rosenkopf, the technological community coevolves with the "technology cycle" in a socio-cultural evolutionary process of variation, selection and retention. The evolutionary dynamics of community organization refer to changes in the actors, linkages between them, and the power held by them. In many cases, a firm's ability to commercialize an innovation may require that its internal resources be utilized in conjunction with the complementary resources of another firm (Brush and Greene, 1996). Complementary assets are defined as resources that are required to capture the benefits associated with a strategy, a technology, or an innovation and thereby gain competitive advantage. They are also defined as distinctive resources of alliance partners that collectively generate greater rents than the sum of those obtained from the individual endowments of each partner (Dyer and Singh, 1998). Another view on "complementarity" focuses on the relatedness between products but allows the links to be created "by" the customer. For example, the value of a car is affected by the aggregate consumption of other cars and the consumption level of the particular brand, since this determines the availability of parts, repairing assistance, gas stations, washing services, and various other related goods and services. Thus the demand for a product is influenced by total demand for the product class or by total demand in a complementary product class. This behavior causes a feedback effect on demand that creates a tendency towards a single network, platform, or standard. Complementary resources include applications developers who may implement, extend, document, and support the standard adoption. Analysis of successful standard adoption and sustenance in network markets indicates the crucial role complementary firms play (Burg, 2001). They create a community of supply structures that are able to mutate quickly as technology develops to standardize new variants and significantly affect the success of a standard. Thus their size and entrepreneurial actions are important in markets where no dominant design or standard has yet emerged.

Standards-based firms are one of the venues for the development, refinement, and sustenance of new products and services based on technical knowledge. In that respect they relate to definitions of technology-based firms as firms that perform in-house research and development (R&D) (Ansoff and Stewart, 1967), as a consequence of being dependent on technology for exploiting business opportunities (Granstrand, 1998), and as high-technology new firms (Oakey, 1994). In this chapter the concept of standards-based firms refers to a recently established firm, independent at start-up, that relies on the development of a technical standard and knowledge of its employees for identifying and exploiting economic opportunities. Standards-based firms may take on different roles in the technological innovation process, either generating new standards, training, and evolution technology communities; extending and servicing standards-based products; or in institutionalization of the standard through government or standard setting bodies. Whether the effects are direct or indirect, the effects of each firm are likely to affect the overall adoption and diffusion of a particular standard.

The entrepreneurial process provides a conception of the activities and contexts that constitute entrepreneurship. In its most general formulation the entrepreneurial process refers to the identification and exploitation of business opportunities. To search for opportunities is an important part of the entrepreneurial process (Khilstrom and Laffont, 1979, Shaver and Scott, 1991). Opportunities are discovered, identified "out of the ambiguities and clouds of an infinite array of alternative prospective futures" (Kirzner, 1973), based on previous knowledge and experience (Shane, 2000). It is not known beforehand whether the exploitation of the opportunity will be profitable or not. The final dimension of the entrepreneurial process is the form of exploitation. Exploitation is the commercial action towards realizing the profits of an opportunity or towards the creation of a profitable opportunity. Compared to the vast amount of studies of growth, there have been relatively few studies of the growth process. Within economics, the growth process has not received much attention, except Penrose's (1959) theory of the growth of the firm. Within strategy and management, the growth process has attracted more attention related to the management of organizational change and development (Chandler, 1962). Organization studies of the growth process have focused on structural changes during growth focusing on the structural changes unfolding according to an internal logic of organizing at different sizes and ages (e.g. Churchill and Lewis, 1983). Scholars studying the economics of innovation have investigated the growth of new technology-based ventures and their impact on industrial dynamics (Granstrand, 1998). Many studies within entrepreneurship research have also investigated technology-based start-ups, trying to explain the conditions for their growth (Autio, 2000, Bhidé, 2000).

In studying organizational evolution, we need to look at both internal as well as external variables such as organizational structure, strategy, and environmental dynamism. Researchers (Chandler and Baucus, 1996) have identified variables relating to venture performance and posited that resources and capabilities are directly related to new venture performance. In addition, specific capabilities are hypothesized to directly relate to the competitive strategies chosen by a firm. Capabilities are a firm's abilities to integrate, build, and reconfigure internal and external assets and competencies so that they enable it to perform distinctive activities (Teece et al., 1997). Firms garner rents by acquiring, developing, and deploying resources such that they provide a distinctive source of advantage in the marketplace. Firms' decisions about selecting, accumulating, and deploying resources are characterized as economically rational within the constraints of information asymmetry, cognitive bias, and causal ambiguity. Brush and Chaganti (1998) propose that combinations of resources are related to survival and the combination of these resources vary across age and size. They examine the influence of human and organizational resources on firm performance. A handful of models have been proposed to explain how resources and capabilities are built up over time (McGrath et al., 1996; Miyazaki, 1995; Oliver, 1997). All these models are empirically grounded; however, they have all followed a factor-oriented, or variance theory, approach. Process theories are less common in the resource-based view of the firm literature, and have yet to be developed for explaining the resource and capability development process in dynamic environments. Process theories focus on sequences of activities to explain how and why particular outcomes evolve over time (Shaw and Jarvenpaa, 1997). All the previous studies have analyzed what can be termed as traditional industries, wherein imitation is a costly process. The literature does not extend to explain the case of new organizations operating in network industries, more so ICT environments where imitation, especially of a standard, is easy. Similar to previous research (Newman and Robey, 1992), we attempt a process model involving antecedent conditions, encounters, episodes, and outcomes over the evolution of standards-based firms in standards (Bluetooth, IEEE 802.1 and Java server J2EE and J2ME environments). Practitioners value process theories, as they are easier to understand and are high in relevance (Shaw and Jarvenpaa, 1997).

Methodology

Since the attempt of this research is to understand how firms evolve in network industries and the process itself is complex and context-specific (Gartner, 1985), a process theory framework is considered more appropriate for the study. A multiple-case design was chosen because multiple cases are regarded as providing more compelling evidence, thus increasing the robustness of the overall research (Yin, 1994). The objective in choosing the case studies is to provide the reader with a broad picture that highlights the diversity among cases, and maintains a reasonable balance in terms of geographic and sectoral representations. The cases presented herein are not a random sample of the projects in existence.

Table 10.1 provides the summary characteristics of sample firms. These firms were founded by "first-generation technocrats", that is, they started their firms with the intention of developing products based on standards. These technocrats had an average prior experience of 7 years. The standards on which they were developing their products and services were all open standards where the entry barriers were low and the standards themselves were continuously evolving. For example, Bluetooth evolved from version 1.0 to 1.2 within the 2 years and had seen a surge of support from 56 firms in 1999 to over 2,000 firms in 2001. Three of our sample firms started working from the beta-release of Bluetooth standard and have evolved to offer products and tools. The key informants for the case sites were the chief executive, company secretary, and senior managers of marketing, and R&D. The interviews were conducted over a 3-month period, with 8–12 hours spent in each firm. The other sources of data included secondary data sources such as company websites, industry experts, press reports, company releases, business plan, analyst reports and promotional material, thereby achieving triangulation of sources and methods triangulation (Patton, 1999). Drafts of the case histories were written and sent to the key informants for accuracy and approvals. We did not attempt to operationalize or measure a concept on an a priori basis; rather, case transcripts were analyzed, interpreted, and coded as a means to identify the dynamic evolution of capabilities and resources. In most cases we used direct quotes from the key informants, because they best reflect the factors under investigation. We used Strauss and Corbin's (1990) coding procedure as they could be usefully employed in our study because of their rigor and systematization. Tentative codes were reviewed and codes that appeared to relate to the same phenomenon were grouped into categories.

Table 10.1   Details of the firms interviewed

Firm	Product focus	Established	Number of employees	Investment
Adamya Tech	Bluetooth, 802.11, UWB	1996	34	$1 million
Impulsesoft	Bluetooth	1998	27	$3 million
Tejas Network	Network solutions	2000	39	$200,000
Jatayu Software	WAP, WLAN	2000	45	$2.5 million
Wilsys Tech	Bluetooth	2001	28	$600,000
Tenet Tech	System solutions	1996	54	$700,000
Pramati	Middleware, J2EE	1996	47	$3.4 million

Results

For want of space, we present two case studies only. We describe the product-market selection, evolution of resources and capabilities of two firms and changes that were brought about in strategy and process.

Case study 1

K. Srikrishna, Baskar Subramanian, M. Chandrasekaran, Karapattu Srinivasan, and Srividhya Baskar, were from the GCT Coimbatore Engineering College and had majored in electronic design automation. They had a burning desire to do something big in their life. After graduation the three joined Bangalore-based Texas Instruments in 1994. "In 1996, we decided to start a company and all we knew was that we wanted to grow big and so we bought a computer and got into the world of e-commerce and the Internet," says Srividya, R&D head. They evaluated many ideas (thirteen technology fields), with digital signal processing (DSP) related business forming a majority of their initial set as all of them had worked on such solutions and earned patents for their former employers. They hired an MBA from the Indian Institute of Management Bangalore (IIMB) to do market research for their technologies and develop strategies for a new player. Broadband technologies emerged as one technological domain where they felt it was easy to compete and sustain, and that led them to Bluetooth and IEEE 801.11 standards.

When the founders came up with the idea of starting the company, "Bluetooth" was still in infancy. Bluetooth was a consortia-owned open standard in the sense that Ericson, Nokia, Intel, IBM, Microsoft, Toshiba, Lucent, and 3Com formed the special interest group (SIG) and through a Bluetooth Qualification Review Board (BQRB) certified products developed by other vendors that met the Bluetooth specifications. The main purpose of the qualification process is to enable interoperability between equipment not only from the same manufacturer but also from different manufacturers. The Bluetooth qualification process helps manufacturers ensure that their product complies with the Bluetooth specification. Qualification is based on conformance testing against a reference test system and functional interoperability testing against another operational Bluetooth product. In addition to testing, the procedure involves the submission of compliance declarations and the assessment of the compliance documentation by a Bluetooth Qualification Body (BQB). A BQB is an individual person recognized by the BQRB to be responsible for checking declarations and documentation against requirements and listing products on the official database of Bluetooth qualified products. BQRB was aggressively promoting its specifications and with several major players involved in standard setting, many new technology firms found the expectations of continuation of support for the standard high. Moreover, the IEEE 802.11 technical committee was seen as responding late with the issue of definitions, protocols, and base band of 802.11 (g) specifications. Thus many new technology firms felt it was safer to bet on Bluetooth as the technology to lead into ultra wideband (UWB) markets with revenues expected to exceed $5 billion by 2007, just for the chipset alone. As Bluetooth Version 1.1 Protocol and base band specifications were announced, and many of the SIG members started signaling new product introductions based on these specs, more stand-alone firms started developing and obtaining BQRB certification. While customers were aware of the limitations of wiring and were looking for technologies that fit these needs but nobody was sure how to implement wireless solutions. Nobody was clear about boundaries and the playing ground. The company was registered in April 1988. With no promoters, the founders had to put in initial funds and they quickly realized customer funding was required to support them. In November 1999 they came out with offering evaluation and other services around DSP, and chip design initially. They initially toyed with the idea of embedded products and Bluetooth solutions for this market, but daunted by the incumbent competition and their lack of resources they chose to focus on the personal computer market. The PC market was big enough and was complicated with the proprietary approach of Microsoft and the open standards approach of other players. Impulsesoft started developing the protocol stack for Bluetooth for PC platforms and pursued innovation, rather than extension, of existing solutions. The product ideas come from a variety of places. These interactions led to development of the Bluetooth serial port adapter (iSPA) reference design and its embedded Bluetooth protocol stack (iBTStack). This product was licensed to Kanebo Ltd, a Japanese consumer manufacturer that would allow Kanebo to offer cable replacement solutions to the Japanese industrial and medical markets.

In January 2001, Impulsesoft became the first company in the world to be a certified Bluetooth Windows solution provider. This was a significant milestone for Impulsesoft which gave them a great advantage over others and recognition from the Bluetooth community. The next milestone was the association with Panasonic, Japan. They are now shipping products with Bluetooth software from Impulsesoft. The third milestone was signing up with Smart Modular, subsidiary of Selectron, the largest manufacturer of electronics goods in the world. Impulsesoft soon realized that the protocol markets are commodity markets with model-based licensing as the predominant approach. It therefore identified the platform-based approach rather than the product-based approach to development. It soon developed Bluetooth software to Sensitron Inc. (San Mateo, CA) to develop wireless patient-monitoring systems and also licensed its ConnectFree prototyping platform to OpenBrain to help the Korean manufacturer develop future Bluetooth applications.

As markets for Bluetooth progressed, Impulsesoft realized it needed to focus on particular applications and to change its product development strategy too. They started studying the weaknesses of the competitors and to develop/extend solutions. The product strategy thus shifted from innovation to imitation. If a competitor provides software that does not support music on PC then they approach their customer and say "we will provide you the software that has the option of having music on the personal computer." This strategy paid immediate dividends in terms of increased revenues from sales of me-too stacks and tools. It also helped the firm in retaining the developers as these small milestones boosted the motivational levels of their product development teams and prepared them for a long-haul development cycle. Meantime, IEEE announced the 802.11G standard as a fully evolved competition for Bluetooth and several industry experts started voicing the limitations of Bluetooth standards for PC applications. Many PC majors including Dell disbanded Bluetooth-based products and started quickly embracing IEEE 802.11 standards into their notebooks.

Opportunities for Bluetooth soon started from unconventional markets such as airports and convention halls. Soon the firm adopted both innovation/imitation strategies to sustain new markets and exploit extension opportunities. From a component-based IP driven model, Impulsesoft started evolving into a complete solution product company. The revenue model started shifting from product sales to sales and services (maintenance and extensions). Impulsesoft had to reorganize its product teams with some focusing on developing novel components and the others bundling existing components (including open source) to deliver a complete solution. It had to emphasize both innovation and imitation across product roadmaps and product platforms.

Case study 2

The following case details concern Pramati, an application server product company that had to evolve with J2EE, Java-based architecture. This firm is also unique because it not only had to develop the products based on open architecture, but also actually competes with leading firms developing the standard BEA and SUN for marketing its product.

Pramati was started by Jay Pullur along with his brother Vijay. Both had held senior level positions at Wipro Infotech gaining global consulting experience. Vijay holds a BTech in Computer Science from Mysore University and an MTech in Computer Science from IIT Kanpur. He had developed one of the first Java products for Intervoice. Middleware was the technology domain they had chosen to operate, the emerging backbone of e-business. They planned to build products that serve the components technology market, while complying with open standards. After examining several technology and domain options (including .NET compatibles such as GNOME), they chose to develop Java-based applications servers. That was the time when Java was more about applets that ran on a desktop. Pramati hoped that server-side Java would take off and discerning customers looking for speed and reliability would look forward to J2EE extensions. By porting the business logic on the server using Java and a Web interface through JSP-like templates, Pramati's application servers received rare reviews. Pramati's products, services, and OEM programs let Enterprise Solution Vendors (ESVs) re-engineer their offerings to J2EE or embed J2EE into their application.

Pramati was the first company in India to license J2EE and among only three companies picked to exhibit Enterprise Java Bean (EJB) technology at Java One in 1999. Another first was when it edged out competitors to become the first company to release products supporting EJB 1 and 2 in 1999 and 2001. "Our focus on research and development and experience in the Java community process, has helped us deliver EJB 2.0 server technology to the market early," says Jay Pullur. The road wasn't easy with Pramati having to endure 15,000 tests from Sun to get the coveted J2EE certification. To ensure high inter-operability, its full-featured Enterprise Application Development product was made compatible with Oracle 9i AS, Bea Weblogic, and IBM Web-sphere – the dominant Application Servers on the market. By August 2001 about 200 server licenses had been sold.

Pramati realized that while it is easy developing extensions of an open standard, to compete successfully in the product markets requires investments in marketing and support. Increased compatibility did not benefit Pramati as more and more customers preferred single vendor solution that runs on IBM AIX, HP UX, Linux, and NT. Moreover, with more components available in public domain as open source products, clients facing increasing price pressures in their markets started demanding low-cost solutions. Also, many software majors threatened by Linux diffusion started bundling other solutions and services with application servers and Pramati had to rethink its strategy completely. From a component-based IP driven model, they started evolving into a complete solution product company, including consulting services on EJB and Java-based architectures. Pramati also started looking at working around solutions for global database vendors who are keen on getting a stronger foothold in the application servers market. It had to emphasize both innovation and imitation across product roadmaps and product platforms.

Case analysis

Impulsesoft's evolution traced in brief above indicates that the evolution process is incremental, enacted and improvised. In sharp contrast to popular books' notion of entrepreneurship that emphasizes founders acting on foresight, the Impulsesoft case study indicates that entrepreneurial process of entry into a technological field, specialization, and product development may not be deliberately directed. It follows an enacted process of improvisation rather than an organized process of selection, development, and execution. Within Bluetooth applications, embedded solutions were attempted but the firm shifted to PC-based applications as it realized better opportunities. Pramati's case study also indicates that technology entrepreneurship is not a very directed, planned activity, but one that follows a more incremental approach as suggested by strategy literature. Signaling and institutionalization activities pursued by standard-setting bodies do influence technological entrepreneurship. Impulsesoft founders evaluated thirteen different options, and chose Bluetooth space influenced by the institutional activism of the sponsor firms. Slow reaction of an established standard-setting firm, IEEE in this case, was perceived to be advantageous for the new standard.

The case analysis reveals that the evolution of firms can be divided into three stages: the formative stage, expansion stage and consolidation stage. Holding for differences in technological fields and entrepreneur's background and other variables, the process of capability development appears to be the same. In the formative years, the firms had limited financial resources and limited organizational and technological capabilities. The first activity that happens is resource pooling. Firms in our sample pursued different sources of knowledge and markets and attempted product innovation and knowledge integration activities across markets extending the protocols from one market space to another. The key resources built/acquired by firms in this stage were product teams, financial resources, and infrastructure. Adamya made considerable efforts to educate its target customers through technical conferences and related marketing activities. The key organizational capabilities at this stage included the recruitment and training of employees. The other key organizational capability was strategy setting.

However, with increased commoditization of the protocol stacks and with increased support for IEEE 802.11 in the case of Adamya and Impulsesoft, and increased bundling in the case of application server markets, the firms realized that this would require a far more flexible approach that required constant experimentation. They found strategic imitation to be a more economic and sustainable option. Both firms initially pursued innovation strategies and later embraced imitation strategies of extending solutions and services. There are several reasons for this. Once a standard (Open) is announced the competition arises within the boundaries of the standard. According to Henderson and Clark (1990), incremental innovations improve component knowledge without any modifications to the architectural knowledge. Therefore, strategic flexibility to respond quickly and effectively to competitive threats becomes important. Experimenting, investing in, leveraging, and co-opting resources inside and outside the firm enabled the firm to develop the capabilities without locking it onto an investment path unsuitable to the unstable economic climate in which it was operating. This stage required an entirely new set of technological capabilities such as quick imitation, strategic extension, and bundling, completely different from what firms had pursued. Product platforms needed to be defined, and people and projects realigned to exploit economies of scope. The importance of marketing and strategic alliances as a key resource was accentuated. In seeking to get the most out of the existing resources, the firms developed a series of initiatives that included leveraging not only their own resources, but co-opting complementary assets available outside the organization. As extensions of the standards emerged and new support from device players started pouring in, firms rediscovered a market to extend innovative products. These products were extensions and rearrangements of technological choices in a novel way. The firms were building capabilities to customize their solutions and integrate their products/services with those of their customers. Table 10.2 details the evolution of the firms with corresponding changes in resources, capabilities and strategies.

Table 10.2 Stages of evolution, strategies, resources, and capabilities developed

Factor	Formative stage	Expansion stage	Consolidation stage
Resources acquired	Financial	Complementary assets	Standards community linkages
Managerial capabilities	Domain knowledge Marketing	Sales and marketing Scanning	Legitimacy and resource leverage
Organizational capabilities	Recruitment of personnel	Alliances and flexibility	Process management
Focus of R&D	Innovation	Strategic imitation	Innovation and imitation
Product markets	Narrow domain, focus on components	Narrow, focus on components	Complete solutions
Intellectual property (IP)	Components meeting standard	Product extensions, low IP	Patents, high IP
Involvement with standard-setting group	Low	Low	High

Conclusions

In this chapter the focus has been on the internal aspects of the process of growth in young technology-based firms at the firm level. The results indicate that the evolution of firms in standards-based industries can be divided into three stages: the formative stage, expansion stage and consolidation stage. Resources, capabilities, interorganizational relationships as well as product development focus seem to vary over the stages. While innovation and financial resources are emphasized in the formative stage, imitation and alliances seem to be the focus in the expansion stage, and finally firms seem to discover the need to engage in innovation and imitation simultaneously to sustain in these markets. This study has a slightly different empirical focus when studying growth than is common in studies of growth in start-ups. Instead of seeking to explain differences in growth rates between two points in time, this study is concerned with the growth process by which recently established firms attain substantial size and how such growth is continued. To empirically analyze growth in this way is a contribution to empirical research on growth. The role of standard-setting bodies becomes central in network industries. They signal the market opportunities, offer "legitimacy," and help build support or user networks.

For managers, the study provides useful insights into how capabilities are developed, managed, and deployed during the formation and sustenance of enterprises in dynamic environments. This chapter offers some first steps in assisting managers in conceptualizing capability as an integrated construct, using it to enhance organizational learning about markets and creating a competitive advantage in stan-dards-based markets. Information-processing and flexibility activities need to be embedded in the very fabric of the organization. Emphasis should be on building appropriate R&D orientation: from innovation to imitation and later to a good mix of both. The case studies underscore the need for managers to develop capabilities to leverage their resources to design flexible processes.

While the study has highlighted three stages of evolution, more research is needed on the sub-processes of evolution. More work is to be done in order to understand how standards-based groups such as the Bluetooth Special Interest Group (SIG) develop the various incentives and signals they employ to persuade the independent software firms to accept the risks of standards-based products and invest in their development, implementation, support and extensions. Of particular interest would be to investigate how evolution of the firm and growth intensity of the technical manpower are related; for example, how changes in growth orientation at the firm level influence individual incentives for technical knowledge seeking. Such work is very challenging and difficult to carry out unless through longitudinal studies includ-ing both individual and firm levels of analysis. The interaction between the process of technical knowledge development and evolution is also an interesting field of inquiry that has not drawn much attention to date.

References

Ansoff, H. I., and Stewart, J. M. 1967. Strategies for a technology-based business. *Harvard Business Review*, 43: 71–83.

Autio, E. 2000. Growth of technology-based new firms. In D. L. Sexton and H. Landström (Eds.), *The Blackwell Handbook of Entrepreneurship*. Oxford: Blackwell, 327–47.

Bhidé, A. V. 2000. *The Origin and Evolution of New Businesses*. Oxford: Oxford University Press.

Brush, C., and Greene, P. 1996. Resources in the new venture creation process: Strategies for acquisition. National Academy of Management Meeting, Cincinnati, OH.

Brush, C. G., and Chaganti, R. 1998. Business without glamour? An analysis of resources on performance by size and age in small service and retail firms. *Journal of Business Venturing*, 14: 233–57.

Burg, V. U. 2001. *The Triumph of Ethernet*. Stanford: Stanford University Press.

Chandler, A. D. 1962. *Strategy and Structure: Chapters in the History of the Industrial Enter-prise*. New York: Anchor Books.

Chandler, G. N., and Baucus, D. A. 1996. Gauging performance in emerging businesses: Lon-gitudinal evidence and growth pattern analysis. In P. Reynolds (Ed.), *Frontiers of Entrepre-neurship Research*. Wellesley, MA: Babson College, 491–504.

Churchill, N. C,. and Lewis, V. L. 1983. The five stages of small business growth. *Harvard Business Review*, May–June: 30–50.

Cooper, A. C. 1993. Challenges in predicting new firm performance. *Journal of Business Venturing*, 8: 241–53.

David, P. A., and Greenstein, S. 1990. The economics of compatibility standards: An intro-duction to recent research. *Economics of Innovation and New Technology*, 1: 3–41.

Dyer, J. H., and Singh, H. 1998. The relational view: Cooperative strategy and sources of interorganizational competitive advantage. *Administrative Science Quarterly*, 23(4): 660–79.

Economides, N. 1989. Desirability of compatibility in the absence of network externalities, *American Economic Review*, 79: 1165–81.

Garnsey, E. 1998. A theory of the early growth of the firm. *Industrial and Corporate Change*, 13(3): 523–56.

Gartner, W. B. 1985. A conceptual framework for describing the phenomenon of new venture creation. *Academy of Management Review*, 10(4): 696–706.

Granstrand, O. 1998. Towards a theory of the technology-based firm. *Research Policy*, 27: 465–89.

Henderson, R. M., and Clark, K. B. 1990. Architectural innovation: The reconfiguration of existing product technologies and the failure of established firms, *Administrative Science Quarterly*, 35: 9–30.

Khilstrom, R., and Laffont, J. 1979. A general equilibrium entrepreneurial theory of firm formation based on risk aversion. *Journal of Political Economy*, 87(4): 719–48.

Kirzner, I. M. 1973. *Competition and Entrepreneurship*. Chicago: The University of Chicago Press.

Miyazaki, K. 1995. *Building Competences in the Firm: Lessons from Japanese and European Optoelectronics*. New York: St. Martin's Press.

McGrath, R. G., Tsai, M. H., Venkataraman, S., and Macmillan, I. 1996. Innovation, competitive advantage, and rent: A model and test. *Management Science*, 42: 389–403.

Newman, M., and Robey, D. 1992. A social process model of user-analyst relationships. *MIS Quarterly*, 16: 249–66.

Oakey, R. 1994. *New Technology-Based Firms in the 1990s*. London: Paul Chapman Publishing Company.

Oliver, C. 1997. Sustainable competitive advantage: Combining institutional and resource-based views. *Strategic Management Journal*, 18(9): 697–713.

Patton, M. Q. 1999. Enhancing the quality and credibility of qualitative analysis. *Health Services Research*, 34(5): 1189–208.

Penrose, E. T. 1959. *The Theory of the Growth of the Firm*. Oxford: Basil Blackwell.

Reynolds, P. D., and White, S. B. 1996. *The Entrepreneurial Process*. Westport, CT: Quorum Books.

Shane, S. 2000. Prior knowledge and the discovery of entrepreneurial opportunities. *Organization Science*, 11(4): 448-69.

Shaver, K. G., and Scott, L. R. 1991. Person, process, and choice: The psychology of new venture creation. *Entrepreneurship Theory and Practice*, Winter: 23–42.

Shaw, T., and Jarvenpaa, S. 1997. Process models in information systems. In A. S. Lee, J. Liebenau, and J. I. DeGross (Eds.), *Information Systems and Qualitative Research*. London: Chapman & Hall, 70–100.

Strauss, A., and Corbin, J. 1990. *Basics of Qualitative Research: Grounded Theory Procedures and Techniques*. Newbury Park, CA: Sage Publications.

Teece, D. J., Pisano, G., and Shuen, A. 1997. Dynamic capabilities and strategic management. *Strategic Management Journal*, 18(7): 509–33.

Tushman, M. L., and Rosenkopf, L. 1992. Organizational determinants of technological change: Towards sociology of technological evolution. In L. Cummings and B. Staw (Eds.), *Research in Organizational Behavior*. Greenwich, CT: JAI Press, 14: 311–47.

Updegrove, A. 1993. Forming, funding and operating standard-setting consortia. *IEEE Micro*, 13(6): 52–61.

Van de Ven, A. H., and Garud, R. 1989. A framework for understanding the emergence of new industries. In R. Rosenbloom and R. Burgleman (Eds.), *Research on Technology, Innovation, Management and Policy*. Oxford: Oxford University Press, 4: 195–225.

Van de Ven, A. H., and Garud, R. 1994. The coevolution of technical and institutional events in the development of an innovation: In J. Baum and J. Singh (Eds.), *Evolutionary Dynamics of Organizations*. Oxford: Oxford University Press, 425–43.

Venkataraman, S. 1997. The distinctive domain of entrepreneurship research. In J. Katz (Ed.), *Advances in Entrepreneurship, Firm Emergence and Growth*. Greenwich, CT: JAI Press, 119–38.

Yin, R. K. 1994. *Case Study Research: Design and Methods*. Thousand Oaks, CA: Sage.

Author Index

Subject Index

Note: "n." after a page reference indicates the number of a note on that page.

Printed in the USA/Agawam, MA
March 18, 2013